T0331504

Efficiency of Social Sector Expenditure in India

Government investment in social sectors has always been an important factor in tackling social issues and facilitating the alleviation of poverty. Hence, for the greatest good, budgetary expenditure for such investment needs to be efficiently allocated and utilized. This book provides an overview of the social sector in India. It looks at fifteen major Indian states between the years 2000 and 2011 to see how these states invested in the social sector and whether they met the criteria of efficient social sector investment.

Using stochastic frontier models, the book provides an efficiency norm, and making use of this normative estimate it compares performance across the fifteen states and suggests important policy implications to improve future performance of the social sector. The various quantitative techniques in the analysis establish that inefficient and inappropriate allocation of inputs was made in both health and education sectors and suggest that future challenges can be overcome by an appropriate mix of emphasis on different activities. This book will provide insight for those who want to learn more about how to build the capacity of the social sector in a more efficient manner.

Brijesh C. Purohit is currently Professor at Madras School of Economics, Chennai, India. He received his doctorate in economics from the University of Mysore Institute for Social and Economic Change, Bangalore, India. Dr. Purohit began his academic career in 1986 and has held various positions. He worked as a Researcher at the Center for Policy Research, New Delhi (1986); an Economist at the National Institute of Public Finance and Policy, New Delhi (1986–90); an Associate Professor at the Indian Institute of Health Management Research, Jaipur (1990–96); South Asian Visiting Scholar at Queen Elizabeth House, University of Oxford (October 1996–March 1997). He has published in various national and international journals in the areas of health economics and financing, and public and corporate finance.

Efficiency of Social Sector Expenditure in India

Brijesh C. Purohit

Routledge
Taylor & Francis Group

LONDON AND NEW YORK

First published 2014
by Routledge
2 Park Square, Milton Park, Abingdon, Oxon OX14 4RN

Simultaneously published in the USA and Canada
by Routledge
711 Third Avenue, New York, NY 10017

Routledge is an imprint of the Taylor & Francis Group, an informa business

British Library Cataloguing in Publication Data
A catalogue record for this book is available from the British Library

Library of Congress Cataloging-in-Publication Data
Purohit, Brijesh C.
    Efficiency of social sector expenditure in India / Brijesh C. Purohit.
        pages cm
    Includes bibliographical references and index.
    1. Expenditures, Public—India.   2. Budget—India.   3. India—Social
policy.   I. Title.
    HJ2005.P8697   2014
    336.3'90954—dc23   2014000003

ISBN: 978-0-415-73626-8 (hbk)
ISBN: 978-1-315-76752-9 (ebk)

Typeset in Times
by Apex CoVantage, LLC

Contents

Tables

Figures

Preface and acknowledgements

It has been globally recognized that public expenditure on social sector services such as health and education plays a significant role in the overall economic and social development of a nation. Keeping in view the vital importance of this sector, ever since independence, Indian planners aimed at an efficient health system encompassing promotive, preventive and curative components. Over the same period, education for all has become a slogan of literacy policy. Studies of efficiency in the health care and education sectors in India, however, are very limited in both numbers and coverage, with the latter restricted to national or state-level efficiency measurements only for health care. None of the studies so far have focused on using quantitative techniques to measure state-level education expenditure efficiency, and few have measured sub-state-level or district-level efficiency in health care. In the Indian context, this book thus fills this gap. It attempts a sub-state-level as well as a state-level analysis covering the period from 2000 to 2011.

The initial chapters provide a synoptic view of the Indian social sector and highlight its achievements and issues. An exhaustive review of mainly nonparametric and parametric studies follows, with a focus on application of data envelopment analysis and frontier estimation techniques conducted in both the developed and the developing world. In the later chapters, an analysis of education and health sector efficiency in India employs nonparametric free disposal hull (FDH) analysis and parametric estimation using a stochastic frontier model. Using both panel data and cross section data at the state level, it carries out an aggregate all-India level and a state-level analysis of health and elementary education system performance. It also covers sub-state-level analysis for the health care sector. At the state level it covers fifteen major rich, middle-income and low-income states. This is followed by a sub-state-level analysis of five states: Punjab, Maharashtra, Karnataka, Madhya Pradesh and West Bengal. This book provides useful inputs for policy makers and researchers as well as contributes towards further debate on the important aspect of efficiency.

This book has grown out of my interest in health economics and financing. I thank all those journals whose copyright agreements permit me to use my own published articles in this volume. Specific journals from which published articles I have used in some portions of chapters in the book include *Review of Urban*

*and Regional Development Studies, Social Work and Public Health, Economic &
Political Weekly* and Online Journal of Health and Allied Sciences.

I am also grateful to my family members and friends who helped me to grow
in my areas of academic interest. Special thanks are due to my elder brother Dr.
Mahesh C. Purohit for his invaluable encouragement in this academic endeavor.

Abbreviations

AIDS = acquired immunodeficiency syndrome
ANM = auxiliary nurse midwife
AP = Andhra Pradesh
BIMARU = Bihar, Madhya Pradesh, Rajasthan and Uttar Pradesh
BPL = below poverty line
CBHI = Central Bureau of Health Intelligence
CCR Model = Charnes, Cooper and Rhodes Model
CDR = Crude Death Rate
CE = Congestion Efficiency
CHC = Community Health Centre
CLS = Corrected Least Squares
CMO = Chief Medical Officer
crore = Indian unit for 10 million
CRS = Constant Returns to Scale
DALE = Debility Adjusted Life Years
DEA = Data Envelopment Analysis
DFA = Deterministic Frontier Analysis
DMU = Decision Making Units
DRG = Diagnostic Related Group
FDH = Free Disposable Hull Analysis
GDI = Gender Development Index
GDP = Gross Domestic product
GoI = Government of India
GoK = Government of Karnataka
GoM = Government of Maharashtra
GoMP = Government of Madhya Pradesh
GoP = Government of Punjab
GoWB = Government of West Bengal
GP = General Practitioner
HDI = Human Development Index
HDR = Human Development Report
HHC = Hospital-Health Centers
HIV = Human Immuno-Deficiency Virus

HMO = Health Maintenance Organization
ICU = Intensive Care Units
IMR = Infant Mortality Rate
INR = Indian rupee
IRS = Increasing Returns to Scale
ISM = Indian System of Medicine
lakh = hundred thousand (an Indian term)
LEXP = Life Expectancy at Birth
LTS = Least Trimmed Squares
MP = Madhya Pradesh
MED = Most Efficient District
MES = Most Efficient State
MI = Malmquist Indices
MLE = Maximum Likelihood estimates
MMR = Maternal Mortality Rate
MP = Madhya Pradesh
MPM = Mortality Probability Models
n.c. = not computed
NDDP = Net District Domestic Product
NFHS = National Family Health Survey
NHP = National Health Policy
NHS = National Health Services
NIS = Newly Independent States
NRHM = National Rural Health Mission
NSDP = Net State Domestic Product
NSSO = National Sample Survey Organization
OECD = Organization for Economic Cooperation and Development
OLS = Ordinary Least Squares
PCI = Per Capita Income
PHC = Primary Health Centre
PHSC = Punjab Health System Corporation
PPP = Purchasing Power Parity
RCH = Reproductive and Child Health
RKS = Rogi Kalyan Samiti (Patient Welfare Society)
S = Strong Disposability of Inputs
SC = Sub Centre
SE = Scale efficiency
SFA = Stochastic Frontier Analysis
SFM = Stochastic Frontier Model
TE = Technical efficiency
TFR = Total Fertility Rate
TN = Tamil Nadu
UK = United Kingdom
UNDP = United Nations Development Programme
UNICEF = United Nations International Children's Education Fund

UP = Uttar Pradesh
USA = United States of America
VRS = Variable Returns to Scale
W = Weak Disposability of Inputs
WB = West Bengal
WHO = World Health Organization
WHR = World Health Report

1 Social sector in India

Achievements and issues

Overview

The social sector occupies an important place in the state budgetary expenditure. It has remained around 5.8 per cent of GDP, and its share in total state expenditure has varied between 36.8 per cent (in 1990–95) and 39.2 per cent (2010–11; Reserve Bank of India, 2012). Within the social sector, the majority (nearly 57%) is being spent on Education, Sports, Art and Culture (46.1%) and Medical and Public Health (10.5%). The other items, which include Family Welfare; Water Supply and Sanitation; Housing; Urban Development; Welfare of Scheduled Castes (SC), Scheduled Tribes (ST) and Other Backward Castes (OBC); Labour and Labour Welfare; Social Security and Welfare; Nutrition; Natural Calamities and the rest, comprise a low percentage, varying from 1.3 per cent (Natural Calamities) to 9.6 per cent (Social Security and Welfare) of the total social sector.

In its 1991 report the United Nations Development Programme (UNDP) introduced three indicators: public expenditure ratio (share of national income accounted for by public expenditure), social allocation ratio (share of public expenditure earmarked for social services) and social priority ratio (share of social services expenditure devoted to human priority concerns, including mainly elementary education, water and sanitation, public health and maternal and child health; UNDP, 1991). These ratios were suggested to be optimal at 25 per cent, 40 per cent and 50 per cent, respectively.

In terms of two of these ratios Figure 1.1 presents the scenario for all the Indian states from 1990 to 2012–13. Overall public expenditure remains 15 per cent, and the social allocation ratio in the latest year touched 40 per cent but remained lower than UNDP's optimal level and varied over the years from 33 to above 39 per cent. Overall, excluding central government expenditure, the Indian states have spent 5.2 per cent to 6.4 per cent of their GDP.

However, this ratio has varied across three categories of states (Figure 1.2). Unlike the all-India state average, non-special and special categories of states have spent in the range of 5.9–7.4 per cent of GDP and 10.8–12.8 per cent of their GDP, respectively.

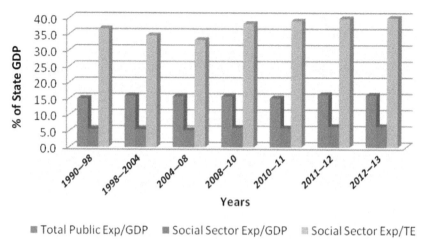

Figure 1.1 Aggregate social sector expenditure of state governments in India

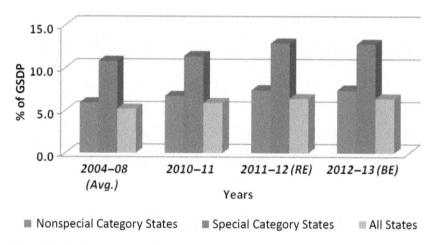

Figure 1.2 Social sector expenditure/GSDP; three categories of states

Within the non-special category of states, there are also notable variations (Figure 1.3). It has varied for the latest year from 5.2 per cent (Haryana) to 12.8 per cent (Bihar). Even within special category states the variation is as much as from 9.2 per cent (Uttarakhand) to 26.1 per cent (Sikkim; Figure 1.4). Overall the social priority ratio, composed of health, education, maternal and child health, nutrition and water and sanitation, has been higher than UNDP's optimal level, and it has remained in the range of 66–80 per cent (Figure 1.5). However, across the major states it remains lowest for Andhra Pradesh (46.34%, Table 1.1). And the highest in 2009–10 is observed for Maharashtra (86.96%).

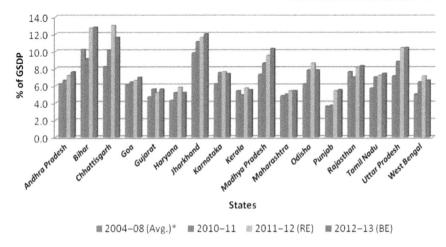

Figure 1.3 Social sector expenditure/GSDP (non-special category states)

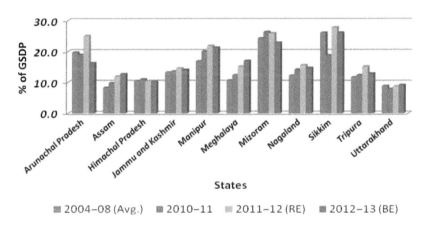

Figure 1.4 Social sector expenditure/GSDP (special category states)

Evolution of the system

The social sector in India includes such important components as health, nutrition, education, water supply, sanitation, housing and welfare. Among these, investment in the health sector has been guided by the priorities laid down in the country's five-year plans. Our first national economic planning exercise, the First Five-Year Plan (1951–56), laid emphasis on health-related issues including malaria control, preventive care in rural areas, maternal and child health (MCH) services, family planning and population control, and water supply and sanitation. Vertical programmes[1] in the form of separate preventive schemes pertaining to malaria, tuberculosis, filariaris, leprosy and venereal diseases were also noted in the priorities listed in the First Five-Year Plan. These vertical

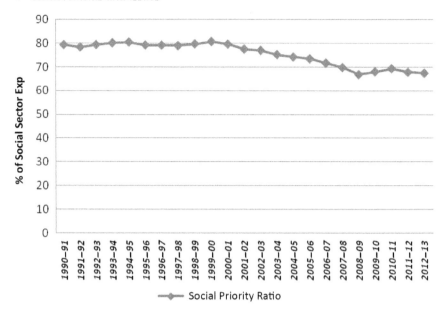

Figure 1.5 Social priority ratio in India, 1990–2013

programmes and other health sector priorities were again listed in the Second Five-Year Plan (1956–61).

As the health system evolved, the subsequent five-year plans had their own focus. Accordingly, a major shift in focus from preventive programmes to family planning was witnessed in the Third Plan (1961–66). The strengthening of the rural primary health centres (PHCs) and existing vertical programmes became the core focus of the Fourth Plan (1969–74). A slight shift in the Fifth Plan (1974–79) occurred with an attempt towards integration of the peripheral staff engaged in vertical health programmes. Further, the Alma Ata declaration in 1978 and the Indian Council of Medical Research/Indian Council of Social Science Research (ICMR/ICSSR) report (ICSSR, 1981) shaped the health sector priorities in the later years. These had an impact on health priorities in the Sixth Plan (1980–84). The policy objective in the Sixth Plan was to integrate the development of the health system into the overall milieu of socio-economic and political change in the country.

A major guideline for the health sector in the country evolved with the formulation of the National Health Policy in 1983. This policy reflected India's commitment to attain the goal of 'Health for All by the Year 2000 AD'. While emphasising the need for universal, comprehensive and primary health services, the policy document provided a list of goals to be attained by 2000. However, achievements were much less than these listed goals.[2]

In the Seventh Plan (1985–90) and the Eighth Plan (1992–97) there was a notable shift, with the major focus being rural health programmes and the private sector's contribution to the health sector. The structural adjustments and

Table 1.1 Social priority ratios (major states), 2001–10

States	Social priority ratios (major states), 2001–10								
	2001–02	2002–03	2003–04	2004–05	2005–06	2006–07	2007–08	2008–09	2009–10
Andhra Pradesh	65.69	65.81	62.04	60.37	64.19	57.96	55.50	49.31	46.34
Bihar	88.88	88.05	85.41	81.80	84.25	85.18	74.20	67.96	76.46
Chhatisgarh	55.74	56.24	62.07	65.58	62.85	59.19	63.07	56.12	54.97
Goa	87.22	86.12	83.89	83.77	78.90	80.50	74.94	80.71	78.20
Gujarat	51.89	69.98	67.08	67.02	65.98	64.39	64.93	58.61	57.19
Haryana	77.66	77.63	78.03	76.72	72.92	73.13	71.96	74.80	75.24
Jharkhand	72.73	76.91	74.43	73.83	80.49	72.80	70.34	69.04	70.27
Karnataka	76.37	75.57	72.31	73.78	70.57	65.92	66.57	68.48	62.62
Kerala	81.73	77.86	82.26	74.79	78.31	80.87	76.52	75.80	73.12
Madhya Pradesh	70.21	62.47	64.01	66.76	64.40	68.49	68.69	69.25	68.00
Maharashtra	80.50	72.55	76.30	79.70	81.62	85.09	91.66	85.80	86.96
Orissa	73.47	75.28	70.88	74.32	70.77	68.34	71.15	66.18	73.41
Punjab	83.28	90.46	87.46	84.65	84.70	75.97	81.56	67.35	70.08
Rajasthan	81.35	79.24	74.07	77.88	80.83	77.34	78.93	79.35	82.86
Tamil Nadu	79.87	76.54	68.22	66.56	65.49	65.99	63.03	59.79	70.74
Uttar Pradesh	84.20	75.60	81.21	74.14	77.74	75.61	68.08	62.08	64.62
West Bengal	76.12	79.52	77.61	77.39	75.80	73.63	70.62	67.28	65.73

Source: RBI (2012).

lesser expenditure on health in the initial plan years coupled with international funding of vertical programmes changed the focus of the Five-Year Plan towards increased private sector participation in the health sector. The subsequent plan periods of 1997–2002 (Ninth Plan) and 2002–07 (Tenth Plan) emphasized primary care, referral services and decentralization in the health care sector. Also in 2002, the Government of India (GoI) brought out a new national health policy (GoI 2002b) which listed the achievements in the health sector between the years 1951 and 2000.[3] Some of the achievements in terms of major indicators are presented in Figures 1.6–1.10. These show considerable improvement in life expectancy (Figure 1.6); reduction in crude birth and death rates and infant mortality rate (IMR) (Figures 1.7–1.8); and significant improvement in health infrastructure in terms of dispensaries and hospitals, number of available of beds (Figure 1.9)

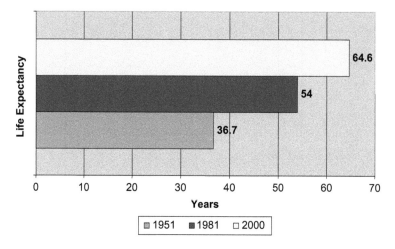

Figure 1.6 Changes in life expectancy in India, 1951–2000

Source: NHP 2002.

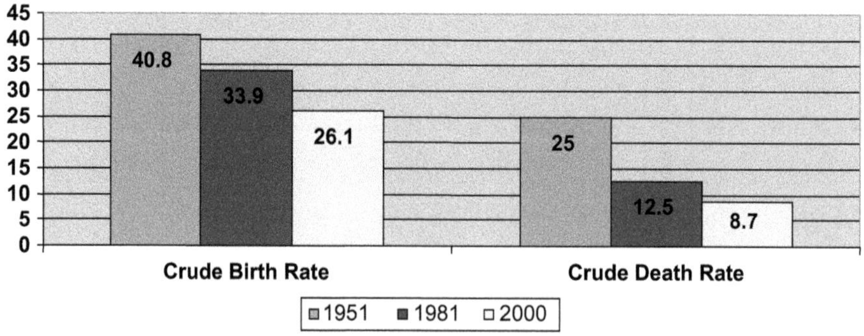

Figure 1.7 Crude birth and death rates in India, 1951–2000

Source: NHP 2002.

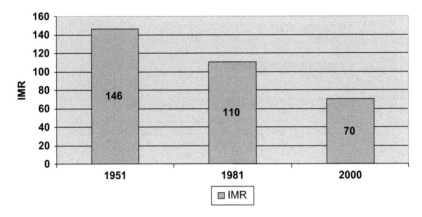

Figure 1.8 Infant mortality rate in India (per thousand), 1951–2000
Source: NHP 2002.

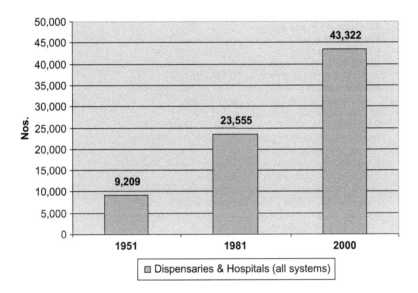

Figure 1.9 Total number of dispensaries and hospitals in India (all systems), 1951–2000
Source: NHP 2002.

and growth in the number of health personnel, including nurses and doctors (Figure 1.10), in the country.

Based on achievements so far and keeping in view new threats from diseases like human immunodeficiency virus (HIV) and acquired immune deficiency syndrome (AIDS), NHP 2002 listed the new goals to be achieved between the years 2000 and 2015 (Table 1.2).

Other notable features of NHP 2002 were recognition of the need for enhanced health facilities and organizational restructuring of the national public health

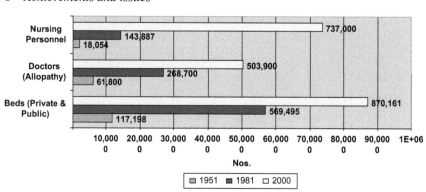

Figure 1.10 Growth in number of beds, doctors and nursing personnel in India, 1951–2000
Source: NHP 2002.

Table 1.2 Goals to be achieved by 2000–15

Eradicate polio and yaws	2005
Eliminate leprosy	2005
Eliminate kala azar	2010
Eliminate lymphatic filariasis	2015
Achieve zero-level growth of HIV/AIDS	2007
Reduce mortality on account of TB, malaria and other vector and waterborne diseases by 50%	2010
Reduce prevalence of blindness to 0.5%	2010
Reduce IMR to 30/1,000 and MMR to 100/100,000	2010
Increase utilization of public health facilities from the current level of <20% to >75%	2010
Establish an integrated system of surveillance, National Health Accounts and health statistics	2005
Increase health expenditure by the government (as a percentage of GDP) from the existing 0.9% to 2.0%	2010
Increase the share of Central grants to constitute at least 25% of total health spending	2010
Increase state sector spending on health from 5.5% to 7% of the budget	2005
Further increase of state sector spending to 8%	2010

Source: GoI (2002b).

initiatives to provide more equitable access to health care facilities; emphasis on control of diseases that contribute to high mortality (e.g. malaria, HIV/AIDS); and the need for designing separate schemes tailor-made to meet the health needs of women, children, aged persons, tribals and other socio-economically challenged sections of society.

Major challenges

Notably, India has achieved important milestones as a result of its sustained planned efforts. As a result, during 1947 to 2004, life expectancy doubled from

32 years to 64.6 years. In addition, IMR has fallen by over 70 per cent, while cases of malaria incidence have been reduced to 20 lakh. Smallpox and guinea worm are nonexistent. Leprosy and polio will soon be eliminated. Despite all these achievements with the prevailing national and state health policies and the systematic Five-Year Plan health sector priorities, there are numerous disconcerting features and new emerging issues in the health care sector in India. The country's total population (16.5% of total global population) accounts for one-fifth of the world's share of diseases; a third of the world's diarrhoeal diseases, TB, respiratory and parasitic infections; a quarter of maternal conditions; a fifth of nutritional deficiencies, diabetes and venereal diseases; and the second largest number of HIV/AIDS cases after South Africa (GoI 2005a,d).

Besides this high disease burden, the overall state financing of the health care sector in India, as noted earlier, has been inadequate, resulting in an unsatisfactory distribution of infrastructure and resources in the health care sector. This has led to undesirable outcomes. There is widespread disparity in health care services in rural and urban areas as well as in poor and rich states and a notable neglect of some of the society's emerging health needs (Purohit 2004, 2008, 2009). As India adopted a health system based on the recommendations of the Bhore Committee (GoI 1946), the major responsibility for the health services should have fallen on the basic infrastructure of public hospitals and PHCs built over the last few decades. However, instead of playing this major role, public sector investment has set up a less efficient health care system, thus providing a major impetus to the private sector for an investment which is more inequitable and less regulated. Even with the low public investment, the largest part (nearly 70%) goes towards recurring expenditures (including wages and salaries). Thus actually a very small amount is spent on medicines and drugs for patients care. After taking inflation into account, real per capita health care expenditure is only INR 120. This overall low spending has affected the availability and quality of health care in the public sector. Based on final outcome indicators, concern is rising regarding efficient utilization of this minimal public sector spending.

According to a study carried out under the aegis of the National Commission on Macroeconomics and Health (NCMH; GoI 2005a), in terms of IMR and safe deliveries, poorly performing states (e.g. Madhya Pradesh, Orissa and Uttar Pradesh) actually spent more (between 45% and 74%) on primary care relative to the better-performing southern states. In terms of international comparisons, countries such as Bangladesh and Indonesia, which spend relatively less on health care than does India, have lower IMR in contrast to India (World Bank 2003). According to data presented in the World Health Report (WHO 2005), India's health-related indicators are indeed lower than those in similarly placed countries like Bangladesh, Sri Lanka and Nepal. In fact, India has a higher IMR per thousand and a lower life expectancy than countries like Sri Lanka and China (Table 1.3).

Thus, not only inefficiency but also overall inadequate and inequitable availability of resources in the public sector have had an adverse impact on the poor.[4]

Consequently, within the country, considerable inequity has emerged in terms of health achievements. Thus, IMR has been higher in rural areas relative to their urban counterparts (Table 1.4). There is a notable disparity between better

Table 1.3 Mortality and life expectancy: India and other Asian countries

	Under-5 mortality (per thousand[1])	Life expectancy (years)
India	87	62
Bangladesh	69	63
Nepal	82	61
Sri Lanka	15	71
China	37	71

Source: UNDP (2006).

[1]Generally mortality is defined in one of the following ways: Under-5 mortality: the probability of dying before the 5th birthday; child mortality: the probability of dying between the 1st and 5th birthdays; Infant mortality: the probability of dying before the 1st birthday; Neonatal mortality: the probability of dying in the 1st month of life; Postneonatal mortality: the probability of dying after the 1st month of life but before the 1st birthday

Table 1.4 Rural-urban and inter-state differentials in health status

	Differentials in health status among states		
	IMR per 1,000 live births (2001–05, NFHS-3)	<5 mortality per thousand (NFHS-2)	Sample Registration System 1999
India	57	94.9	57	70
Rural	62.2	103.7	62.2	75
Urban	41.5	63.1	41.5	44
Kerala	15.3	18.8	15.3	14
Maharashtra	37.5	58.1	37.5	48
Tamil Nadu	30.4	63.3	30.4	52
Orissa	64.7	104.4	64.7	97
Bihar	61.7	105.1	61.7	63
Rajasthan	65.3	114.9	65.3	81
Uttar Pradesh	72.7	122.5	72.7	84
Madhya Pradesh	69.5	137.6	69.5	90

Sources: International Institute for Population Sciences and Macro International (2007); GoI (2001a).

performing States like Kerala, Maharashtra and Tamil Nadu and lower performers like Orissa, Bihar, Rajasthan, Uttar Pradesh and Madhya Pradesh (Table 1.4).

Benefits from the public health system have also been uneven across different segments of the society. In particular, women, children and socially disadvantaged populations such as scheduled castes and scheduled tribes have not received health benefits in an equitable manner, and this is reflected in higher values of IMR for these groups (Table 1.5).

Thus, over the years the inefficiency and inadequacy of public sector health care services have been propelling factors in the expansion of private sector services. Indeed, the private sector in India has gained prominence, particularly after

Table 1.5 Differentials in health status among socio-economic groups in India

	NFHS-3	NHP-2002
Indicator	IMR/1,000	IMR/1,000
India	57	70
Scheduled castes	66.4	83
Scheduled tribes	62.1	84.2
Other disadvantaged	56.6	76
Others	48.9	61.8

Sources: International Institute for Population Sciences and Macro International (2007); (GoI 2002b).

liberalization (Purohit 2001a; NCMH 2005a). It has catered to every segment of the health sector, namely provision of medical services, general and specialized care, diagnostics, hospital planning and construction, pharmaceuticals, technology development, training and education. An estimated 98.68 per cent of private institutions, however, remain in the for-profit sector (GoI 2005a). In terms of total investment, a study by CII-McKinsey (2002) estimated it to have an overall worth of INR 69,000 crores, which was projected to double by 2012. This investment is further supported by an additional health insurance of Rs. 39,000. As such, the private sector currently absorbs nearly three-quarters of human resources and technology, 68 per cent of 15,047 hospitals and 37 per cent of 623,819 beds in the country (GoI 2005a).

In view of its potential, a considerable investment is being made by nonresident Indian (NRI) and industrial/ pharmaceutical companies (Purohit 2001a). Popular hospital networks and chains of diagnostic services have come up, including such brand names as Apollo, Hindujas, Wockhardt, CDR, Mediciti, Max and Escorts, and L.V. In the absence of satisfactory public-sector performance in providing health care, health services from these private providers are expanding at a fast pace, and these are becoming the providers of health care for upper-income groups. With their high-tech care, these providers are also making India a potential hub for medical tourism. However, this trend in health insurance and the growing role of corporate hospitals may result in an overall increase in the cost of health care. This may further lead to increased dependence of the poor and lower-middle-income groups on the public health sector.

Moreover, there has been a major policy directive that curative care can be left to the market forces and resources thus released can be dedicated to primary care. This is observed in both the National Health Policies of 1983 and 2002 (GoI 1983, 2002b). The same emphasis in health policy is seen on the part of the central and state governments, which have extended a number of exemptions in the last decade and half. These have been mainly in the form of excise and import duty exemptions, land subsidy and concessional bank credit. However, this argument in favour of encouragement to the private sector has not really been supported by the recent empirical study based on a sample survey of eight median districts. The study indicates that such a reliance on the private sector, even for curative care, could be contrary to the objectives of health policy. Some of the survey's pertinent findings, for instance, suggest that private health care is marked by such factors as fragmentation of provider market; near absence of private-sector providers in the poorest blocks; overall small size of outpatient (OPD) clinics; urban concentration of these providers; abysmally low per capita ratio of doctors; a high proliferation of technology-intensive machines including ultrasound, Doppler machines and CT scans; low bed occupancy ratio in relation to public facilities; substandard treatment; high cost of care and concentration of three-quarters of specialists and technology in few towns (GoI 2005c).

If we presume that the private, for-profit sector is going to be a replacement for the public-sector provider in the delivery of curative health care, the findings

Table A1.1 Health care sector achievements in India, 1951–2000

Indicator	1951	1981	2000
Demographic changes			
Life expectancy (years)	36.7	54	64.6 (RGI)
Crude birth rate per thousand of population	40.8	33.9 (SRS)	26.1 (99 SRS)
Crude death rate per thousand of population	25	12.5 (SRS)	8.7 (99 SRS)
Infant mortality rate (IMR)	146	110	70 (99 SRS)
Epidemiological shifts			
Malaria (cases in millions)	75	2.7	2.2
Leprosy cases per 10,000 of population	38.1	57.3	3.74
Smallpox (no. of cases)	>44,887	Eradicated	
Guinea worm (no. of cases)		>39,792	Eradicated
Polio (no. of cases)		29,709	265
Infrastructure			
SC/PHC/CHC	725	57,363	1,63,181 (99-RHS)
Dispensaries and hospitals (all)	9,209	23,555	43,322 (95–96-CBHI)
Beds (private and public)	117,198	569,495	8,70,161(95-96-CBHI)
Doctors (allopathy)	61,800	2,68,700	5,03,900 (98-99-MCI)
Nursing personnel	18,054	1,43,887	7,37,000(99-INC)

Source: GoI (2002b).

Note: CBHI = Central Bureau of Health Intelligence; INC = Indian Nursing Council; MCI = Medical Council of India; RGI = Registrar General of India; RHS = Rural Health Statistics; SC/PHC/CHC = sub-centre/primary health centre/community health centre; SRS = Sample Registration System.

of this study restrict such optimism and possibly indicate a high cost even in the presence of universal insurance. Given the equity, efficiency and cost implications of sole dependence for health care on the private sector, it is pertinent to look into the possibility of enhancing efficiency in the public sector or achieving an optimal mix of public and private sector funding as well as other alternatives, such as not-for-profit community-based organizations charged with bringing better health care facilities to the country.

Evolution of water and sanitation sector programmes

Water supply and sanitation were added to the Indian national agenda during the first five-year planning period (1951–56). In 1954, the first national water supply programme was launched as part of the government's health plan. This was funded by both central and state administrations through equal funding. The initial years were marked by limited achievements due to lack of a qualified workforce and short supply of materials. In the subsequent five-year plans, more funding was allocated for the development and strengthening of state public health engineering departments. In 1968, states were granted limited financial authority to sanction rural water supply schemes. In this duration (1954–68), the programme aimed at local community development and the welfare of the backward classes. A major policy initiative, namely, the National Water Policy, was enunciated in 1987 to guide the planning and development of water resources throughout the country. This policy led the Indian states to focus on (a) water resource management, with a top priority being domestic water supply; (b) design standards for structures to protect groundwater sources; (c) water-quality monitoring and mapping and (d) data management and valuation. Another National Water Policy adopted in 2002 emphasized drinking water. As a result some states, such as Karnataka, Madhya Pradesh, Orissa, Rajasthan and Tamil Nadu, also enunciated state-level policies. Thus the national policy guiding the water and sanitation sector in India in the Eighth Five-Year Plan (1992–97) emphasized that 'safe drinking water and basic sanitation are vital human needs for health and efficiency' and acknowledged that 'death and disease, particularly of children, . . . and the drudgery of women are directly attributable to the lack of these essentials' (GoI 1992a). High priority was given to serving villages that did not have adequate sources of safe water and to improving the level of service for villages classified as only partially covered.[5] The Ninth and Tenth Plans also broadly followed the directions set by the Eighth Plan.

The primary responsibility for providing drinking water and sanitation facilities in the country rests with the state governments,[6] and, more specifically, the local bodies in the urban areas. The Centre provides or allocates funds and also ensures that funds are provided in state budgets, and progressively larger allocations have been made for water supply and sanitation in the various Five-Year Plans.

Overall, India's approach to water supply and sanitation in the Eighth, Ninth and Tenth Plans broadly follows the New Delhi declaration, adopted by the United Nations General Assembly in December 1990, which emphasizes protection of the environment and safeguarding of health through the integrated management of water resources and liquid and solid waste as well as other pertinent features.[7] Over the years, the focus in the rural sector in both water and sanitation has been on decentralization, demand responsiveness and a people-centred approach, increasingly taking the government from being a direct service provider to being a facilitator. In the urban sector, over the plan periods, an emphasis on Urban Water Supply and Sanitation (UWSS) and reforms mark notable improvements in the policy.[8] At present, states generally plan, design and execute water supply schemes (and often continue to operate them) through their State Public Health Engineering Departments (or Panchayati Raj Engineering Departments or Rural Development Engineering Departments) and Water Boards. In addition, a variety of different government institutions at the Centre have a role in the management of drinking water supply, pollution control and financing of infrastructure development. For instance, the Central Water Commission (CWC) in the Ministry of Water Resources (MoWR) has responsibilities for regulating the use of surface water for irrigation, industrial use and drinking water. The Central Groundwater Board (CGWB) of the same ministry has oversight responsibility for the monitoring of groundwater levels and rates of depletion as well as production of water resource inventories and maps. The National Rivers Conservation Directorate (NRCD) under the Ministry of Environment and Forests (MoEF) oversees the implementation of action plans to improve the quality of the nation's rivers (previously their activities were confined to the Ganga Action Plan but now extend to the polluted stretches of 27 major rivers, with works spread over 149 towns in 16 states). Likewise, the Central Pollution Control Board (CPCB) promotes basin-wide pollution control strategies. The CPCB liaises with State Water Pollution Control Boards and lays down standards for treatment of sewage and effluents. The board is also responsible for action in the case of noncompliance.[9]

Ministry of Urban Development (MoUD) launched the Accelerated Urban Water Supply Programme (AUWSP) in 1993–94 to implement water supply schemes in towns with populations below 20,000 (as per the 1991 census). Under this programme, 50 per cent of the estimated cost of the schemes is provided by the ministry as a grant based on detailed project report and the remaining 50 per cent by the state government, including a 5 per cent beneficiary/town contribution. In special cases, 100 per cent financing is available as the central share.[10] There has also been a centrally supported water quality monitoring programme, again with substantial funding for water quality laboratories and monitoring staff in each state. The NHP 2002 adopted by the ministry recognizes that water supply and sanitation are part of an interconnected set of factors that need to be addressed holistically and in coordination among various institutions.

At the state level, most states have separate public health engineering departments charged with planning, investigation and design. Following the Third Five-Year Plan recommendation to form statutory water and sewerage boards, in some states (such as Gujarat, Kerala, Maharashtra and Tamil Nadu) the Water Supply and Sewerage Boards (WSS boards) or corporation (for instance, in Uttar Pradesh) have been constituted to handle urban and rural water. With the recent move towards decentralization, a mix of agencies have evolved, including state public health engineering departments, state boards and district engineering agencies.[11]

Additionally, nongovernmental organizations (NGOs), both national and international, have played a significant role in India's social sector over the past three decades. They have exhibited comparative advantages that other organizations lack.[12] Further, private initiatives also continue to drive the construction and maintenance of traditional open wells and household toilets. Nationwide, the number of privately constructed toilets is almost twice the number constructed through government programmes. During the Eleventh Five-Year Plan, the government has identified 100 per cent sanitation as a goal. In October 2008, the government of India also announced a national urban sanitation policy. The ultimate objective is that all urban dwellers will have access to and be able to use safe and hygienic sanitation facilities and arrangements so that no one defecates in the open. The vision of the policy is for all Indian cities and towns to become totally sanitized, healthy and liveable and to ensure and sustain good public health and environmental outcomes for all citizens with a special focus on hygienic and affordable sanitation facilities for the urban poor and women. The focus of the policy is on behavioural changes by generating awareness amongst communities and institutions about sanitation and its linkages with public and environmental health, and also promoting mechanisms to bring about and sustain behavioural changes aimed at adoption of healthy sanitation practices.

Despite this concerted planning effort in India, a recent study by UNICEF (2008) indicates that even with the progress of water supply in relation to Millennium Development Goals (MDG) targets being on track, nearly 4 per cent of its urban population and 14 per cent of its rural population use unimproved sources of water. In terms of sanitation, nearly 18 per cent in urban areas and 58 per cent in rural areas are devoid of any facility. In fact in 2006, only 28 per cent of people in rural areas, who make up two-thirds of India's billion-plus people, had access to toilets. In urban areas, 30.66 million households, or 35.49 per cent of urban households, suffer inadequate access to sanitation facilities; 7.87 per cent of households defecate in the open, 5.48 per cent use community latrines and 19.49 per cent use shared latrines. More than 37 per cent of the human excreta generated is disposed of unsafely. The percentage of notified and nonnotified slums without latrines is 17 per cent and 51 per cent, respectively.[13] In addition, there are districts in different states which continue to be known as diarrhoea endemic.[14]

Education system

India's education system is divided into different levels which include education at pre-primary, primary, elementary and secondary levels as well as undergraduate and postgraduate levels. The government has laid emphasis on primary education up to the age of 14 years, referred to as elementary education. In fact, 80 per cent of all recognized schools at the elementary stage are government run or supported, making it the largest provider of education in the country.

Official figures in 2011 showed 5,816,673 elementary school teachers and 2,127,000 secondary school teachers in India. From time to time, there have been efforts to enhance quality in education. One of these, the District Education Revitalization Programme (DERP), was launched in 1994 with an aim to universalize primary education in India by reforming and vitalising the existing primary education system. Eighty-five per cent of DERP was funded by the central government and the remaining 15 per cent was funded by the states. This programme led to 160,000 new schools, including 84,000 delivering alternative education to approximately 3.5 million children. It was also partly supported by UNICEF and other international programmes.

Besides an improved high gross enrolment ratio of 93–95 per cent for the last three years in some states, DERP also emphasized improvement in staffing and enrolment of girls. Another widely publicized current scheme for universalization of education is the Sarva Shiksha Abhiyan (SSA), one of the largest education initiatives in the world.

Owing to quality or availability factors, nearly 27 per cent of Indian children are privately educated, and this percentage is much higher in urban areas. According to the latest District Information System for Education (DISE survey), a considerable percentage of teachers in private schools are untrained (parateachers; 54.91%), compared to 44.88 per cent in government schools. However, the number of private schools in India is still low; the share of private institutions is 7 per cent (upper primary 21% and secondary 32%).

Secondary education

Secondary education covers children aged 14–18 years and nearly 88.5 million children fall in this category, according to the 2001 census (GoI 2001b). The National Policy on Education, 1986 (GoI 1998c), has provided for environmental awareness, science and technology education and introduction of traditional elements such as yoga into the Indian secondary school system. A significant emphasis in India's secondary schools is on inclusion of the disadvantaged sections of society. The SSA initiative has also been extended to secondary education in the form of the Madhyamik Shiksha Abhiyan.

To provide uniform education in institutions, following the same syllabus at the same pace regardless of the location to which the central government employee's family has been transferred, the government also started the Kendriya Vidyalaya project in 1965.

Higher education: undergraduate and postgraduate levels

After passing the Higher Secondary Examination (the grade 12 examination), students may enrol in general degree programmes such as a bachelor's degree in arts, commerce or science, or professional degree programmes such as engineering, law or medicine. India's higher-education system is the third largest in the world, after those of China and the United States. The main governing body at the tertiary level is the University Grants Commission (India), which enforces its standards, advises the government and helps coordinate between the centre and the state. Accreditation for higher learning is overseen by twelve autonomous institutions established by the University Grants Commission.

As of 2009, India has twenty central universities, 215 state universities, 100 deemed universities, five institutions established and functioning under the State Act, and thirty-three institutes of national importance. Other institutions include 16,000 colleges, including 1,800 exclusive women's colleges, functioning under these universities and institutions. The emphasis in the tertiary level of education has been on science and technology, and thus Indian educational institutions by 2004 consisted of a large number of technology institutes. Distance learning is also a feature of the Indian higher-education system. Yet another scheme, Rashtriya Uchattar Shiksha Abhiyan, uses strategic funding to promote higher-level educational institutions, covering 316 state public universities and 13,024 colleges.

Technical education

India offers the largest pool of technically skilled graduates in the world, with the number of graduates coming out of technical colleges increasing to more than 700,000 in 2011 from 550,000 in FY 2010. India's National Policy on Education provisioned for a body to regulate and develop higher technical education, which came into being as the All India Council for Technical Education (AICTE) in 1987. At the central level, the Indian Institutes of Technology, the Indian Institute of Space Science and Technology, the National Institutes of Technology, the Indian Institutes of Information Technology and Rajiv Gandhi Institute of Petroleum Technology are deemed of national importance. Some of the central universities, such as Banaras Hindu University, Jamia Millia Islamia University, Delhi University, Mumbai University and the University of Calcutta, are also pioneers of technical education in the country.

In addition to levels of education previously mentioned, there has been an initiative for open and distance learning as well. For instance, at the primary and secondary school levels, the National Institute of Open Schooling (NIOS) provides opportunities for continuing education to those who missed completing school education. Nearly 14 lakh (1.4 million) students have been enrolled at the secondary and higher secondary levels through open and distance learning. In 2012, many state governments also introduced state open schools to provide distance education.

At higher-education level, Indira Gandhi National Open University (IGNOU) coordinates distance learning. It has a cumulative enrolment of about 15 lakhs, serviced through fifty-three regional centres and 1,400 study centres with 25,000 counsellors. The Distance Education Council (DEC), an authority of IGNOU, coordinates thirteen state open universities and 119 institutions of correspondence courses in conventional universities.

Education in rural India has lower rates of completion than in urban areas. A gender gap also exists within the schools; 18 per cent of males earn a high school diploma compared with only 10 per cent of females. The estimated number of children who have never attended school in India is near 100 million, a figure which reflects the low completion levels.

Further, following India's independence a number of rules were formulated to provide special reservations for the Scheduled Castes, Other Backward Castes and Scheduled Tribes of India, such as 15 per cent and 7.5 per cent in Kendriya Vidyalaya for SC and ST respectively; at the university level, reservations and concessions in merit are also given for SC, ST and OBC candidates.

India's minorities, especially the ones considered 'educationally backward' by the government, are provided for in the 1992 amendment of the Indian National Policy on Education. The government initiated the Scheme of Area Intensive Programmes for Educationally Backward Minorities and the Scheme of Financial Assistance or Modernization of Madarsa Education as part of its revised Programme of Action (1992). Both these schemes were started nationwide by 1994. In 2004 the Indian parliament passed an act which enabled minority education establishments to seek university affiliations if they passed the required norms.

Welfare schemes for aging

The constitution of India provides direction for government's role at both the central and state levels.[15] For instance, one provision (entry 24 in list III of schedule VII) deals with the 'Welfare of Labour, including condition of work, Provident Fund, livelihood for workmen compensation, invalidity and old age pension and maternity benefits'. In a similar vein, other provisions (item 9 of the state list and items 20, 23 and 24 of the concurrent list) relate to old age pension, social security, social insurance and economic and social planning. Another (article 41 of directive principles of state policy), dealing with the state's role in providing social security to the aged, mentions that 'the state shall, within the limits of its economic capacity and development, make effective provision for the right to employment, education and public assistance in case of unemployment, old age, sickness and disablement, and in other cases of underserved want' (GoI 1996). These directions in the constitution are partly reflected in some of the economic security schemes which we discuss below.

Public sector

At present in India, a number of public schemes are directed to the economic security of older persons. Some are initiated by the central government, others by state governments. These include the National Old Age Pension Scheme (NOAP), the old age and widows' pension in Maharashtra, and the widows' pension in Karnataka, West-Bengal and Kerala. These state schemes provide different and paltry amounts to their elderly populations.

Under NOAP, central government assistance of Rs. 75 per month is provided to anyone aged 65 or older who is destitute and has no regular means of subsistence, either from his/her own income or through support from family members or others. Overall nearly 78.5 per cent of potential beneficiaries are covered by the scheme and the extent of inadequate coverage varies between 5 and 87.9 per cent, 19–37 per cent and 14–35.6 per cent across high-, middle- and low-income categories of states (Alam 2004). The NOAP is implemented in the states and union territories through rural and urban local bodies also called as panchayats and municipalities, respectively. They in turn are encouraged to involve voluntary organizations in benefiting the destitute elderly. The main lacunae of the scheme are the inadequate and low amount of coverage resulting from lack of effective administration.

Old-age pensions provided by different state governments are also very low. The amount of pension per month for the aged varies between Rs. 100 and 275, Rs. 100 and 150 and Rs. 75 and 300 across high-, medium- and low-income states (Purohit 2003). The eligibility age also varies across states between 60 and 65 years. Some states, such as Maharashtra, Punjab, Uttar Pradesh and Madhya Pradesh, have lower ages of eligibility for females relative to males by 5 years (Purohit 2003).

The 2007 budget speech announced the New Pension Scheme (NPS), which seeks to provide old-age security for all individuals, including the unorganized sector, by creating a mechanism which enables them to save throughout their working lives. Under NPS, every subscriber will have an individual pension account, portable across job changes. The amount (including income on the investments) will be available to individuals at the age of 60 years, with at least 40 per cent to be converted into monthly payments for the rest of their lives. Another measure for the aged in the 2007 budget was the introduction of reverse mortgages for older adults by the National Housing Bank (NHB). The scheme allows older-adult borrowers to mortgage their house property to a lender who then makes periodic payments to the borrowers throughout the remainder of their lives.

Currently existing publicly mandated and supported schemes include the Employees' Provident Fund (EPF), the Employees' Pension Scheme (EPS), and the Public Provident Fund (PPF).The Employees' Deposit Linked Income Scheme provides an additional payment in the event of death or permanent disability of a worker while in service. The EPF and EPS are meant for organized sector employees only. At present, 171 industries and classes of establishments are covered by the EPF Act of 1952. Organizations employing twenty or more persons are mandated to subscribe to the EPF or EPS plus the Employees' Deposit Linked Income Scheme. These schemes are managed by the EPF organization. All told, only 34 million, or less than 11 per cent, of the working population is eligible to participate in EPS or EPF. Other mandated Provident funds are the Coal Mines Provident Fund, the Seaman's Provident Fund, the Assam Tea Plantation Provident Fund, and the J&K Provident Fund.

The EPF scheme is a defined-contribution, publicly managed plan under which accumulations are paid to workers as lump sums on retirement. The EPS is a publicly managed defined-benefit plan paying workers a monthly pension after retirement. It also has elements of a defined-contribution plan and is fully funded. All employees covered by these schemes and drawing salaries below Rs. 5,000 per month are required to participate and contribute. An equal contribution from employers and employees provides between 20 and 24 per cent of wages towards the EPF and EPS. From the employer's contribution of 10 to 12 per cent, 8.33 per cent is diverted to the EPS while the balance is pooled into the Provident Fund (PF) accounts of employees. The government contributes another 1.16 per cent of wages into employees' PF accounts. Thus, overall, more than 25 per cent of wages under the scheme goes to retirement benefits. This high contribution leaves employees very little scope for saving for other contingencies.

Other weaknesses of the schemes are that they provide poor retirement benefits because of the ease of premature withdrawals permitted as well as highly inadequate final accumulations.[16] The EPS, by contrast, provides defined benefits of up to a maximum of 50 per cent of the average of the last 12 months' salary. The contribution rates under EPS vary across industries and classes of establishments. Premature withdrawals and final payments are taxed.

The PPF, introduced in 1968–69 for employees of the unorganized sector, covers less than 1 per cent of the working population. It operates through maintaining individual accounts (PPF accounts) with either some designated nationalized bank or post offices. The PPF account allows an accretion of a minimum of Rs. 100 and a maximum of Rs. 70,000 per member per year. Both the accretions and withdrawals under PPF are tax-exempt. An individual with a PPF account can withdraw a partial amount after 5 years; full maturity is attained after 15 years. The main weaknesses of the scheme include premature withdrawals with tax exemptions and lack of professional investment of the annual deposits. The result here, too, is little positive impact on old-age security.

Private sector

Private plans include the pension schemes of the Life Insurance Corporation of India (LIC), the Unit Trust of India (UTI), Kothari Pioneer Pension Plan and pension plans by some of the banks including Housing Development Finance Corporation (HDFC) and Industrial Credit and Investment Corporation of India (ICICI). The LIC offers three schemes: Jeevan Akshay, New Jeevan Suraksha (NJS) and New Jeevan Dhara (NJD). Each defines a maximum and minimum entry age, purchase price and minimum annuity payment. At present, the minimum annual annuity in Jeevan Akshay is Rs. 200 for a minimum purchase price of Rs. 25,000; the minimum and maximum entry ages are, respectively, 40 years and 79 years. NJS and NJD prescribe minimum and maximum ages for entry into the schemes of 18 and 65 years. These schemes provide an annuity for life, along with 25 per cent notional cash options, which include a basic sum plus a guaranteed addition of Rs. 75 per thousand of rupees paid per year and loyalty additions (a percentage of the premium paid back to the individual, depending on the number of years the policy has been held before maturity or death). The NJS offers variable returns, and the pension rates payable against any given accumulation can also vary from those prevailing at the time of purchase. The annuity rate payable against any given accumulation will be that prevailing under Jeevan Akshay.

The UTI Retirement Plan (RBP) is an open-ended notified pension plan (one that has been mentioned or specified in the official *Gazette* of the central government). The scheme, initiated in 1994, permits any resident or nonresident Indian between 18 and 60 years of age to invest a minimum amount of Rs. 10,000; there is no restriction on the maximum amount that can be invested. At the age of 58, the individual must choose between a monthly pension plan and a lump sum withdrawal. Premature withdrawal before age 58 is permitted by selling the UTI assets at a discount of 10 per cent of the prevailing net asset value. The contributions made to the plan are eligible for a tax credit of 20 per cent of the amount up to a ceiling of Rs. 6000.

Currently, one of the private-sector mutual funds in India with a notified pension plan is known as Kothari Pioneer Pension Plan. It is an open-ended, debt-oriented balanced fund. The scheme requires a minimum investment of Rs. 10,000 with no ceiling on the maximum. A minimum of a three-year lock-in period is required to receive the benefits under the scheme. Four options are available for an investor after attaining an age of 58 years: a pension plan, a lump-sum option, a combination pension and lump-sum option, and a flexible option. Under the flexible option, an investor can withdraw a fixed amount every month for a specified length of time. In recent years other schemes initiated recently by banks like HDFC and ICICI also run, by and large, on the similar lines.

Others

A recent national scheme, Annapurna, envisages the distribution of free grains, up to 10 kg per month, to destitute older persons who may be eligible for the old-age pension under the NOAP but are not receiving it, and whose sons are not residing with them. The below poverty line (BPL) families which also include older persons are provided food grains at the rate of 35 kg per family per month. The food grains are issued at the rate of INR 3 per kilogram of rice and INR 2 per kilogram of wheat. People aged 60 years and older from the BPL category are given priority for identification. Instructions have been issued to state governments for giving priority to the ration card holders who are over 60 years of age in fair price shops for issue of rations.

Various tax concessions are also provided to older persons under different tax legislation. For instance, a rebate is available to those who are aged 65 or older. A deduction of up to Rs. 15,000 is permissible for medical insurance premiums and up to Rs. 40,000 for medical treatment. The Ministry of Finance extends the income tax rebate up to an income of Rs. 1.85 lakh (185 thousand) per year, and higher rates of interest are offered to senior citizens on the deposits they make in post offices.

The Ministry of Road Transport and Highways also extends a reservation of two seats for senior citizens in the front row of buses of the State Road Transport Undertakings. Some state governments give fare concessions to senior citizens in those same buses and are introducing bus models, which are convenient to the elderly. In most of the states, various concessions, usually ranging from 25 per cent to 50 per cent, are provided to older persons for travel by bus, rail or airline. For instance, Rajasthan provides a discount of 25 per cent on buses operated by the state transport; Chandigarh and Maharasthra provide 50 per cent in state road transport. In Punjab, women over 60 years of age are exempted from paying for travel by bus.

Indian Railways (Ministry of Railways) provides 30 per cent fare concessions in all Mail/Express trains, including Rajdhani/Shatabadi/Jan Shatabadi trains, for individuals aged 60 years and above. It also offers separate counters for older adults for the purchase, booking and cancellation of tickets. Other concessions extended by Indian Railways include wheelchairs for use by needy individuals, including older adults, at all junctions, district headquarters and other important stations; wheelchair ramps at the entrances to important stations; specially designed coaches with space for wheelchairs; handrails and specially designed toilets for people with special needs.

The Ministry of Civil Aviation, through Indian Airlines, provides a 50 per cent discount on normal economy class fare for all domestic flights to Indian senior citizens – men aged 65 and older and women aged 63 and older, subject to certain conditions. Similarly, Air India offers discounts to senior citizens aged 60 and older on flights to the United States, the United Kingdom and Europe as well as on domestic routes. Others, such as Sahara Airlines, offer a 50 per cent discount on basic fare for economy class travel on domestic flights to people aged 62 and older.

The Ministry of Health and Family Welfare provides for separate queues for older persons in hospitals for registration and clinical examination. The Department of Telecommunications (DOT) gives priority to senior citizens who register faults or complaints by assigning their cases to a special high-priority. Senior citizens are also allowed to register telephone connection by DOT under its priority category.

At the local government level, the Municipal Corporation of Delhi, for instance, operates a separate counter to facilitate senior citizens' submission of their property tax bills. The corporation allows a rebate of 30 per cent of the property tax, due on the covered space of a building up to 100m^2, in the case of any self-occupied residential building singly owned by a man who is 65 years of age or older.

In fact, the Ministry of Social Justice and Empowerment, being the nodal ministry, is also implementing schemes (under the plan budget) such as the Integrated Programme for Older Persons, which has replaced the earlier scheme of Assistance to Voluntary Organizations for Programmes Relating to the Welfare of the Aged. Under the Integrated Programme, financial assistance up to 90 per cent of the project cost is provided to NGOs for establishing and maintaining old age homes, day care centres and mobile medicare units and providing non-institutional services to older persons. It also implements another scheme (under non-plan budget) called the Scheme of Assistance to Panchayati Raj Institutions/Voluntary Organizations/Self Help Groups for Construction of Old Age Homes/Multi-Service Centers for Older Persons. Under this scheme, one-time construction grants for elderly housing and multiservice centres are provided to NGOs on the recommendation of state governments and UTI administrations.

At the judiciary level, courts in the country accord priority to cases involving older persons and ensure their expeditious disposal. In 2007 GoI introduced a bill in Parliament known as the Parents and Senior Citizens Bill which attempts to mandate the care of elderly citizens in law and envisions the establishment of tribunals to ensure its functioning. The legislation seeks to make it a legal obligation for children and heirs to provide maintenance to senior citizens. It also permits state governments to establish old-age homes in every district. The purpose of the bill is to secure financial stability for parents who are unable to support themselves. The constitution, through its directive principles, directs the state, not private citizens, to make effective provision for the support of senior citizens. Two acts, namely the Code of Criminal Procedure of 1973 and the Hindu Adoption and Maintenance Act of 1956, currently mandate that children care for their parents if they are unable to care for themselves. In the 2007 bill too, the onus has been placed on children and relatives of senior citizens. However, while it allows state governments to establish old-age homes, the bill does not make it mandatory, nor does it address the needs of senior citizens who do not have either children or property (Parker 2007).

A number of Indian states, including Himachal Pradesh, Maharashtra and Goa, have also enacted 'parents' maintenance bills,' which provide for maintenance to be extended to parents whose children are neglectful. These bills authorize the appropriate provincial and judicial authorities to establish a maintenance allowance and serve as the appellate authority. Such legislation is expected to help needy older persons through the quick disposal of cases. However, the political will to assure implementation is lacking.

The role of the central government

At the central government level in India, the Ministry of Social Justice and Empowerment (MSJE) is responsible for old-age provisions. In recent years, the Indian government has taken four broad steps to enhance the welfare of older persons:

1 The development of a national policy on older persons
2 The establishment of a National Council for Older Persons (NCOP)
3 The launch of a project called 'Old Age Social and Income Security' (OASIS)
4 The revision of existing Ministry schemes

The national policy on older persons

During the 1999 International Year of Older Persons, the government of India promulgated a national policy on older persons (NCOP). The policy provides a broad framework for intersectoral collaboration and cooperation both within the government as well as between the government and NGOs. The policy has identified a number of areas for intervention, including economic security, health care and nutrition, shelter, education, welfare and the protection of life and property. A notable feature has been the proposal to develop a mandatory, contributory pension scheme for all self-employed and salaried persons in the existing pension scheme, as well as to provide some support for all those living below the poverty line. The goal is to cover the elderly who are not currently covered by any existing schemes. The proposal does not, however, specify any time frame or budgetary allocation for implementation, and it does not dwell on the adequacy or effectiveness of the existing old-age pension scheme in meeting the needs of older persons.

The National Council for Older Persons

To put the national policy into operation, the MSJE has constituted the National Council for Older Persons (NCOP). It consists of thirty-nine members and a seven-member working group. Its objectives are to advise the government on policies and programs for older persons; provide feedback on specific initiatives and the national policy on older persons; advocate for the aged; lobby for concessions, rebates, and discounts for older persons; represent the collective opinion of older persons to the government and suggest steps and measures to enhance the quality of intergenerational relationships and make old age productive and interesting. Ironically, older persons are not required to be represented on this body.

The OASIS project

The growing concern for social and income security among older citizens led the social defence bureau under the MSJE to commission a national project known as OASIS (Old Age Social and Income Security). It consists of an eight-member expert committee charged with recommending actions to the government of India that will encourage young workers in the unorganized sector to build up enough savings during their working lives to support them in their retirement years – thus reducing the burden on government. An expert committee attached to OASIS has produced a detailed report providing recommendations for enhancing coverage, improving the rate of return and bringing about improvements in customer service in the publicly supported Provident Fund, the Employees' Provident fund, and the annuity plans of the LIC, UTI and other companies (GoI 2002e). The recommendations focus on improving existing provisions and propose expanded pension coverage for excluded workers who are capable of saving even modest amounts and converting these savings into income for old age. It is envisaged that this new pension system would incorporate an individual retirement account (IRA) through which individuals would start saving early in their careers, with a minimum INR 100(US$2) per contribution and INR500 (US$10) as the total accumulation each year. It is proposed that the plan work through myriad locations all over India, such as in post offices, bank branches and the like (GoI 2002e). In light of these recommendations, the government of India had recently launched a scheme under the OASIS project that could enable the aged to generate an earning stream by saving even very small amounts.

Revision of existing schemes

In the wake of the national policy, the MSJE has revised many of the existing schemes, including the following:

- The enhancement of grants from INR 5.00 Lakhs (US$10,244) to INR 30.00 Lakhs (US$61,463) to panchayat institutions for the construction of old-age homes and multiservice centres for older persons
- An integrated program of assistance to voluntary organizations to empower and improve the quality of life of older persons through reinforcing and

strengthening the capabilities and commitment of the family; fostering amiable multigenerational relationships; generating greater public awareness of issues pertaining to the older population; popularising the concept of lifelong preparation for old age; facilitating productive aging; promoting health care; meeting the housing and income security needs of elder persons; providing care to destitute older persons and strengthening capabilities to deal with issues pertaining to older persons at the local or other institutional level

• Financial assistance of 90 per cent of project costs for establishing and maintaining old-age homes, day care centres, mobile medicine units, and non-institutional services

Other important central government initiatives already implemented, pertaining to pension schemes other than NOAP, include the enhancement of survivors' pensions and the incorporation of a 'dearness' allowance (an adjustment for inflation) and gratuity (a second-tier lump sum retirement benefit over and above a first-tier lump sum benefit provided by a Provident Fund). These benefit older persons by enhancing payments received to either 50 per cent (individual pension) or 30 per cent (survivors' pension) of the basic pay last drawn by the retired employee.

Steps already taken for implementation of NPOP

So far MSJE has taken a number of steps for implementation of NPOP, which include the following:

i   Reconstituting the NCOP in the year 2005 under the chairmanship of the Minister for Social Justice and Empowerment to advise and aid the government on policies and programmes for older persons and also to provide feedback to the government on the implementation of the National Policy on Older Persons as well as on specific programme initiatives for older persons. The NCOP is the highest-level body to advise and coordinate with the government in formulating and implementing policy and programmes for the welfare of the aged. Presently, it has thirty-seven members. It has emphasized certain areas of concern:

   a   Establishing a uniform age of 60 and older for extending facilities/ benefits to senior citizens
   b   Helping to assure financial security among the elderly population by (1) proposing tax benefits and higher interest rates for senior citizens; (2) promoting long-term savings in both rural and urban areas; (3) increasing coverage and revising old-age pension schemes for the destitute elderly and (4) Facilitating prompt settlements of pension, provident fund, gratuity and other retirement benefits
   c   Meeting the health care and nutritional needs of elderly populations by (1) strengthening the primary health care system, (2) providing training and orientation to medical and paramedical personnel in the health care of the elderly, (3) promoting the concept of healthy aging, (4) helping

societies produce and distribute material on geriatric care and (5) providing separate queues and reservation of beds for elderly patients

d   Providing food security and shelter by (1) increasing coverage under the Antyodaya scheme, with emphasis on provisions for the benefit of older persons, especially the destitute and marginalized sections; (2) earmarking 10 per cent of houses/house sites for older persons and (3) creating barrier-free environment for the disabled and elderly persons

e   Meeting the education, training and information needs of older persons

f   Identifying the most vulnerable among the older population and working for their welfare

g   Realising the crucial role the media play in highlighting the situation of older persons and emphasising their continued importance in society

h   Protecting the lives and property of elderly citizens

ii   Setting up an Inter-Ministerial Committee headed by the secretary of Social Justice and Empowerment and composed of twenty-two ministries or departments and a representative of state governments and UT administrations. It is meant for ensuring speedy implementation of the decisions of the National Council for Older Persons and also reviewing the progress of actual implementation by the appropriate ministries and departments. This committee essentially coordinates the combined effort by all the ministries and departments to implement the National Policy on Older Persons.

The role of the private sector

Some private insurance schemes incorporating a medical component have been initiated in the last few years specifically targeting older persons. These include Jeevan Dhara, Jeevan Akshay, Jeevan Samiksha, Beema Nivesh, Senior Citizen Unit Plan, Medi-Claim, Group Medical Insurance Scheme and Jan Arogaya. These schemes cater to different segments of the older population and can be initiated early in an individual's work life with a very low premium, ranging from INR 100 (US$2) or a small lump sum payment of INR 10,000 (US$205). Most of these schemes are eligible for tax concessions and run by either the LIC of India or New India Assurance and its subsidiaries.

All of these schemes have maximum age limits. For instance, Medi-Claim has an age limit of 80 years, and the Jan Arogya scheme uses 70 as the limit. Thus, insurance may not be available when it is most needed. In addition, the many tests required at age 50 or 60 in order to obtain, for example, a Medi-Claim policy serve as a disincentive to apply. Older persons also lack sufficient access and mobility to execute the demands of insurance companies (e.g. increasing premiums, limited selection of hospitals), even if the companies were inclined to offer coverage. Recently, however, a high-level panel on health insurance setup by Insurance Regulatory and Development Authority (IRDA) has made a number of recommendations, including health insurance access to all senior citizens, guaranteed renewal of insurance without any upper-age limit, portability of health insurance plans and progressivity in income tax concessions meant for health insurance (*The Economic Times* 2007). If implemented these recommendations might alleviate some of the aforementioned flaws of the health insurance system as it pertains to older citizens.

Notes

1 Starting with the first plan, it was thought that it would take a long time to implement all the recommendations of the Bhore Committee (or the Health Survey and Development Committee), which was appointed by the Government of India in October 1943 to make (a) a broad survey of the present position in regard to health conditions and health organization in British India, and (b) recommendations for future developments. Therefore, national vertical programmes were started, which later became the centre of focus. These were run and monitored by the central government. These included a malaria control programme and programmes for the control of tuberculosis, filariasis, leprosy and venereal diseases. Health personnel were to take part in vertical programmes. However, by introducing verticality, the first plan failed to create an integrated system. One of the main bottlenecks to the effective delivery of comprehensive healthcare services at the community level has been the multiplicity of vertical national health programmes. While all these programmes have depended upon the lowly multipurpose health worker (officially called the Auxiliary Nurse Midwife [ANM]) for their implementation, the programmes' different planning, monitoring and supervisory systems bring about a very uneven pattern of service delivery.

2 The current status with regard to these goals is presented in Appendix Table 1.1.

3 For details of achievements as provided by NHP (GoI 2002b), see Appendix Table 1.1.

4 As indicated in the 52nd round of NSS (National Sample Survey), among the poor (in 1995–96), 61 per cent used public facilities compared to 33 per cent among the rich. In addition, overall utilization of government hospitals by the upper quintiles accounted for a higher share in total health care; utilization by the rural poor declined between 1986–87 and 1995–96.

5 The Eighth Five-Year Plan also identified several points of emphasis, including management of water as a commodity, delivery of water services based on principles of effective demand and standards of service corresponding to the level that users are willing to maintain.

6 Water supply and sanitation is a state responsibility under the constitution of India, and following the seventy-third and seventh-fourth constitutional amendments, the states may give the responsibility and powers to the Panchayati Raj institutions (PRIs) and urban local bodies (ULBs).

7 These include (a) organization of reforms, promoting an integrated approach that includes changes in procedures, attitudes and behaviour as well as the full participation of women at all levels; (b) community management of services, backed by measures to strengthen local institutions in implementing and sustaining water and sanitation programmes; and (c) sound financial practices, achieved by better management of existing assets and extensive use of appropriate technologies. The Tenth Plan envisages 100 per cent coverage of rural and urban population with safe drinking water as per the stipulated norms and standards (40 litres per capita per day (lpcd) of safe drinking water within a walking distance of 1.6 km or elevation difference of 100 m in hilly areas, to be relaxed as per field conditions; at least one hand pump/spot source for every 250 persons).

8 For instance, in the Tenth Plan, the objectives of universal coverage, adequacy in terms of minimum per capita consumption norms, regularity of supply, avoidance of excessive withdrawal leading to depletion and inaccessibility of water sources and the need to conserve and make conjunctive use of water resources are highlighted. The plan recognizes that unsatisfactory service standards have led to low tariff structures, which in

turn result in poor resource positions, maintenance and service – a vicious circle – and that while surveys show consumer willingness to pay higher tariffs, such increases in tariff structures would have to be accompanied by substantial improvements in service quality. The plan also recognizes that given that vicious circle, the main problem in the financing of UWSS is the (un)sustainability of the current model, which is heavily dependent on state governments' willingness to provide guarantees for institutional finance and meeting the state share of project costs.

9   Other government agencies involved either directly or indirectly with water supply and sanitation in India include the Ministry of Agriculture (MoA), which is involved in planning, formulating, monitoring and reviewing various watersheds based developmental project activities. At the national level, the RGNDWM (Rajiv Gandhi National Drinking Water Mission, under the Department of Drinking Water Supply, MoRD) formulates guiding policy, sets standards, and provides funds and technical assistance to the states for rural water supply and sanitation (RWSS). It allocates funds under the centrally sponsored Accelerated Rural Water Supply Programme (ARWSP) and supervises the Restructured Centrally Sponsored Rural Sanitation Programme (RCRSP). The RGNDWM has also a National Human Resource Development Programme (NHRDP, launched in 1994), which aims at training at a grass-roots level. The Human Resource Development (HRD) programme also aims at empowering PRIs/local bodies to take up operation and maintenance activities related to rural water supply systems. It also aims at capacity building of local communities by giving requisite training to mechanics, health motivators, masons and the like, especially women, to operate and maintain hand pumps and other components of water supply systems as well as to generate demand for adequate sanitation facilities. Under the NHRDP, several states have set up state-level HRD cells for planning, designing, implementing, monitoring and evaluating an appropriate and need-based HRD programme in villages through district-level trainers who in turn may be trained at selected institutions, forming the Indian Training Network (ITN). The MoUD is the nodal ministry for policy formulation and guidance for the UWSS sector. The ministry's responsibilities include broad policy formulation, institutional and legal frameworks, setting standards and norms, monitoring, promotion of new strategies, coordination and support to state programmes through institutional expertise and finance. The ministry is also responsible for managing international sources of finance. The Central Public Health and Environmental Engineering Organization (CPHEEO), created in 1953, is the technical wing of the MoUD, which advises the ministry on all technical matters and collaborates with the state agencies in water supply and sanitation activities. The CPHEEO plays a critical role in agreeing on (giving technical sanction to) externally funded and special programmes and those parts funded by the Life Insurance Corporation of India (LIC) and also plays a central role in setting design standards and norms for urban water supply and sanitation. The ministry also supports the states by sponsoring research relevant to the sector, largely through the National Environmental Engineering Research Institute (NEERI) in Nagpur, Maharashtra. Areas of research include compost plants, urban water treatment plant evaluations, urban water supply tariffs, water distribution system performance evaluation, low-cost methods of flocculation, optimization of water treatment, drinking water in urban slums and leak detection equipment.

10   The AUWSP is administered through the CPHEEO at the Centre. Another major area of central government assistance to the states is in human resources development. Concern with human resources development led to the Public Health Engineering (PHE) Training Programme, starting in 1956. The programme trains 108 in-service engineers every year through eleven postgraduate courses in engineering. By 1996, a total of 1,950 had completed this training. In addition, the CPHEEO arranges short-term courses. The ministry has also jointly sponsored a management programme for senior public health officials with DFID (Department for International Development) funding for the past 25 years. In addition to the countrywide HRD programmes, the Ministry

is also supporting the establishment of HRD and training cells for the water sector in each state with a one-third grant for capital costs where proposals are approved.

11 In some states, the organizational matrix is complicated. For example in Maharashtra, the Groundwater Survey and Development Agency is responsible for hand pump programmes, the Maharashtra Water Supply and Sanitation Board is responsible for piped water supply, the district is responsible for operating and maintaining all drinking water installations and the Irrigation Department is responsible for drinking water sources downstream of command areas. Despite the apparent organizational complexity, the national trend is to decentralize capital investment responsibilities to Zilla Parishad engineering departments at district and block levels, and operations and maintenance activities to district and, in many cases, gram panchayat levels. Andhra Pradesh is the only state in which water supply and sanitation is the exclusive responsibility of the Panchayat Raj engineering department. At the local levels, gram panchayats are the lowest tier in the local administrative framework and may be responsible for one or more villages or habitations. The block is the intermediate tier in the local administration framework, serving, in the vast majority of states, a population ranging between 100,000 and 150,000. The district is the top tier of local government. Hygiene education is largely delivered via the education departments and the school sanitation programme, and via RGNDWM's programmes on IEC (Information, Education and Communication), especially in the TSC (Total Sanitation Campaign) areas.

12 These include the capacity to (a) reach the rural poor and remote areas, (b) promote local participation, (c) operate at low costs and (d) adapt and be innovative when needed. The initial involvement of NGOs in the sector came in the 1960s with the famines in Bihar (1964) and Maharashtra (1969). In this early period, NGOs functioned as drilling contractors to state governments and donor-financed programmes. The efforts of these NGOs convinced the donor community and the government to invest in hand pump programmes for drinking water, especially in the chronically drought-prone areas of the country. More recently, NGOs have operated successfully within donor-assisted projects where the institutional context is conducive, such as the World Bank–funded project in Karnataka and the World Bank–assisted Uttar Pradesh RWSS (Rural Water Supply and Sanitation) project. In these projects, NGOs have been used mostly as an intermediary between the community and the water agency, facilitating project activities related to community mobilization, cost sharing, health education and other nontechnical activities.

13 All areas in a town or city designated as a 'slum' by the state, union territories administration or local government under any act including a 'slum act' are considered notified slums.

14 Sulabh International Social Service Organization 2007, p. 96.

15 The constitution of India is one of the bulkiest constitutions in the world, consisting of 444 articles divided into 26 parts and 12 schedules. The schedules provide a detailed list of subjects that are, in turn, divided into three lists: a union (federal) list, a state list and a concurrent list (including subjects that can be legislated by both the national government and the states). Finally, the constitution includes directive principles of state policy, which the national government must consider when formulating policy.

16 In fact, in 1997–98 EPF distributed an average final payment of less than Rs. 25,000 per member and only Rs. 17,000 per member for premature withdrawal.

2 Policy issues in financing

Sources and options for financing

Policy issues and initiatives

In the recent past, like many other developing countries, India chose to adopt the path of structural adjustment in the early 1990s (Cornia, Jolly and Stewart 1988). The process implied a liberalization of the Indian economy and it simultaneously aimed at reducing the budgetary deficit. Consequently the governmental expenditure on the social sector had to be curtailed (Prabhu 1996). The impact of these measures is also being felt in the health care sector.

Although there are three tiers of government, namely central, states and local, which contribute to overall public sector spending on health care, the primary responsibility for health care in the Indian constitution rests with the states. In general, a major chunk of public expenditure (almost 90%) in the health care sector in the country comes through the states' budgets. In this regard, however, the states maintain a certain degree of financial dependence on the centre. First, through central funding the states run family planning programmes and centrally sponsored schemes such as national disease control programmes including leprosy, malaria, tuberculosis, immunization and nutrition schemes and the components of primary healthcare, rural water supply and sanitation which fall under the minimum needs programme of the centre. The funding from the central government to the states comes either as cent per cent grants or partly through matching grants. In the latter instance, the states have to contribute through a matching contribution from their budgets. Second, the central government bears the full cost of medical research and education in the centrally funded institutions.

In the period before liberalization, 1974–82, the grants to the states from the central government for the health sector made up 19.9 per cent of the states' health expenditure. However, following liberalization, this component of central grants fell to 5.8 per cent (in 1982–89) and further to 3.3 per cent (in 1992–93; Duggal, Nandraj & Vadair 1995a, 1995b; National Institute of Public Finance and Policy [NIPFP] 1993; Tulasidhar 1993). This decline was most noticeable in the case of specific-purpose central grants for public health and disease-control programs.[1] The central component for public health dropped from 27.92 per cent (in 1984–85) to 17.7 per cent (in 1992–93). Over the same period the central component for disease-control programs declined from 41.47 per cent to 18.50 per cent. Even the other component of health expenditure, family welfare, faced a decline in central grants, from 99 per cent to 88.59 per cent over the same duration.

This falling share of central grants had a more pronounced impact on the poorer states,[2] which found it more difficult to raise local resources. As depicted in Figure 2.1, this trend in decline in grants from the central government through the Ministry of Health and Family Welfare continued from 1991 to 2004 and has led to a continuous decline in overall public capital expenditure in India's health sector.

The likelihood of increased state expenditure on the health care sector is further limited in future with the continued pace of reforms. As a result a number of notable health care trends are appearing in the private sector. These private initiatives include an increasing investment by nonresident Indians (NRIs) in the hospital industry, a spurt in corporatization in the states of NRIs' original domicile and increasing participation by multinationals keen to explore the health insurance market in India. Some of these developments in policy and market forces have begun recently or have been reinforced in the wake of structural adjustment. Likely with the aim of mobilizing resources based on recent private initiatives, some of the states have been trying to shift the responsibility to the private sector through various policy measures. These include, for instance, strategies to attract private-sector participation and management in primary health care centres, privatization or semi-privatization of public health facilities such as nonclinical facilities in public hospitals, innovative ways to finance public health facilities through nonbudgetary measures, and tax incentives by the state governments to

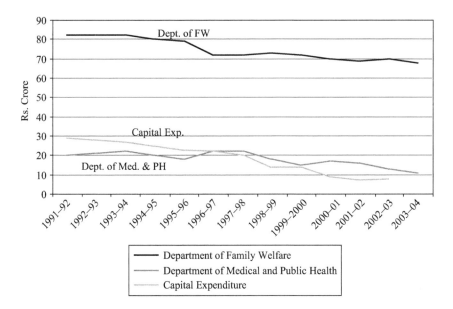

Figure 2.1 Trends in grants-in-aid allocation by Ministry of Health and Family Welfare to states and declining capital expenditure

encourage private-sector investment in the health sector. Bearing in mind, however, the vital importance of such initiatives in the private sector and the government's responses in shaping the future health care in India, our objective in this chapter is to examine in detail both of these aspects and their implications for the Indian health care sector. This chapter is based on published information available from governmental and other agencies. The former of these categories includes budgetary documents, publications of the Ministry of Health, and studies carried out for governmental agencies. The latter includes various publications of independent agencies working in the area of health.

This chapter is divided into five sections. The next section explores various options for financing health care and their relative merits and demerits in light of empirical studies. Recent market force developments that have had a direct bearing on the health care sector in the country have been elaborated in third section. This is followed by the policy measures that various state governments have recently initiated or reinforced. The final section brings forth the policy options and welfare implications emerging from our analysis.

Sources and options for financing

Four approaches could augment the resource base of the health care sector: (i) adopting the cost recovery system at the secondary- and tertiary-level health institutions (World Bank 1993, 1995); (ii) adopting other innovative financing mechanisms including specific taxes, cesses, local levies and community-level endowment funds supplementing public funding and provision of public health services; (iii) initiating suitable health insurance coverage with an appropriate public-private mix and (iv) adopting another mode of health care delivery wherein the government encourages private-sector participation by taking up the role of public purchaser of private services rather than remaining a provider per se. The suitability of each of these strategies in the Indian context is, however, an empirical question. There is only fragmentary evidence in the Indian context relative to these health care financing issues. It is thus both interesting and necessary to explore the various issues pertaining to the feasibility and efficacy of various resource mobilization measures in the health care sector by analysing the experience of various countries which either have adopted structural adjustment policies or have otherwise reformed their health care sectors.

Keeping in view the significance of learning from the innovative nature of such developments and the possibility of applying these ideas to the Indian situation, we carry out a detailed review of relevant experiences in health services financing in developing as well as developed countries. We will bear in mind the interrelationship between finance and other supply aspects of health care services, namely the planning, organization, availability and delivery of health care services. Related demand-side questions of access, utilization and quality of care are also evaluated. These issues lead us to ethical questions: should health be provided to all by the government, or should it be considered a commodity best left to market forces?

We first discuss user fees, different insurance mechanisms and health financing reforms, especially those pertaining to decentralization and privatization. This is followed by a synthesis of the relative merits and demerits of different health financing innovations. Keeping in view the relevance of different financing mechanisms to health services availability, efficiency in production and consumption of health services and the applicability in the Indian context, we explore policy implications.

User fees

In earlier World Bank studies of user fees, Vogel (1988a) studied Botswana, Burkina Faso, Brunei, Cote d'Ivoire, Malawi, Mozambique, Zimbabwe, Ethiopia, Ghana, Kenya, Lesotho and Rwanda. Recent studies in the African subcontinent have covered some new aspects of user fees in Burundi, Cameroon, Egypt, Guinea, Kenya, Nigeria, Uganda and Zambia[3] (see Appendix 2.1).

User charges are generally advocated to fund recurrent costs, and they remain the most controversial funding method. The possibility of their implementation in the public sector was put on the policy agenda following the World Bank's policy document *Financing Health Services in Developing Countries: An Agenda for Reform* in 1987. The idea got a further thrust from the Bomako Initiatives promoted by UNICEF and endorsed by WHO and African leaders in the same year. The economic rationale behind the imposition of user fees emphasizes that (i) payments for services will discourage frivolous use of health facilities, (ii) by making payments consumers will become conscious of quality and will demand it and (iii) the greater availability of funds raised through user fees at the point of service will increase both the availability and quality of services (Griffin 1987). However, in practice the positive benefits envisaged through user charges did not materialize or were overshadowed by other, negative unintended outcomes. The socially regressive impact of user fees in particular has been prominently highlighted in the experience of most developing countries.

The exhaustive reviews by Griffin (1987) and Creese (1991) summarize the experiences that many Asian and African countries have had with user fees. It has been found that owing to exemptions for the indigent and the poor, user fees cannot recover the entire recurrent costs. Cost recovery in terms of gross yield varies between 5 per cent and 15 per cent in African countries. In terms of the total health ministry budget, for instance, the collections from user fees may be as low as 3 per cent (Quick et al. 1993).

Studies in different countries for the most part indicate a dampening impact of user fees on the utilization of health services. For example, in Zaïre it was observed that a price increase in health services overall led to a fall in utilization rate from 37 per cent to 31 per cent (De Bethune, Alfani and Lahaye 1989). The decline in prenatal contacts was around 11 per cent. Generally it is the poor who tend to respond negatively to price increases, thereby affecting equity. A study contrasting rural and urban responses in Ghana found that an increase in the price of health care in rural areas led to a decline that sustained even after 2 years.

By contrast, in urban areas, the attendance over this period sustained. Moreover, there was a diversion of rural demand to unlicensed sellers of drugs (Waddington and Enyimayew 1989, 1990). However, in Cameroon user charges did not lead to reduction in demand (Litvack and Bodart 1993). In a more recent study it was found that in Kenya the introduction of the fee in a phased manner also led to a fall in outpatient (OPD) visits from 14,000 to 10,000 per month (Mwabu and Wang'ombe 1995). The study results indicate higher sensitivity to the costs of diagnostic services relative to registration fees.

Further, the vulnerability resulting from user fees has focused on certain age groups and types of diseases. For instance, in Lesotho, the impact of an increase in fees was greatest on the 0–5 years age group (Bennett 1989). Even in Lesotho (Byrne and Gertler 1990), it was observed that children in general and adults with cardiovascular and genito-urinary conditions were at greater risk of reduced access to health care due to increases in fees (Byrne and Gertler 1990). Likewise, in Swaziland, a decline in the use of government services for sexually transmitted diseases and respiratory diseases was suspected (Yoder 1989). In Bangladesh, it seemed to deter patients with communicable diseases (Creese 1991). Following reforms in the 1980s, in China the emphasis on user fees to obtain self-sufficiency in health service finance has also been associated with both a regressive impact on utilization and wasteful investment on inappropriate high-tech equipment (Liu, Hsiao, Li, Liu, and Ren 1995).

The study by McPake, Hanson and Mills (1993) found that in most countries examined the incentives created by the pricing structure of these initiatives and the lack of appropriate exemption mechanisms to protect vulnerable groups were the problem areas. The travel and other costs pertaining to the use of higher-level facilities led to problems with patients being unable to afford the services under Bomako initiatives. As Creese (1991: 318) opines, 'Fees in the health sector are thus not an instrument of health policy, but a means of fiscal policy, with the health ministry being a tax collecting agency.'

However, efforts have been made to overcome some of the problems associated with user fees. For instance, in another study in Kenya by Collins, Quick, Musau, Kraushaar and Hussein (1996), it was indicated that the implementation of user fees in phases according to the level of facility (national, provincial, district and subdistrict hospitals and health centres) led to better acceptance by both providers and patients. The phased implementation backed by the development of better management systems helped to reduce the decline in demand, and revenue collections improved. The improved management system included steps such as the preparation of cost-sharing operation manuals, and staff training for procedures pertaining to patients' claims, cash collections, waivers, exemptions, accounting and reporting. Likewise, anomalies in exemptions such as free services to civil servants were replaced by new medical allowances to the civil servants. The phased implementation, downward from the apex referral hospital, as well as the retention incentive created by appropriate management training helped to improve collections. However, the results of the management training input did not indicate a consistent improvement in quality of services (Collins et al. 1996).

Cost increases to patients via user charges can be partly mitigated by supply-side cost sharing, i.e. cost control and containment measures. Ellis and McGuire (1993) and Hodgkin and McGuire (1994) pointed out that to pay providers in advance on the basis of the average cost of treating groups of diagnostically related illnesses would make providers more cost conscious, and therefore cost reduction or containment will take place.

Nonetheless, the experience of user fees has been so far found to be unsatisfactory with respect to either the quality or the accessibility of services (Creese 1991). Further, the literature remains obscure on the question of the impacts of different payment systems such as flat fees, differentiated fees, fees per episode or per item of service and prepayment versus payment at times of use (Creese 1991). The limitations of user fees for financing supervision, logistical support, referral linkages and evaluation have been also recognized (Abel-Smith and Dua 1988), and thus the implementation of user fees is best considered an imperfect and partial solution to the problem of increasing health service resources (Stinson 1984).

Later studies have analyzed the policy moves of removing user charges mainly after the year 2000. For instance, Prinja, Aggarwal, Kumar and Kanavos (2012) assessed the effect of user charges on inpatient hospitalizations rate and equity in Haryana State. The inpatient department (IPD) statistics of the public-sector facilities in Yamuna Nagar district where user charges had been introduced were analyzed and compared with Rohtak district, which did not have user charges between 2000 and 2006. The National Sample Survey data of Haryana for 2004–05 were analyzed to compare utilization of public-sector facilities for hospitalization, cost of hospitalization, and prevalence of catastrophic out-of-pocket (OOP) expenditure by income quintiles in three districts which had user charges and seventeen districts of Haryana which did not levy user charges. It was found that during 2000 and 2006, hospital admissions declined by 23.8 per cent in Yamuna Nagar district, where user charges had been introduced, compared to an almost static hospitalization rate in Rohtak district, which did not have user charges ($P = 0.01$). Public-sector hospital utilization for inpatient services had a pro-rich (concentration index 0.144) distribution in the three districts with user charges and pro-poor (concentration index –0.047) in the seventeen districts without user charges. Significantly higher prevalence of catastrophic health expenditure was observed in public-sector institutions with user charges (48%) compared to those without user charges (35.4%; $P = 0.001$). The findings showed that user charges had a negative infiuence on hospitalizations in Haryana, especially among the poor, and public policies for revenue generation should avoid user charges.

The study by James et al. (2006) analyzes the experience of many low- and middle-income countries and provides some reflections on the recent debate about user fees in the health sector and relates the debate to the wider issue of access to adequate healthcare. It is argued that, from the wealth of evidence on user fees and other health system reforms, a broad consensus is emerging. First, user fees are an important barrier to accessing health services, especially for poor people. They also negatively impact adherence to long-term expensive treatments.

However, this is offset to some extent by potentially positive impacts on quality. Second, user fees are not the only barrier that the poor face. As well as other cost barriers, a number of quality, information and cultural barriers must also be overcome before the poor can access adequate health services. Third, initial evidence on fee abolition in Uganda suggests that this policy has improved access to outpatient services for the poor. For this to be sustainable and effective in reaching the poor, fee removal needs to be part of a broader package of reforms that includes increased budgets to offset lost fee revenue (as was the case in Uganda). Fourth, implementation matters: if fees are to be abolished, this policy needs clear communication with a broad stakeholder buy-in, careful monitoring to ensure that official fees are not replaced by informal fees, and appropriate management of the alternative financing mechanisms that are replacing user fees. Fifth, context is crucial. For instance, immediate fee removal in Cambodia would be inappropriate given that fees replaced irregular and often high informal fees. In this context, equity funds and eventual expansion of health insurance are perhaps more viable policy options. Conversely, in countries where user fees have had significant adverse effects on access and generated only limited benefits, fee abolition is probably a more attractive policy option. Removing user fees has the potential to improve access to health services, especially for the poor, but it is not appropriate in all contexts. Analysis should move on from broad evaluations of user fees towards exploring how best to dismantle the multiple barriers to access in specific contexts.

A study by Lagarde and Palmer (2008) tried to assess the effects of user charges on the uptake of health services in low- and middle-income countries, focusing on sixteen studies with experimental or quasi-experimental study designs, including cluster randomized controlled trials (C-RCT), controlled 'before and after' (CBA) studies and interrupted time series (ITS) studies. Papers were assessed in which the effect of the intervention was measured in terms of changes in service utilization (including equity outcomes), household expenditure or health outcomes. Only studies reporting effects on health service utilization, sometimes across socio-economic groups, were identified. Removing or reducing user fees was found to increase the utilization of curative services and perhaps preventive services as well but may have negatively impacted service quality. Introducing or increasing fees reduced the utilization of some curative services, although quality improvements may have helped maintain utilization in some cases. When fees were either introduced or removed, the impact was immediate and abrupt. Studies did not adequately show whether such an increase or reduction in utilization was sustained over the longer term. In addition, most of the studies were given low-quality ratings based on criteria adapted from those of the Cochrane Collaboration's Effective Practice and Organization of Care group. Thus the authors concluded that there is a need for more high-quality research examining the effects of changes in user fees for health services in low- and middle-income countries.

A study by Nanda (2002) highlights the implications of user fees for women's utilization of health care services by focusing on selected studies in Africa. It suggests that lack of access to resources and inequitable decision-making power constrains poor women to face OOP costs such as user fees to make the cost of care out of reach. Even though many poor women may be exempt from fees, there is little incentive for providers to apply exemptions, as they too are constrained by restrictive economic and health service conditions. If user fees and other OOP costs are to be retained in resource-poor settings, there is a need to demonstrate how they can be successfully and equitably implemented. The lack of hard evidence on the impact of user fees on women's health outcomes and reproductive health service utilization points to the urgent need to examine how women cope with health care costs and what trade-offs they make in order to pay for health care. Such studies need to collect gender-disaggregated data in relation to women's health service utilization and in relation to the range of reproductive health services, taking into account OOP fees charged by not only public health providers but also by private and traditional providers.

A study by the Research Group published by the Japan International Cooperation Agency (2006) after the examination of 2 years of experience of user fees policy and fee exemption measures in Madagascar suggests that a variety of problematic issues had arisen at the policy implementation level, indicating that further input is needed in the process to make this implementation more robust. It suggested training for policy implementers, such as health administrators, health service providers and community participants, to impart the necessary skills to implement the policy effectively; information on and communication about the policy so people would be aware of and better understand the policy objectives and contents; and conducting monitoring and evaluation of the policy to assess policy performance and effectiveness.

A study by the International Rescue Committee (IRC 2012) suggests that eliminating fees only for vulnerable users will be insufficient to improve the health of the population overall. Rather, to be effective, fee elimination should be an important policy in a package of broad health system reforms, which also includes such steps as improving the quality of health services, increasing resources (including the drug supply), adequately and consistently paying salaries for health personnel, expanding the network of health facilities and personnel available to respond to the sick and increasing state funding dedicated to health. The IRC opined that an effective way to reach these goals is to remove cost as a barrier to care for pregnant women and children less than 5 years old. In the late 1980s, careful and evidence-based health policy was not pursued when widespread application of cost-recovery schemes were applied, and the resulting harmful effects are now evident. As health policy, user fees amount to a consumption tax on health care services. In the context of the Democratic Republic of Congo (DRC), this is a regressive burden shouldered by the poorest citizens when they are the most vulnerable. The IRC believes the elimination of user fees to be the appropriate strategy for the DRC if the country is to take steps towards the widespread utilization of health services and the reduction of preventable illness and death in the population.

Uneke et al. (2008) conducted a quantitative and qualitative survey in various parts of eastern Nigeria to assess the opinion of the Nigerian general public on the institution or abolition of user fees in health services. Of the 910 study participants, 520 (57.1%) supported the institution of user fees while 390 (42.9%) supported their abolition. The majority of study participants would prefer paying user fees if they were affordable and would guarantee efficient and quality service. The greater percentage of those advocating for abolition of user fees were nonliterate persons, the unemployed and the aged. If user fees are to be instituted, a mechanism is needed that will provide some concessions such as appropriate systems of waivers and exemptions to these categories of individuals so that no one is denied access to basic health care.

A multicountry review by Meessen et al. (2009, 2011) for the United Nations Children's Fund (UNICEF) observed that momentum is currently building up at national and international levels with respect to user fee removal. African political leaders have shown their willingness to take strong action to remove financial barriers for vulnerable groups, especially pregnant women and children. They are ready to do so by using national resources. Aid mechanisms – and the Highly Indebted Poor Countries Initiative in particular – seem to be supportive of such initiatives. Models adopted by governments vary. The different contexts and traditions in Francophone and Anglophone Africa lead to different orientations and strategies. One of the key issues deserving greater attention in the future, at both the policy and scientific levels, is the remuneration model of health care providers (input- versus output-based arrangements). Another important finding is that the lack of consultation, coupled sometimes with the unexpected character of the decisions political authorities make, resulted in insufficient preparation of several user fee removal reforms, resulting in weaknesses in the design, formulation and implementation of the reform. The most worrisome omissions or mistakes observed are a lack of attention to other bottlenecks in supply and demand; too basic initial estimations of the impact of the reform on the utilization by the population and its consequences in terms of extra burdens on frontline health staff and on the public budget; insufficient commitment, allocation or disbursement of resources to finance the increase in utilization; poor understanding of incentive issues; low implication of frontline health workers in the design; poor communication towards frontline health workers at the launch of the reform and insufficient effort in monitoring, enforcement and evaluation. These weaknesses were spread unevenly across countries, which suggests that it might already be possible to improve reform practice in low-income countries by organizing more exchanges at the regional level. In most countries, it was observed that program managers were doing their utmost to keep the system afloat while taking action to fine-tune the reform. A primary constraint for successful reform could be the limited availability of technical expertise in health care financing in most countries. International actors have usually not come to the rescue; especially during the formulation and implementation stages of the reform their support was missed. This could be the consequence of a tradition of focusing on one's own aid framework and project. International actors campaigning for user fee removal should also consider shifting their focus from agenda setting to technical support. Possible strategies are provision of technical expertise, pilot experiments, support to regional networks, better coordination between agencies, technical guidelines and translation of material available only in English.

The study by Hardeman et al. (2004) analyzes a scheme in Cambodia called the Health Equity Fund that identifies the poor and pays the user charges on their behalf. It presents the experience of one such fund, managed by a local NGO, in Sotnikum, Cambodia and investigates its effects on the constraints to equitable health services. In the initial 2 years of operation, the study found that the health equity fund supported 16 per cent of hospitalized patients. The four major constraints to access that were identified included financial, geographical, informational and intra-household. The results of the study show that the health equity fund effectively improves financial access for the poor but that the poor continue to face many constraints to timely access. The study also found that the health equity fund as set up in Sotnikum was very cost effective, with minimal leakage to the nonpoor. Its being managed by a local NGO seems to constitute a promising channel for donors who want to invest in poverty reduction. However, further research and experimentation are recommended in different contexts and with different set-ups.

Health insurance

The health insurance mechanism provides a way by which risk sharing within society may take place (Akin 1987). Those who do not fall sick but participate in the insurance schemes contribute towards the expenses of health care of other members of the community. Simultaneously, the insurance provides all citizens security that in times of illness their care will be paid for by a third party. The experience of risk sharing in developing countries has been very limited. Generally large-scale health insurance schemes do not exist there in either public or private sectors. According to one survey by the World Bank, the population covered by insurance in 1985–86, except for China and Korea, varied between 0.3 per cent in Papua New Guinea and 34.8 per cent in the Philippines. In China and Korea, the population covered remained 59.3 per cent and 56.5 per cent respectively (Griffin 1992). In another survey by the World Bank, Vogel (1990a, 1990b) studied twenty-three sub-Saharan African countries. Among these, only twelve had formal insurance. The percentage of the total population insured ranged from 11.4 per cent (in Kenya) to merely .001 per cent (in Ethiopia). Besides these, the other five countries which had insurance included Burkina Faso, Burundi, Cote d'Ivoire, Mali, Nigeria, Senegal, Sudan, Zambia and Zimbabwe. The share of public insurance in the total recurrent health expenditure in these countries varied between .043 per cent (in Cote d'Ivoire) to 24.1 per cent (in Zambia). In the same group of countries, the corresponding share of private insurance remained in the interval of .02 per cent (in Ethiopia) to 16.51 per cent (in Zimbabwe).

The findings of this survey indicate that in the existing set-up of insurance the main beneficiaries are the relatively small middle classes. Vogel concludes, 'Development of health insurance to date in sub-Saharan Africa has not promoted greater equity in the access to health services by the poor, nor has it permitted greater access' (Vogel 1990a, pp. 22–23). In most of these countries, the lack of deductibles and coinsurance results in inefficiency in consumption of health services. Similarly, on the production side, the system, being based on open-ended, cost-based retrospective payments, had a perverse effect on providers. The latter have no incentive to minimize costs, and therefore medical costs tend to escalate.

However, there are case studies of different types of insurance schemes having relatively low coverage. Prior to the reforms of the 1980s in the Asian subcontinent, the Chinese health care system in fact provided an excellent example of successful insurance schemes in rural areas. Since the 1950s exhaustive health insurance coverage had existed in China for the different tiers of its health care system, namely village, township and county. In the postreform period, however, the coverage has fallen drastically in rural areas. Currently, three types of insurance operate in China. These are known as Gogfei Yiliao, or Publicly Funded Medical Care; Laobao Yiliao, or Labor Insurance Medical Care; and Cooperative Medical Care Scheme (Ho Lok 1995). Among these, Publicly Funded Medical Care is funded from the government budget. It provides coverage for civil servants, workers in public agencies, universities, handicapped military officials above a certain ranking and university students. By the end of 1993 the scheme covered some 29 million people. Labor Insurance Medical Care is financed at the enterprise level from welfare funds of the enterprises. It provides coverage for employees in state and collective enterprises and their immediate family members. By the end of 1993 it covered 144 million people. The Cooperative Medical Care Scheme is practiced in rural areas. Before the reforms, in 1978–79, nearly 80–90 per cent of the rural population was covered. In the post reform era, this coverage declined sharply, and in 1993 only 20 per cent of workers in the agriculture sector were covered.

Before the agricultural reforms in the 1980s, health services in rural China were organized and financed through the cooperative medical system (CMS). By the end of 1983, the collective system of agricultural communes was almost replaced by individual household farming systems whereby each household leased its own land and retained all the earnings. It is noteworthy that China's remarkable achievement in terms of its IMR falling from 200 per 1,000 live births (in 1949) to 47 per 1,000 live births (1973–75) and increased life expectancy from 35 to about 65 years (or in other words its 'first health care revolution' [Ho Lok 1995]) had its roots in the successful CMS. The CMS was characterized by collective financing, prepayment and a three-tier organization of health services (Hsiao 1984; Halstead et al. 1985). Under the CMS, village health stations, township health centres and county hospitals provided a closely interrelated referral system. After the collapse of the CMS, each of these became independent institutions.

In India, a good example is provided by the ESIS (Employees State Insurance Scheme) in urban areas meant for industrial workers. This scheme has been in existence since 1952. It covers nearly 25 million people, which is larger than many national systems in Latin America. Yet research showed that ESIS had been incurring losses. These were due to its coverage, which extends beyond health care alone. Being a social security scheme, ESIS provides for wage compensation against sickness and also allows cash payments for partial disability and occasions such as marriages and funerals. In fact, the amount of money sanctioned under the cash benefit component of the ESIS brought about substantial operational inefficiency in the scheme (Indian Institute of Management 1987). Now ESIS is operational without losses. Other employment-based schemes in India include the Central Government Health Scheme (CGHS), the Railways Health Scheme, and schemes for defence employees, ex-servicemen and mining and plantation workers. Overall coverage in all these schemes in the year 2005 was around 4.3 million, 8 million, 6.6 million, 7.5 million and 4 million respectively (Gupta and Trivedi 2005). It is also suggested that some of these schemes, for instance CGHS, are fraught with equity implications since it accounts for nearly 14 per cent of total expenditure of the health department with a miniscule coverage of 0.3 per cent of the working population (Gupta and Trivedi 2005).

Likewise case studies of small-scale insurance schemes operated by NGOs in different parts of India have been documented (Dave 1991). Case studies of insurance card schemes in some Asian as well as African countries also exist. Typically, these card schemes have problems of low coverage, poor quality of services and administrative and financial problems.

In Thailand, for instance, a voluntary health card scheme has been operative since 1983. It has only 5 per cent coverage of the population. People are reluctant to buy insurance cards unless there is some unavoidable expenditure such as expected delivery. The scheme depends heavily on government subsidies, and cardholders complain of getting less attention than do non-cardholders (Piyaratn 1994). In another card scheme in Vietnam running since 1993, the coverage is less than 5 per cent of the population. Problems in the scheme's implementation include high dependence on government subsidies, poor quality of services, doctors asking for bribes and discrimination against cardholders (Abel-Smith 1993). In a card scheme implemented in Burundi and in operation since 1984, coverage is 23 per cent of households. Yet revenue from card sales covers only one third of the drug costs. Many households did not participate due to poverty. Problems such as a 50 per cent higher utilization of health services by cardholders as compared to the general population, cardholders receiving less attention, low quality of services and drugs frequently being out of stock are reported. In Burundi, responses from female respondents also indicated their impressions that the card was good for (i) poor families or families with seasonal income and (ii) women with husbands who drink (Arhin 1994).

In most developed countries, except the UK, Scandinavia and Japan, which started full coverage through their national health services in 1948 (UK) and 1960 respectively (Scandinavia and Japan); the full coverage was started in 1955, 1956, 1956, 1961 and 1964 in Sweden, Iceland, Norway, Denmark and Finland respectively. In other developed countries the full coverage began as recently as the 1970s or 1980s.[4] The experience of these six developed countries indicates that initially there were problems in formulating health insurance to cover the self-employed (e.g. farmers, fishermen and other people with low earnings). The various approaches to overcoming this difficulty included (i) cross-subsidizing the low-income self-employed with other funds; (ii) subsidizing such insurance with public funds (Powell and Anesaki 1990) and (iii) trying to collect some contribution from farmers by land tax according to potential profit (e.g. in Italy), by a health tax on agricultural produce (e.g. in Brazil) or by a contribution as part of the income tax (e.g. in the Netherlands, France and Belgium). A variety of means were adopted to cover the unemployed, the elderly and the disabled. These included, for instance, considering the elderly as dependent on insured persons and having the central or local government agency responsible for contributing funds for those dependent on social assistance.

Likewise, as Hurst (1991) observed, the organizational pattern of insurance funds in the developed countries also had a number of variants which included (i) one insurance fund in which powers are delegated to local areas, which simplifies administration when people change employers or places of residence; (ii) a series of local funds; (iii) a mandatory set of certain defined benefits to be provided by all funds, whether these funds are centralized or decentralized (this is the pattern existing currently in Germany, Japan and South Korea) and (iv) competition between funds for members, with a central body collecting the contributions and distributing them among the chosen insurers according to the risks of their members (this is the current model in the Netherlands). Similarly, health insurance systems can be distinguished in terms of direct and indirect systems. In direct systems, e.g. those in East European countries, salaried professionals have their own hospitals and health centres. In indirect systems, such as those prevailing in Belgium, Canada, France, Japan, Luxembourg and Germany, health insurance funds contract all services, paying private doctors on a fee-for-service basis. However, in countries with national health insurance systems, the services of private profit-making insurers are not used. The central governments in most of these countries play a crucial role in regulating nonprofit insurers (Abel-Smith 1992).

Further, as it prevails in Europe, essentially the third-party payment takes place in one of three forms distinguished as (i) the reimbursement model, (ii) the contract model or (iii) the integrated model (Hurst 1991). In the reimbursement model, there is no direct connection between the insurers and the providers. Consumers pay the premium to the insurers and providers are also paid by the consumers, who in turn get their payment reimbursed. In the contract model, insurers pay the providers directly based on a contract. In the integrated model, insurers pay the providers directly in a vertically integrated organization of providers and financiers. This is done, for instance, by global budgets and salaries. In countries such as the UK, New Zealand and Sweden, a trend towards separation between purchasers and providers is replacing the earlier vertically integrated system. The trend is moving towards integrated health care organizations like health maintenance organizations (HMOs) in the USA. However, in the situation exemplified by the USA, where there are multiple third-party payers, the notion of price competition among providers and third-party payers becomes important. This leads to four basic models involving providers and insurers in different situations of the presence or absence of price competition (Table 2.1).

In all, through a combination of these four basic models, there could be ten different models of health insurance (Table 2.2).

Table 2.1 Four basic models of health care markets with third-party payers (insurers) and providers of care

Third-party payers	Providers of care	
	Price competition	No price competition
Price competition	1	3
No price competition	2	4

Table 2.2 Different models of the relation between the third-party payers (insurers) and the providers of health care

Third-party payers	Providers of care	
	Price competition	No price competition
Price competition	1a Competitive reimbursement model 1b Competitive contract model 1c Competitive integrated model	3a Monopolistic provider reimbursement model 3b Monopolistic contract model
No price competition	2a Competitive reimbursement model 2b Monopsonistic contract model	4a Noncompetitive provider model 4b Bilateral monopolistic contract model 4c Monopolistic integrated model

However, in any model involving competition among insurers, the tendency towards cream skimming has to be avoided. Cream skimming is nonexistent in a monopsonistic compulsory health insurance market. This market also has the advantage of lower transaction costs as compared to a competitive market since providers need to conclude a contract with a single payer only. However, there are certain disadvantages in monopsonistic compulsory health insurance: (i) if it is a private monopsony, it may exercise monopsony power in the medical service market, and it may augment the monopoly rent of a private insurer with market power in the insurance market; and (ii) it may not be able to provide incentives for the third-party purchaser to act as an agent on behalf of the health care consumers. To overcome this problem a system of regulatory incentives and monitoring needs to be developed to ensure that the single third-party purchaser acts in the best public interest.

Currently the UK health care system has been moving away from a monopolistic integrated model (4c) towards a monopsonistic contract model (2b), i.e. replacing a vertically integrated finance and delivery system with a system of contracts between a third-party purchaser and competing providers. The Dutch health care system is poised to adopt a competitive contract model (1b) with compulsory health insurance. At present it is a combination of a bilateral monopolistic contract model (4b; nearly 60% of its population is buying health insurance from a regionally based sickness fund) and a monopolistic provider reimbursement model with competing private health insurers (3a).

The recent amendments in New Zealand have replaced a monopolistic integrated model (4c) with a monopsonistic contract model (2b). In Belgium, there is a move to introduce a competitive contract model (1b; Nonneman and Van Doorslaer 1994). Price competition among sickness funds is also on the agenda in Germany (Schulenburg 1994). Thus, keeping in view the basic objectives of enhancing equity and efficiency, many countries in the Organization for Economic Co-operation and Development (OECD) have adopted different types of reforms. Some forms of insurance reforms have tended to be better in certain respects than others:

i   The countries which relied mainly on the contract model as well as global budgeting did not have an increase in their health expenditure in relation to their GDP. For instance, in Germany and the Netherlands, which adopted this kind of reform, health expenditure (as a proportion of GDP) remained almost the same, although their real per capita GDP rose by almost 14 per cent. Yet the countries which relied mainly on the integrated model had similar outcomes.

ii   Countries such as Belgium and France, which adopted a combination of reimbursement and partial global budgets, had a rise in the share of their health expenditure, but it was lower than the rise in their real per capita income (OECD 1992).

iii   The introduction of market components in the health care systems in these countries might have produced adverse consequences for equity in terms of allocation of internal resources geographically and across patient groups (Scotton 1994).

iv   In the countries with public integrated systems, there has been concern about under-service as well as inflexible and ineffective management systems (OECD 1993).

v   In the reimbursement or contract model, where it is presumed that money follows patients, anxiety about unnecessary care partly led to supplier-induced demand. In such systems, concern is also voiced about excessive regulation. Thus, each of these systems has its own merits and demerits. However, the numerous possible forms and combinations of insurance coverage indicate an evolving state of knowledge and policy in this area. It cannot be said that the right options have been implemented everywhere. Choices about one system or the other is a matter of both political ideology and people's needs. The perceptions about the latter tend to be more dynamic in nature. However, as Abel-Smith (1992, pp. 225–226) put it, 'There is a very strong case for trying out new models in one local area before applying them nationally. The transition may well take several years and cannot be hurried.'

Privatization and decentralization

Experience has revealed that besides direct financing mechanisms, other resource mobilization measures in the health care sector are important as well, in particular privatization and decentralization. The distinction between privatization and decentralization is central in a discussion of these experiences. The former aims at passing the provision of certain services from the government to the private sector. The latter implies the transfer of responsibility for planning, management and resource generation and allocation from the central government and its agencies to other levels of government or public authorities (Rondinelli 1981).

Many of the recent reforms in developed countries, for instance in the UK, are geared towards privatization. Policy changes in favour of privatization cater to regulated markets in which greater reliance is placed on market mechanisms, with government regulation imposed only to prevent market failure. Here the health care market may be opened to private providers, and the price mechanism is a critical tool for balancing supply and demand.

Generally it is presumed that managed markets, especially in the hospital sector, will increase supply-side efficiency by increasing competition among providers, and there will be increased transparency in trading or hospital business (Broomberg 1994). Thus, efficient managed markets in welfare services like health presuppose (i) competition between suppliers, (ii) definable outputs for which consumer valuation could be made and (iii) lower transaction costs compared to an existing set of costs (Sappington and Stiglitz 1988). In some types of reforms, some of these conditions are not satisfied. For instance, reforms in the UK have been associated with substantial transaction costs which include the costs of writing contracts, additional managerial staff deployment at various levels, monitoring their implementation and thus overall higher administrative costs in the post-reform phase (Le Grand 1994). It is estimated that following the reforms, administrative and management overhead costs in the National Health Services (NHS) in the UK doubled from their earlier 5–6 per cent of total health service expenditure (Health Policy Network 1995).

There may be other costs associated with managed markets. These include (i) the loss of monopsony purchasing power by the state in health care, especially skilled staff such as medical doctors; (ii) the sacrifice of equity and probable concentration of profitable services and selection of low-risk patients (Le Grand 1991) and (iii) the impact of private providers, especially private hospitals, on public hospitals, providing incentives for the latter to behave like a for-profit provider, which concentrates on profitable services and avoids essential but nonprofitable services (von Otter and Saltman 1992).

In the case of developing countries, doubts have been expressed about the applicability and generalization of managed markets in health care. In these countries the nature of health-sector institutions, market conditions and other crucial parameters are very different from their counterparts in developed countries. Simultaneously, most of the conditions necessary for successful implementation of such market-oriented reforms (e.g. high competition among providers, information availability and transparency and management capacity) often do not exist in developing countries (Broomberg 1994). Nonetheless, as articulated in the World Development Reports of 1987 and 1993, the World Bank has been emphasizing that the private sector can be a more efficient producer of secondary and tertiary levels of health care, and therefore that the government budget can be diverted to primary health care or to a minimum package of care (World Bank 1993). But in fact in some developing countries the private sector is already playing a major role in providing health care. In India, for instance, nearly 80 per cent of expenditure is being incurred in the private sector.

Despite the virtual absence of the basic conditions for success, privatization has been attempted even in developing countries. These efforts fall into one of three types: (i) divestiture (i.e. change in the ownership of an enterprise from the public to private sector), (ii) liberalization or deregulation or (iii) franchising or contracting out. Generally, the latter two forms of privatization have been more popular in developing countries (Cook and Kirkpatrick 1988).

The experience of some of the developing countries has been quite adverse. In certain social insurance schemes in Latin America and Asia, clinical care has been contracted out (McGreevey 1990; Griffin 1990; Bennett and Mills 1993). For example in Chile the privatization drive in 1973, accompanied by efforts to encourage new private health insurance schemes, did not produce encouraging results. Due probably to lack of demand, caused by a severe recession that continued until the mid-1980s, only about 3 per cent of the population had private insurance coverage (Viveros-Long 1986). By contrast, the newly industrialized Korea owes its rapid privatization in the health care sector to high growth in GNP (Yang 1990). In some countries, as in Mexico, international agencies like US Agency for International Development (USAID) have successfully encouraged privatization of nonclinical elements of health services including drug sales, family planning, water supply and sanitation (Lewis and Kenney 1988; Lewis and Miller 1987). In many Latin American countries, such as Brazil, Columbia and Peru, social security schemes have started buying from both public and private providers (Gwynne and Zschock 1989).

In general, an exploitation of the consumer (i.e. the patient) will take place with sole reliance on the private-for-profit sector since a patient may commonly not have anything approaching perfect information (Arrow 1963). The private sector then generally serves the urban elite, thus exacerbating the problem of equity.

To encourage private providers to serve in rural areas, countries including Mexico, Malaysia, Zimbabwe and India have tried to subsidize such providers through tax relief (WHO 1991). Experiments in increasing the income levels of public-sector doctors (e.g. in Iran) and pay clinics (e.g. in India and Mozambique) have also been effected. The contracting out of services such as laundry (in Zimbabwe and India), radiotherapy, CT scans and X-rays (in Malaysia) has also been successful.

However, problems with contracting out are also not uncommon. For example after contracting out hospital laundering, laundry costs in Zimbabwe increased fourfold. Similarly the cost of medical equipment maintenance doubled after being contracting out, without quality improvements. In Malaysia, owing to large capital requirements, the private firms did not show much willingness to contract for rubbish disposal. Moreover, one study in South Africa observed that these contracts often favour the same contractor (Broomberg 1994). This may owe to lack of capacity and required information for design, negotiations, implementation and monitoring of efficient contracts (McPake and Ngalanda Banda 1994).

Besides the lack of necessary conditions for successful privatization in developing countries, a sharp distinction between the reforms in Western Europe and developing countries has been pointed out by Bennett (1992). It is, namely, that the Western European countries have maintained and moved towards universalizing the public finance of health care and have created competition among a great diversity of providers (OECD 1990). By contrast, the current emphasis in developing countries on privatization is primarily a short-term move for extra funds that ignores the long-term wasteful and pluralistic nature of such moves. It makes government financing less comprehensive. It does not take care of the long-term implications of such moves (Bennett 1992).

Decentralization, like privatization, cannot overcome all the resource constraints in the health care sector. At times, it may even have the contrary effect of increasing levels of inequity. An interesting example is provided by the Chinese reform, in which in the early 1980s an overall decentralization of the public financing system took place (World Bank 1990). As a result, tax revenue for all levels of governments decreased from 34 per cent of GDP in 1978 to 20 per cent in 1988. With the new system, the central government gradually increased the retention rates in most provinces. This step was aimed at creating an incentive for the provinces to collect taxes, thus increasing tax compliance, and at the same time providing the provinces with a greater share. Another step was to introduce a provincial contracting system in 1988. This allowed the provinces to contract with the centre for a fixed revenue-sharing quota. A certain base quota must be transferred to the central government, and the province may keep all the revenues above this quota. So far, seven relatively prosperous provinces have been allowed to contract in this manner, leading to a serious reduction in the central government's revenue-raising ability and its ability to distribute to poor provinces. This has resulted in further regional, provincial and urban/rural disparities in income and wealth – an unintended effect of decentralization.

This decentralization of financial power in China has been coupled with fees for access to the service system, a plurality of ownership in rural areas and competition among health care units working in the countryside, and transfer of control and management of township hospitals from country health bureaus to township governments. Further, self-sufficiency and cost recovery at each level is emphasized (Bogg et al. 1996; State Council of the Republic of China 1985). Consequently, many traditional Chinese medicine (TCM) hospitals have problems of viability since the nature of their treatment does not allow for variation in their source of income. They mainly rely on sales of medicines. Thus, the decentralization policy in China, in making local officials responsible for local health expenditure, is likely to lead to an undue concentration of investment in medical technology, especially equipment, without consideration of efficiency, effectiveness or appropriate use (Zheng and Hillier 1995). Further, it is not certain that medical insurance, decentralization of decision making and financial autonomy will improve efficiency. In fact, 'Much depends on the institutional setup . . . decision makers are conditioned by the constraints they face (both market and institutional constraints) and their interests need not coincide with the broader interest of the society' (Ho Lok 1995).

In this regard, reflecting on the transformations in the Chinese rural health care system, Liu et al. (1995) make some very pertinent observations. They point out that 'more than ten years have elapsed since China changed its economic system and China is still struggling to find an equitable, efficient and sustainable way for financing and organizing health services for its rural population.' They note that

> the Chinese experience demonstrated the need to understand the limits of market forces and refine the role of government in rural health care under a market economy . . . However, under a market economy, the government still has a responsibility to provide sanitation, clean water, prevention, health education and primary care. In China, the government reduced its financial support for basic public health in rural areas and the controllable communicable diseases increased.

Similarly, the failure of decentralization in overcoming health financing constraints has been noted in Papua New Guinea, where political immaturity and lack of financial management know-how at lower levels of government could not enhance resources for health services despite potential finance-raising powers endowed by the constitution (Thomason, Newbrander, and Kolehmainen-Aitken 1991).

International experiences and lessons for India

The foregoing analysis indicates that a range of financing mechanisms exists in the health care sector. The feasibility of any type of financing mechanism, however, is intimately linked to questions of equity and efficiency in regard to supply and demand in the sector. On one hand, these questions thus impinge upon supply aspects like planning, organization and delivery. On the other, the demand side aspects regarding utilization and quality of care also become pertinent. Simultaneously, the feasibility of any financing alternative cannot be divested from social, economic, demographic and institutional realities embedded in a country-specific context. In a country such as India, significant disparities exist across the states, and therefore the feasibility of any policy measure is constrained by state-specific factors. Indian health-finance strategies might be desegregated for three groups of rich, middle-income and poor states. As indicated in the earlier discussion, so far the global experience of user charges has been associated with their dampening impact on demand for health services.

Though user charges are currently being deployed in most of the teaching and district hospitals in India, their revenue potential and their impact on demand have not been analyzed. Case studies in some of the states indicate that efforts to capture equity considerations by means of exemption for the poor as well as bureaucratic delays in rate revisions have hampered the revenue potential of user charges even for the diagnostic facilities (Purohit and Siddiqui 1995a). Besides developing adequate information bases pertaining to cost structures of various facilities for individual states, the administrative efficiency of this mechanism is far from satisfactory.

More recent initiatives to retain the funds collected by means of user charges at the site of the facilities has, however, improved the financial autonomy of hospitals and resulted in some improvement in quality of services (NCMH; GoI 2005a). Such benefits at present are reported in some seven Indian states only.[5] Nonetheless, legislative measures are necessary to overcome impediments to user fees collections and their utilization in all the states (Purohit and Mohan 1996). Further, keeping in view the relevant experience of some of the African countries, appropriate management training, especially in collection and financial techniques, is necessary.

Likewise, supply-side efficiency needs enhancing through measures aimed at cost containment and controls. Evidence in this regard, limited to case studies of teaching hospitals in Rajasthan, indicates that there is scope for resource mobilization through enhancing operating efficiency (Purohit and Rai 1992). Further studies should provide a database for the cost and financing structures of different health procedures. Moreover, a focus on the particular aspect of the impact on demand of the implementation of user fees in public-sector health facilities would be useful so that the equity implications of this mechanism in the country can be judged. At present, the studies in this regard are marked by their absence. Similarly, more information is necessary to look into the feasibility of the health insurance mechanism. Presumably the social safety nets associated with structural adjustment could be used to experiment with a localized monopolistic integrative model, especially in poorer states. In richer states, however, scope for initial experimentation with other models of insurance could be studied in greater detail. Bearing in mind that the insurance schemes in the public sector have been unpopular so far owing to their low coverage and numerous administrative complexities, attempts could be made to overcome these factors. At the same time, health insurance comprises merely 1 per cent of the total business of insurance companies, so it lacks aggressive campaigning by them. It would be possible, therefore, to stimulate insurance in health by initiating reforms such as the following:

i   Covering the unorganized sector using the experience of other countries with suitable adaptation for the Indian situation. This could be done, for instance, by keeping in view the experience of the countries such as Italy, Brazil, the Netherlands, France and Belgium, which in their earlier phases moved towards universal coverage by means of such taxes as the land tax, a tax on agricultural produce and contributions as part of the income tax.

ii Initiating a series of studies to gather adequate information about the willingness and ability of citizens in different state income categories to contribute
towards different kinds of insurance coverage of different social groups. Any
such set of information will be a valuable contribution, especially before
the government embarking upon any new small- or large-scale insurance
schemes.

The form of insurance sought to be encouraged may have its own long-term
effects on the production and consumption of health care services, however. Open-
ended insurance without specific deductibles or coinsurance, as the experience in
some African countries indicates (Vogel 1988a), may have adverse consequences
in terms of users' choosing only private providers and frivolous use of care. Similarly, the issue of revenue mobilization by means of insurance or cost recovery
should not ignore the important aspect of equity. Besides questions of inter- and
intrastate equity and intersectoral equity, equity issues in health care have to be
tackled more carefully. More specifically, the type of equity most desirable in the
long run has to be clear. From a theoretical perspective at least seven different
notions of equity in health care can be distinguished. These include the concepts
of (i) equal expenditure per capita; (ii) equal inputs per capita; (iii) equal inputs
for equal needs; (iv) equal financial access for equal needs; (v) equal utilization
for equal needs; (vi) equal marginal net need and (vii) equal health status (Menzel
1983). If adopted, each one of these notions would have different implications
with regard to resource requirements specified over a time horizon.[6]

One of the important conclusions related to the finance and delivery of health
care is privatization. In India, the need exists not so much to privatize but to
regulate the private health care sector. A vast private sector currently exists in
health care. For instance at present about 70 per cent of hospitals and 50 per cent
of hospital beds are in the private for-profit and nonprofit sector. This sector also
employs about 70 per cent of qualified doctors (Jesani and Ananthram 1989).
In this context, it is important that the medical council play an important role in
regulating the medical education, which in the private sector requires large sums
for admission; this in turn is creating commercially minded doctors. Further, there
is also a need to create a system in which doctors entering into private practice
are guided to avoid wasteful practices such as overprescription of drugs and lab
tests and no adherence to standards.[7] However, currently these institutions seem
to lack the necessary infrastructure and do not have a set of standard norms for
general and approved practices in the country. The state and local governments
from time to time have enacted various regulations and guidelines.[8] Studies also
indicate a low awareness among private doctors about the various regulative acts
(Bhat 1996).[9] More steps are necessary, therefore, to create an appropriate regulatory environment for the private health care sector in India.

Besides regulating the for-profit private sector, a more supportive role from
the nonprofit private sector, namely NGOs, could be envisioned. In many remote
rural areas, these organizations have been successful in mobilizing resources and
public support for health care (Purohit 1995). It is important that appropriate

attention be focused on the role and long-term sustainability of this sector (Purohit 1996a, 1996b, 1996c).

Currently there is a move towards more decentralization through revival of the Panchayati raj institutions, the third tier of government. To overcome the resource crunch at lower-level health institutions (i.e. primary health centres and subcentres) an interesting step could be to empower these local-level institutions with the capacity to levy specific taxes or cesses to be used for health care services. This may, however, require a constitutional amendment so that specific taxes could be retained at the local-level institutions.

Corporatization of the health care sector

Bearing in mind the pros and cons of the various financing options, it is pertinent here to highlight the most significant trends emerging in India in the wake of liberalization and the recent years. Most notable is the vigorous new entry of corporate hospitals and multinationals into the health care scenario. The reason for this new tempo is the potential which India offers to nonresident Indians (NRIs) and multinationals. With the current ratio of population to all types of beds being 1,300:1, it has been estimated a huge demand-supply gap exists, and it may require nearly 3.6 million beds to overcome it (Sushi 1997).[10] Taking into account the requirements of primary and secondary health care, the shortfall is estimated to be around 3.9 million beds. In the tertiary level of health care, the gap may be somewhere around 20 per cent of the preceding total, which amounts to some 0.58 million. To overcome this gap, the resource requirements may be quite enormous.[11] It is estimated that India needs US$32–$50 billion to reach half of China's current bed per 10,000 population over 10 years (India Brand Equity Foundation [IBEF] 2006). Further, it is also estimated from a survey conducted by McKinsey & Company for Confederation of Private Sector Initiatives in Health Care that against a requirement of 60,000 super-specialty beds each year, only 3,000 multispecialty beds are being planned in India, and these may cost around Rs. 7.2 billion over the next few years (McKinsey & Company and CII 2012).

Nonresident Indians in the hospital industry

Realizing the need as well as the potential for profit and desiring to develop the states where they once lived, many NRIs from the USA and UK have taken interest in the development of health care diagnostics or super-specialty hospitals in their hometowns. From August 1991 to August 2002, the Foreign Investment Promotion Board (FIPB) approved 117 foreign direct investment (FDI) proposals worth Rs. 81.84 billion in the Indian health care sector (India Investment Centre 2007). The major chunk of this FDI (Rs. 11.6 billion) came to Delhi[12] to help in the development of super-specialty hospitals and diagnostic centres. The other places in the country that this NRI investment benefited include Guntur in Andhra Pradesh, Bhuwaneshwar in Orissa (Rs. 30 million), Calcutta in West Bengal (Rs. 80 million) and Bangalore in Karnataka (Rs. 0.6 million).[13] These investments in states other than Delhi are mostly focused on diagnostic centres and bring with them high-tech care, advanced medical technology and trained Indian medical manpower. This trend is further strengthened by a recent policy initiative to allow 100 per cent FDI through an automatic route (IBEF 2006). This is partly halting and even reversing the trend of brain drain of medical personnel.

Multinational corporations in the hospital industry

Health care is emerging as a blue-chip industry and in recent years it has attracted the investment of both domestic and foreign companies. Unlike the earlier direction of the private sector, which focused mainly on nursing homes and polyclinics, the new market orientation is towards super-specialty care (*The Hindu* 1997). In this regard, although the pioneering efforts were made in 1983 by an organization known as the Apollo Group,[14] a number of other companies have now entered the market. Notable among these are the successful domestic and foreign companies CDR, Wockhardt, Medinova, Duncan, Ispat, Escorts, Mediciti, Kamineni, Parkway, Jardine, Nicholas and Sedgwick, Pacific Health Care and Columbia Asia (IBEF 2006; Pal and Viswanathan 1997; Viswanathan 1997). It is reported that at least 20 international players are vying for a piece of the Indian hospital market. The entry of so many of these companies has added towards the overall corporatization of the health care industry with a focus on high profit margin, super-specialty and diagnostic care. Mostly these companies have expanded their network in major metropolitan centres of the country.

The domestic pathology industry in the country is estimated to have an investment of US$1 billion, and it has been growing currently at an annual rate of 15 per cent. With an estimated 40,000 pathology laboratories in India, this industry makes up nearly 2.5 per cent of the overall health care delivery market (Express Healthcare 2008; 2011). As an offshoot of this growth in diagnostics, the outsourcing of pathology tests by foreign hospitals is becoming a huge opportunity, which may amount to nearly US$800 million in business from the UK alone.

This proliferation of technology in health diagnostics has brought India into the international arena, and its quality is considered second to none. Foreign nationals have also noticed the cost advantage. It is observed that costs in India are on an average one-eighth to one-fifth those of comparable treatments in the West. This has resulted into about 1,80 thousand patients from across the globe coming to India for medical treatment. This phenomenon, called medical tourism, has brought forth an estimated US$333 million in 2004. With a growth rate of about 30 per cent, it will be a US$2 billion industry by 2015. Moreover, some companies from the West have outsourced health care business process to Indian health care BPOs (Business Process Outsourcing units), providing a cost advantage of 20–30 per cent. As a result it is estimated that this outsourcing of BPO to Indian companies may create 100,000 new medical BPO jobs every year – up from 18,000 in 2012 – with a turnover of about US$4–5 billion coming from the US markets (BPO Watch 2012).

Given the rising cost of health care in last few years,[15] foreign companies are aiming to capture the potential health insurance market consisting of the nearly

135 million upper-middle-income citizens who can afford private health care, a
market estimated to range between Rs. 6500 million and Rs. 275 billion. This
is significantly larger than the current annual health insurance premium market
represented by General Insurance Company (GIC) and its subsidiaries of Rs 1
billion and covering merely 1.6 million people. Keeping in view the opening of
the health insurance market to multinationals, many foreign companies have initiated steps such as setting up representative offices or entering into ties with Indian
companies.[16] These multinationals aim at devising health insurance schemes
suited to the Indian situation; improving coverage by incorporating payments
for general physicians, medical tests and specialist charges; and containing costs
through appropriate controlling systems. As a result, estimates suggest that individuals covered under private health plans increased from 4–5 million in 2000 to
over 12 million in 2006. Industry analysts suggest that health insurance premiums
steadily increased from US$385 million in 2004–05 to US$777.8 million in 2007
(Purohit 2009).

Besides health insurance, the high-tech medical electronic equipment industry
has been the other area attracting MNC investment following liberalization. This
is a result of the high-tech nature of modern diagnostics, which is based largely
on foreign technology that has a high obsolescence rate of around 5 years, a char-
acteristic that results in a need for regular replacement. In general, a reduction
of import duties on individual components and high rates of import duties (up to
31%–37%) on high-tech finished products (e.g. CT scanners) have encouraged
multinationals to have the imported components assembled in India rather than
manufacture the medical equipment in the country. Moreover, the demand for
high-tech medical devices in India is growing annually between 12 per cent and
15 per cent. This is due to changing disease profiles and clinical needs as well as
the growth in medical tourism. Overall, high-tech products constitute nearly 80
per cent of the overall medical device market. This market is expected to grow
from US$1.2 billion in 2005 to US$5 billion by 2012, with a yearly expansion
rate of nearly 15 per cent (India Briefing 2012).

Policy measures: incentives to private-sector participation

In the last few years a number of state governments have become increasingly
aware of potential policy measures that could enhance resource availability to
the health care sector through either economic or institutional reforms. These
include policy initiatives to attract private-sector participation and management
inputs in running primary health care centres, privatization or semi-privatization
of public-sector health facilities, innovative nontax measures to finance public
health facilities and tax incentive measures to attract private-sector investment
in healthcare (Table 2.3). Some of the state governments have even initiated
moves to reorganize their health directorates into public-sector undertakings.[17]
More often, however, this has been done with the assistance and insistence of
the World Bank. In this section we do not intend to go into this aspect of reor-
ganization, but rather we focus on the other previously mentioned measures.

Table 2.3 Innovations by states for the provision of health care services, 1995–2000

Area of innovation	Broad direction of the innovation and initial innovators
Public-private partnerships	Handing over management of public facilities to NGOs (Gujarat, Karnataka); contracting private specialist services and outsourcing hospital ancillary services, IEC, etc. (most states)
Decentralization	Transfer of budgets to and involvement of local bodies (Kerala, Karnataka, Himachal Pradesh, Orissa); Management Boards of Health Facilities (Rajasthan, Madhya Pradesh, Andhra Pradesh)
Human resources	Contracting professionals for service delivery – ANMs, doctors, surveillance, auditing, etc. (all states); multiskilling, pre-internship training, mandatory pre-postgraduate rural service (Orissa)
Financing	User fees and financial autonomy to hospitals (Madhya Pradesh, Rajasthan, Andhra Pradesh, Karnataka, Punjab, West Bengal, Maharashtra); health insurance (Andhra Pradesh, Karnataka, West Bengal); direct transfer of funds from GOI to districts under NHPs; financial delegation of powers to PHCs, CHCs and district CMOs (Tamil Nadu, Gujarat)
Accountability	Delegation of powers to district-level officials (Gujarat, Tamil Nadu); rationalizing responsibilities for better accountability, performance-based monitoring (Andhra Pradesh, Gujarat)
Community mobilization	Link couple schemes (Gujarat, Rajasthan); village planning and community health workers (Madhya Pradesh, Uttar Pradesh)
Regulation/standard setting	Quality control circles (Gujarat); blood transfusion standards (NACO); ISO certification (Karnataka, Himachal Pradesh); ensuring essential drugs at health facilities under the Panch Byadhi chikitsa scheme (Orissa); centralized drug procurement (Tamil Nadu, Orissa, Andhra Pradesh, Rajasthan)

Source: Initiatives from Nine States, GoI (2004).

Notes: ANM = auxiliary nurse-midwife; NGO = non-governmental organization; IEC = information, education and communication; ISO = International Standards Organization; NACO = National AIDS Control Organization; NHP = National Health Programme.

Measures to attract private-sector inputs in public health centres and privatization

Because resources are scarce, the existing public health system has been unable to provide care to all. At present nearly 135 million Indians do not have access to health services (World Bank 1996) and 80 per cent of Indians who live in poor areas do not have access to even the fifteen essential drugs needed at the primary health care level (Pandit 2006). In fact WHO has labelled India as a Group A country, which means that less than 30 per cent of its population has regular access to essential drugs. Despite the Bhore Committee's 1946 recommendations of one health centre for every 20,000 people, the country currently has one PHC per 31,000 population (World Bank 1996; GoI 1946). Even the existing public health facilities are run with an abysmally low availability of resources; presently an average Indian PHC budgets only Rs. 1 per capita for drugs. Thus, apparently prompted by the desire to increase access to more people, some of the state governments have favoured increasing participation of the private sector in running the existing public health facilities (*Times of India* 1997; Hamine 1998).

In this regard two distinct strategies with differing implications have been adopted. One strategy has been to attract direct private investment on a purely philanthropic basis while the bureaucracy of the existing health care facility maintains the management. The private companies' expenditure qualifies as charitable spending and can be claimed as a tax exemption. However, beyond the tax exemption, there is no additional element of benefit to private parties. This strategy has been adopted in Tamil Nadu, where the state government has called for private-sector participation by inviting private investment in the public health infrastructure.[18] Thus the efforts of Tamil Nadu are geared towards pooling public and private resources for social purposes and impose more social obligations on industry. The success of such pilot projects depends upon continual profitability of companies participating in the scheme and successful mixing of two different work cultures, namely public and private.

Another strategy has been to increase private-sector participation by handing over the management of public-sector facilities to a private party working on a not-for-profit basis with the core funding from the government. In the state of Maharashtra, the state government appointed a committee in July 1997 whose recommendations were available the following October. The committee suggested some 30 guidelines for the transfer of PHCs to registered private NGOs that are capable of providing necessary services in remote and hilly areas. These guidelines emphasize the capabilities of the private organizations willing to take over the functioning of PHCs, the functions they will perform after the takeover and the amount and method to be adopted for grants to be received by these organizations. The committee should ascertain that the NGO in question has the requisite manpower, expertise in providing basic health services in remote and hilly areas, vehicles and capacity of providing specialized extension services and medical aid in cases where patients need to be moved. Generally these private agencies will have the right to retain the existing staff or effect changes in the workforce while adhering to prescribed government norms. In either case the agency will receive wage expenses for its employees from the government. The agency taking over the PHCs shall also be responsible for providing residential quarters for its staff, training, miscellaneous repairs and sanitation. As per the committee's recommendation a grant of Rs. 12,000 per PHC will be provided to these agencies. The grant for construction of the health centre and residential quarters for the staff will be a reimbursement based on certification from the public works department of Zilla Parishads. In the case of implementation of various health schemes and programs, the agency shall be eligible to receive grants, medicines and other equipment. However, expenses incurred for program implementation and administration will be initially borne by the agency and will be reimbursed based on actuals after every 3 months. The committee has suggested that the private agencies shall be allowed to charge medical fees from patients only in accordance with government rules. The money collected from such fees shall be deposited in a separate account that the agency can use for repairs and upgrades to its services. Thus the Maharashtra Committee guidelines take care of crucial issues involving private-sector management of public-sector health facilities. The fixing of user fees at the existing government levels ensures that the poor do not suffer and the resources are used to improve provision of services for all. This development of transparent policies and legislation can help bring about private-sector involvement in the health delivery system in a socially desirable manner.[19]

Besides the previously discussed strategies for increasing private-sector participation, in many states the policy initiatives have called for contracting out some specific services in the public hospitals (Purohit and Mohan 1996; Table 2.3). The involvement of the private sector in the health care education system has also been tried in some states.

The previously mentioned strategies pertaining to increasing private-sector participation in public health facilities share a common objective in making the private sector a partner with the government to shoulder social responsibility. However, the success of any of the approaches will depend on their implementation. In the first strategy, attracting private investment on a philanthropic basis, the main considerations will be continued profitability of the company, its geographical location, screening of companies based on their past record of social responsibility, the extent of financial responsibility shouldered by the company and the applicability of tax incentives. However, this kind of support would depend on the company's continued profitability. Fluctuations in trading activity may sometimes lead a company to retrench its funds from social positions. The government should arrange for an alternative private-sector party available in such instances so as not to cause undue delay in providing the requisite care in the service area.

In the case of the second strategy, the crucial considerations would be procedures pertaining to an effective delegation of powers within the existing bureaucratic framework and mechanism of coordination between lower-level (PHC) and upper-level (district) authorities. Performance following the private-sector adoption of a PHC would still depend crucially upon the cooperation of bureaucracy in various ways. In the absence of clear autonomy in hiring personnel as well as wage and rate fixation while taking into account the ability to pay of poorer people in the area, the chances of success of such collaborations between public and private sectors may be slim. This kind of autonomy might require a modification of rules and procedures which itself may be a time-consuming process, and political interference may further slow it down.

Innovative nontax financing

Some of the states have initiated some innovative financing measures to mobilize private resources for the public health delivery system (Table 2.3). This is done through establishment of an autonomous committee or society that is entrusted with all the funds, including user charges, visiting fees, outpatient ticket fees and the like. This committee has its own bank account and can determine the allocation of funds.[20] Another innovative method that has been established in Himachal Pradesh is a scheme called Vikas Me Jan Sahyog (People's participation in development). This scheme envisages the people contributing 20 per cent of funds and the state government contributing the remaining 80 per cent. The scheme covers the construction of hospitals, subcentres and ayurvedic hospitals in an area. In Kerala, an innovative measure to raise resources for cancer control involved the community in a unique manner. The state announced that 25 per cent of the total collections from Indira Vikas Patra[21] would be earmarked for early detection and prevention of cancer. This resulted in an enormous positive response from the public, and instead of the planned collection of Rs. 100 to 120 million, Rs. 760 million was collected under the scheme. In fact, 25 per cent of this collection, earmarked for cancer control and an early detection program, was nearly equivalent to 10 years of the sanctioned budget.

Tax incentive measures

A number of tax concessions have been extended to the hospital industry in recent years. These include measures at both the central and state levels. At the state level, these concessions are available in the allotment of land and investment allowances in medical equipment. The Rajasthan government, for instance, allots land for hospitals at concessional prices and gives subsidies for investment in medical equipment (Lakhotia 1997). To extend these facilities the private entrepreneurs have been classified into different categories,[22] some of which could entitle the private company a reduction of 25–50 per cent on the market price of agricultural lands in rural areas and residential lands in urban areas up to a certain ceiling. However, if the land allotted to build a medical institution is not put to use within 2 years of the date of allotment, the government may take it back. If the medical institutions are set up by the deadline stipulated by the act, however, the eligible health care institution will be exempted from local levies and state sales tax on medical equipment, plants and machinery, whether imported from abroad or outside the state or purchased within the state. Similarly, many of these incentives as well as financial help from banks are made available to private hospitals in other states, including Andhra Pradesh (AP) and Delhi.

In return for these concessions, however, these corporate hospitals and diagnostic centres are required to render free OPD and inpatient services to at least 40 per cent of their patients who may be poor, identified as such by either government hospitals or other entities. The idea behind this provision is to cross-subsidize the poor partly through the government subsidy and partly through the higher rates charged paid by well-to-do patients at these hospitals. In practice, however, these hospitals have been observed as not following their agreement. Thus, some of the branches of the Indian Medical Council (e.g. in Vijayawada in Andhra Pradesh) have demanded that the government make it mandatory for these hospitals to display a board on their premises informing the public about the free facilities clause (*The Hindu* 1998). Likewise, the council suggested that government hospitals refer patients identified as poor for treatment to these hospitals.

However, coordination on this aspect between the private hospitals and the concerned state governments remains problematic.[23] At the central level, these hospitals have the advantage of the concessional duty for imports of medical equipment. At present, import duties have reduced to an average level of 15 per cent for medical equipment and there is no duty on lifesaving equipment (*The Pioneer* January 31, 1998). At the aggregate level these imports in value terms contribute 50 per cent of the total requirement of the medical equipment in the country. Hospitals have been accorded infrastructure status, which attracts lower tariff, and higher depreciation is also permissible on depreciation of medical equipment. Moreover income tax exemptions for 5 years are allowed for hospitals established in rural areas.

This kind of import liberalization in health care equipment on the one hand is accelerating the growth in the domestic production of medical supplies[24] and on the other is being spurred by the affluent, consumer-oriented middle-income population, which is demanding quality health care that employs high-tech equipment.[25]

Policy options and welfare implications

Many of the merits and problems associated with recent policy measures and market forces as applicable to a developing country seem to be equally relevant for the Indian health care sector. The main thrust of the policy in the postliberalized period has been to encourage market forces. However, there are limits to market forces unless appropriate refinement in the role of government is attempted. In last few years, many of the recent reforms in both developed and developing countries, for instance, are geared towards privatization or increasing private-sector participation in public health care (Purohit 1997). As noted earlier, with increasing private-sector participation it is presumed that managed markets, especially in the hospital sector, will increase supply-side efficiency by increasing competition among providers, and there will be increased transparency in trading or hospital business (Broomberg 1994). Also, the efficient managed markets in welfare services such as health presuppose (i) competition between suppliers, (ii) definable outputs for which consumer valuation could be made and (iii) lower transaction costs compared to an existing set of costs (Sappington and Stiglitz 1988). In some types of recent reforms some of these conditions are not satisfied, and one of the consequences has been a rise in costs.[26] Nonetheless, it has been emphasized that the private sector can be a more efficient producer of secondary and tertiary levels of health care, and therefore the government budget can be diverted to primary health or to a minimum package of care (Broomberg 1994; World Bank 1987, 1993). In general, the experiences of other developing countries indicate that an exploitation of the consumer (i.e. the patient) will take place with sole reliance on the private-for-profit sector since it will serve mainly the better-off strata of society in the urban areas and thus exacerbating the problem of equity.[27] In fact, such adverse implications of liberalization are also observed through a comparison of two official estimates for 1995–96 and 2004 on utilization of health care facilities published by the National Sample Survey Organization (NSSO) of India (GoI 1998a, 2006b). The NSSO estimates indicate, for instance, that the number of untreated ailing persons in the rural areas increased by 3 per cent (from 9% to 12%) due to nonavailability of medical facility and by 4 per cent (from 24% to 28%) for financial reasons. By contrast, in urban areas there was a decline in untreated spells due to lack of affordability by 1 per cent (from 21% to 20%), with no change in untreated spells at 1 per cent due to nonavailability of medical facility.

Thus, even though the newly evolving atmosphere initially seems to be promising, considerable apprehensions remain. Foremost is that all the measures aimed at privatization of public-sector health facilities should not be construed as a pretext for government shunning its essential responsibility to provide basic health facilities. Failure to refine the role of government and a greater reliance on market forces may be counterproductive to health status (Liu et al. 1995).

The welfare implications of recent trends in the postliberalization period thus depend to a great extent upon deft regulatory mechanisms to encourage market forces and simultaneously avoid adverse outcomes such as rising costs, increasing inequity and consumer exploitation. One of the adverse implications of increasing corporatization and supplier-induced high-tech care has been the rising cost of health care, and it is necessary to provide shelter to the poor against it. This may further necessitate the development of a proper mix of public and private health insurance suitable for providing adequate coverage to all. Given the present status of minuscule health insurance coverage through the government-owned General Insurance Corporation and its subsidiaries, an important step has been to open up the insurance market to multinationals. As mentioned earlier in this chapter, already some multinationals are exploring the potential market in India, and they have partnered with domestic companies. In contrast to coverage of 1.6 million people by GIC and its subsidiaries, the MNCs in 2006 covered nearly 12 million. In this regard, the role of the Insurance Regulatory and Development Authority (IRDA)[28] is crucial in regulating future development of the insurance business and allowing health insurance coverage to grow substantially over time.

However, the health insurance as envisaged by the multinationals is not a panacea to all the problems of resource constraints, as it is initially likely to cater to the people in the organized sector only. As a matter of fact, a vast majority of India's population live in rural and underserved areas and many get their livelihood in the unorganized sector. This segment will continue to need the same type of public-sector health facilities for quite some time in near future. Therefore the mushrooming growth of corporate hospitals may still not be a workable substitute for adequate budgetary spending on the health care sector. The apprehension is that the lack of a more suitable policy to enhance government support to existing public health facilities may lead to increasing inequity between the levels of health care facilities available to the well-off and poorer strata of the society.

With a view to mobilising more resources for public-sector health institutions, there are merits to attracting private-sector participation in public health facilities. This strategy has the underlying objective of not only increasing the availability of resources through the pooling of public and private funds for social purposes, but also partly shifting the responsibility of a hitherto state welfare activity onto a profit-making enterprise. The success of such a scheme depends, however, upon the continued profitability of the private enterprise. This also requires an adjustment of the bureaucracy and private parties with regard to various details pertaining to scale and level of activities. The cooperation in procedures of approvals and reimbursements from different government functionaries will greatly determine the successful outcomes of such schemes in near future. Thus, only over time will we know if the move to attract private-sector participation in maintaining PHCs in the Indian states is successful. If outcomes of such schemes are positive, other states may follow suit. Meanwhile the current situation of scarcity of resources aggravated by budgetary cuts from the central government may continue to leave the poor without proper public health facilities. As with the initiatives discussed previously involving the private sector through financial or manpower inputs, initiatives to contract out nonclinical services have been rather more successful and hold more promise for future.

It is likely that with greater proliferation of private health institutions in urban areas, doctors will have further incentives and opportunities to avoid government services in rural areas. The real solution to this problem may lie with bridging the gap in the various infrastructural aspects between rural and urban areas. So far, the positive outcomes in terms of increasing per capita income as a result of enhanced business and trading activities in the postliberalization era have a strong urban bias. Consequently the prevalent rural-urban disparity in the country may further increase and may most likely affect the government's attempts to provide better availability of doctors in remote rural areas. In this regard, the involvement of NGOs could be a more successful strategy. In view of the significant support the NGOs have been able to provide for dysfunctional or nonexistent government health and medical manpower facilities in the rural areas of various states, the policy initiatives should focus on long-term sustainability of these NGOs.[29]

Another step in the direction of increasing health facilities in rural areas may be encouraging entrepreneurs by means of concessions such as tax holidays for investment in the health sector in backward areas. Simultaneously, to derive greater advantages of liberalization for the health sector, efforts should also be made to provide fiscal incentives for encouraging indigenous manufacturers of medical equipment.[30] This will help in saving the foreign exchange and furthering the development of the medical equipment industry. The latter in due course will help in providing better-quality care at lower cost. The current problems in providing tax subsidies to corporate hospitals in urban areas, such as the confusion over free treatments in lieu of tax subsidies, need to be overcome in the preparation and implementation of contracts between the corporate entrepreneur and respective state governments. Such problems indeed defeat the very objective of helping the poor.[31] There is also a need for a strong administrative system or social audit which could compel these private hospitals to provide adequate information access to the public regarding these clauses and the extent of their utilization in their respective hospitals.

Further, so far only a few states, including Andhra Pradesh, Rajasthan, and Delhi, have been trying to extend the tax concessions to hospital entrepreneurs. It will be notable if other states also try similar kinds of tax concessions to attract adequate investment in the sector. Care should be exercised, however, in extending such concessions to a particular sector like health. Without an overall resource impact of such measures having yet been determined, in the long run chances remain of a suboptimal resource allocation across various welfare sectors.

To sum up, the current policy options pertaining to the health care sector in the postliberalization period in India require a fine-tuning of government policies that can avoid consumer exploitation, increase equity and provide coverage against the rising costs of care.

Public expenditure on education in India

In recent times, several major announcements were made about policies to develop the education sector in India, the most notable of these being the National Common Minimum Programme (NCMP) of the United Progressive Alliance (UPA) government. The policies included (a) progressively increasing expenditure on education to around 6 per cent of GDP; (b) to support this increase in expenditure and increase the quality of education, imposing an education cess over all central government taxes; (c) ensuring that no one is denied education because of economic backwardness and poverty; (d) making education a fundamental right for all children in 6–14 years of age and (e) universalising education through flagship programmes such as Sarva Siksha Abhiyan and Mid Day Meal.

Although the country targeted devoting a 6 per cent share of the GDP towards the educational sector, actual performance has definitely fallen short of expectations. Expenditure on education has steadily risen from 0.64 per cent of GDP in 1951–52 to 2.31 per cent in 1970–71 and thereafter reached the peak of 4.26 per cent in 2000–01. It declined to 3.49 per cent in 2004–05. There is a definite need to step up again. As a proportion of total government expenditure, it has declined from around 11.1 per cent in 2000–01 to around 9.98 per cent during UPA rule, even though ideally it should be around 20 per cent of the total budget.

Due to a declining priority of education in the public policy paradigm in India, there has been exponential growth in private expenditure on education also. According to available information, private, out-of-pocket expenditure by the working-class population for the education of their children in India has increased by around 12.5 times over the last decade. During the financial year 2011–12, the Central Government of India allocated Rs 38,957 crores for the Department of School Education and Literacy, the main department dealing with primary education in India. Within this allocation, a major share of Rs 21,000 crores is for the flagship programme Sarva Siksha Abhiyan. However, budgetary allocation of Rs 21,000 crores is considered very low relative to the Anil Bordia Committee recommendation of Rs 35,659 for the year 2011–12. This higher allocation was required to implement the 2009 Right of Children to Free and Compulsory Education Act.

India has one of the largest higher-education systems in the world and has been witnessing healthy growth in its number of institutions and enrolment in the last few decades. The number of universities has grown more than six times in India: more than 33,000 colleges exist, with one-third of the last four decades' total of colleges having been set up in the last 5 years.

Over the past few years, India's higher-education sector has witnessed tremendous growth. Today the country has the largest higher-education system in the world in terms of number of institutions. It is the second-largest in terms of enrolment. While India has shown impressive growth in the number of institutions and enrolment in the country, it still faces challenges on several fronts, including low and inequitable access to higher education, shortage of faculty, deficient infrastructure and low-quality and inadequate research. Today a key concern for India is the creation of an employable workforce to harness its demographic dividend to the maximum extent. To achieve this, the country needs an education system that can deliver quality in terms of a skilled and industry-ready workforce, without diluting focus on world-class research and innovation.

The Twelfth Five Year Plan (2012–17) recognizes the challenges facing India's higher-education system and proposes several initiatives to resolve these, such as through increased funding for disadvantaged groups, deployment of cutting-edge technologies, faculty development programmes, improved governance structures and provision of incentives for research.

The government intends to achieve enrolment of 35.9 million students in higher-education institutions, with a gross enrolment ratio (GER) of 25.2 per cent, through these initiatives by the end of the plan period. It also intends to significantly improve the quality of the system while enabling the coexistence of multiple types of institutions, including research-centric, teaching and vocation-focused ones. The private sector can be expected to play an instrumental role in achieving these outcomes through the creation of knowledge networks, research and innovation centres, corporate-backed institutions, and support for faculty development.

India's education sector, with 25.9 million students enrolled in more than 45,000 degree and diploma institutions in the country, has witnessed particularly high growth in the last decade, with enrolment of students increasing at a Compund Annual Growth Rate (CAGR) of 10.8 per cent and institutions at a CAGR of 9 per cent. The private sector has played an instrumental role in this growth, with private institutions now accounting for 64 per cent of the total number of institutions and 59 per cent of enrolment in the country, as compared to 43 per cent and 33 per cent, respectively, a decade ago.

The government has also given the required thrust to the sector in its Five Year Plans. During the Eleventh Plan period (2007–12), India achieved a GER of 17.9 per cent, up from 12.3 per cent at the beginning of the plan period. Various legislative actions were also taken during this period, including the introduction of the Higher Education and Research Bill.

Appendix 2.1

Table A2.1 Evidence on implementation of user fees and their impact on access (for both the poor and the general population)

Country	Study	Impact on access: positive, negative or mixed?	Main finding (with further details in italics)
Benin	Soucat et al. (1997)	Positive	Utilization of both preventive and curative care rose following user fees introduction, due to improved quality. *Following implementation of the Bamako Initiative, which included introducing user fees, utilisation increases were observed for both preventive and curative care, due to better quality care (especially greater drug availability).*
Burkina Faso	Ridde (2003)	Negative	Utilization of curative care fell after user fees introduction. *Primary-level health and welfare centres charging user fees recorded an average annual decrease of 15.4% in new consultations for curative care, as compared with a 30.5% annual increase for those not charging fees.*
Burundi	Bate and Witter (2003)	Negative	Ineffective exemption mechanisms for user fees. *No clear criteria for exemptions, with only a small fraction of the population benefiting (4% of sample had cards, with only half of these benefiting from cards).*
Cambodia	Akashi et al. (2004)	Positive	Utilization increased following user fees introduction, as they replaced informal payments. *Before user fees, informal payments were used to boost salaries. After fees, revenues were retained by the hospital.*
Cambodia	Barber et al. (2004)	Positive	Utilization increased following user fees introduction, as they replaced informal payments. *User fees guaranteed fixed prices for services, with utilization increasing by greater than 50% for inpatient and surgical care.*
Cambodia	Jacobs and Price (2004)	Negative	User fees, whilst not adversely affecting overall utilization, did adversely affect the poor. *Increases in user fees created a 'medical poverty trap', with some of the poor deterred from seeking care.*

(*Continued*)

Table A2.1 (Continued)

Country	Study	Impact on access: positive, negative or mixed?	Main finding (with further details in italics)
Cameroon	Litvack et al. (1993)	Positive	Utilization increased following user fees introduction, through improved quality. *User fees ensured better quality of services through enhanced drug availability, with increases in utilization extending to the poor.*
China	Liu and Mills (2002)	Negative	User fees, whilst improving public sector productivity, reduced take-up of preventive services. *The increased reliance on user fees worsened allocative efficiency, with over-provision of unnecessary services and under-provision of socially desirable services.*
Democratic Republic of Congo	Haddad and Fournier (1995)	Negative	Utilization fell after user fees introduction, despite improvements in quality. *In 1987–91, service utilization fell by 40%, with 18%–32% of this decrease is explained by cost, despite improvements in drug availability, staff skills and better medical equipment.*
Ethiopia	Russell and Abdella (2002)	Negative	Ineffective exemption mechanisms for user fees. *Exemption mechanisms limited in breadth (based on income thresholds, yet much subsistence in economy) and depth (only cover minor registration fees and not the more important drug costs).*
Ghana	Nyonator and Kutzin (1999)	Negative	Exemption mechanisms for user fees are largely nonfunctional.
Guinea	Soucat et al. (1997)	Positive	Utilization of both preventive and curative care rose following user fees introduction, due to improved quality. [See details on Benin above].
Kenya	Collins et al. (1996)	Negative (Neutral)	Utilization fell after user fees introduction, although by much less after phased implementation.

	Author (Year)	Effect	Findings
	Mbugua et al. (1995)	Negative	The initial 1989 registration fee led to an average reduction of 27% at provincial hospitals, 45% at district hospitals and 33% at health centres. In contrast, the outpatient treatment fee re-introduced in 1992 was associated with much smaller decreases in utilization. Utilization fell after user fees introduction, with exemption mechanisms being ineffective. Attendance for outpatient and inpatient care in government facilities was lower when registration fees were charged, as compared with when fees were removed. Utilization by children, exempt from fees, followed a similar pattern
Mali	Mariko (2003)	Positive (Neutral)	Increases in user fees are likely to have only had a minor effect on utilization of services. Quality of care is an important determinant of demand, with price increases only having a minor effect on utilization. These could be offset if policymakers improve both the structural and process quality of care
Mauritania	Audibert and Mathonnat (2000)	Positive	Utilization increased following user fees introduction, through improved quality.
Niger	Chawla and Ellis (2000)	Positive (Neutral)	Increases in utilization were observed following user fee introduction, due to better drug availability, with no evidence of severe negative equity effects. User fees only had a negligible negative impact on utilization of healthcare. No evidence of serious reductions in access following increases in formal user fee charges, due to improved quality of care.
Niger	Diop et al. (1995)	Positive	Utilization increased following user fees introduction, especially when combined with an annual tax. Utilization increased markedly in district with small fee plus an annual tax, as compared with a pure fee-for-service method (negligible utilization impact) and control district without fees (utilisation fell).
Niger	Meuwissen (2002)	Negative	Utilization fell after user fees introduction, following nationwide implementation.

(Continued)

Table A2.1 (Continued)

Country	Study	Impact on access: positive, negative or mixed?	Main finding (with further details in italics)
			Although previous pilot studies had shown that user fees would not adversely affect access, due to improved quality, nationwide implementation led to more severe drops in utilization in a number of health centres.
Nigeria	Uzochukwu et al. (2004)	Mixed	Utilization of malaria services increased following user fees introduction, although the rich and educated benefited the most. Utilization of malaria services increased despite the introduction of user fees, due to improved quality (training of health workers and better drug availability), although the rich and educated were the principal beneficiaries.
Sierra Leone	Fabricant et al. (1999)	Negative	The rural poor are disproportionately disadvantaged by fees, with exemption mechanisms ineffective. The burden of curative treatment costs came mainly from private and NGO providers, with the rural poor facing a high financial burden.
Sudan	Abdu et al. (2004)	N/A	Introduction of effective exemption mechanisms significantly increased utilization. Exemptions (financed by the government) from fees for all pregnant women and under-5s with malaria resulted in significant utilization increases for both population groups.
Tanzania	Hussein and Mujinja (1997)	Negative	Utilization of outpatient services fell following user fees introduction. Utilization of outpatient services in government-owned district hospitals fell by over 50%, following introduction of user charges. Private facility use remained constant, mainly because employers typically paid for private facility users.
Tanzania	Laterveer et al. (2004)	Negative	Ineffective exemption mechanisms for user fees.

Uganda	Kipp et al. (2001)	Negative	Blanket exemption mechanisms (for under-5s, maternal and child health services, patients with selected conditions) are not working properly. Utilization of outpatient services fell following user fees introduction, although not universally. Utilization dropped by 21.3%, although it increased in facilities located in remote areas due to better drug supply and other community projects.
Zambia	Blas and Limbambala (2001)	Mixed	Utilization fell for most services where user fees were payable, but rose for fee-exempted services. Hospitals and health centres experienced an approximately 1/3 decrease for general attendances over a 2-year period, but decreases were less marked afterwards. However health centre admissions increased by 25%, and fee-exempt measles vaccinations and deliveries increased by 40% and 60% respectively.
Zimbabwe	Zigora et al. (1996)	Negative	Utilization fell following user fees introduction.

Source: James et al. (2006).

The Twelfth Plan recognizes the challenges and issues of higher education in India and proposes several initiatives around six focus areas to address them. These are expansion – augmenting capacity in existing institutions; equity – creating targeted schemes for backward and minority communities; excellence – building excellence through research and innovation, faculty development and internationalization; governance – enhancing institutional autonomy and transparency; funding – increasing public and private funding and linking them to outcomes; and implementation and monitoring – improving coordination across ministries and agencies.

As of 2011–12, there were 12,748 diploma-granting institutions. Student enrolment in higher educational institute (HEIs) has grown 12 times in the last four decades and in higher education it reached close to 18 per cent in 2011–12. General courses account for the larger share of HEIs and overall student enrolment.

Notes

1 See for instance Duggal et al 1995a; NIPFP 1993.
2 The impact of this falling share of central grants on different groups of states, namely poor, middle-income and rich states as depicted by the revenue expenditure indices, indicated that between 1990 and 1993 poor states fell from 100 to 93, 98, 75, 79 and 95 respectively for the budgetary heads of medical and public health and its components, namely medical, public health, prevention and control of diseases, and family welfare. The decline was highest (i.e. from 100 to 75) for the poor states on the item of public health. In case of middle-income states, the decline below the 1990s level was more noticeable for prevention and control of diseases and for family welfare, which declined respectively from 100 to 84 and 83. Rich states saw a much lower decline, from 100 to 97 for both the items of public health and disease control (Tulasidhar 1993). In the study cited here, Bihar, Madhya Pradesh, Orissa, Rajasthan and Uttar Pradesh were included in the poor category, Andhra Pradesh, Assam, Karnakata, Kerala, Tamil Nadu and West Bengal were considered middle-income states and Gujarat, Haryana, Maharastra and Punjab were in the rich category (Tulasidhar 1993).
3 See for instance Forsberg et al. 1992; Quick et al. 1993; Litvack and Bodart 1993; McPake, Hanson, and Mills 1993; Ellis, McInnes and Stephenson 1994; Collins, Quick, Musau, Kraushaar and Hussein 1996; Mwabu and Wang'ombe 1995.
4 For instance, full coverage was started in the 1970s in Canada. It began in the 1980s in Italy, Spain, South Korea and Portugal.
5 These are Karanataka, Maharashtra, Punjab and Rajasthan (see Table 2.3).
6 For example, equal utilization for equal needs has greater resource implications than equal financial access for equal needs. Equal inputs for equal needs implies that the additional year that a 55-year-old may live as a result of having medical care has the same value as the 54 years that a 1-year-old might live after having received care. Equal health status implies a different time frame than equal expenditure per capita. Moreover, equity in the provision of health care must also be considered with respect to equity in the finance of the health care. For example, if a country did provide equal health expenditure per capita and thus achieved equity in provision but financed the health care by means of a regressive tax system, then equity still would not have been achieved. One beginning operational definition of equity for cost recovery in the health sector in developing countries might be "equal financial and physical access for equal needs" where the tax system is proportional to income. This definition would correspond to the public finance concept of vertical equity on the expenditure side of the equation, but not on the tax side (Vogel 1988a, 1988b).

7 As Bhat (1996) suggests, there is an urgent need to initiate a separate registration system which could provide structural information on the types of equipment, location, number of medical and paramedical staff and the like in a practice. Such an information base is crucial in private practice. Presumably the state should play an important role in regulating this sector. In India, however, state regulation has been very lax. Even regulatory bodies such as medical associations and medical councils have been lethargic. Generally the responsibility for governing medical practices through the formulation of proper codes and their effective implementation lies with the medical associations and councils.

8 These include the Indian Medical Council Act, Code of Ethics, International Code of Ethics, Declaration of Geneva, Consumer Protection Act, Drugs and Cosmetics Act, Dangerous Drug Act, Drug Control Act, Drug Price Control Act, Pharmacy Act, Nursing Home Act, Bureau of Indian Standards and Public Nuisances Act.

9 It has been also observed that private-sector institutions in India lack strong peer pressure, standards for appropriate and general practices and a strong mechanism to implement the existing guidelines (Bhat 1996).

10 Of the country's 0.81 million total hospital beds, currently 32 per cent belong to 150 private-sector corporate hospitals. The private sector in fact employs nearly 80 per cent of the country's medical personnel.

11 It is estimated that investment cost per bed including land, building, equipment, support system and medical consumable cost per year ranges from Rs. 0.7 million to Rs. 3.5 million, which varies with the nature of specialty. Thus the resource requirements may be much larger.

12 This funding came through Indraprastha Medical Corporation and TWL Holdings of Mauritius. The latter has invested Rs. 25 million for a 30 per cent equity in a 600-bed super-speciality hospital built by the Indraprastha Corporation. Likewise another NRI from the USA has decided to invest Rs. 27 million for setting up an advanced diagnostic centre in Delhi, his place of original domicile, Delhi.

13 Guntur in Andhra Pradesh, for instance, will benefit from a joint venture of Indian Hospital Corporation Limited and NRI-owned Soumya Medicare International through a 250-bed super-specialty hospital.

14 The Apollo hospitals were pioneers starting back in 1983, with its super-specialty hospitals covering some 50 medical specialties and a turnover of Rs. 161,020 million in 1996. This group has expanded in major towns including Chennai, Hyderabad, New Delhi, Ranchi, Madurai and Nellore. It aims at opening hospitals by mid-1998 in Mumbai, Pune and Ahmedabad. The group has earmarked about Rs. 12.5 billion to build more 100 hospitals in 16 metros – 32 specialty care hospitals in big cities and others in smaller towns. The fact that Apollo has very well utilized the market potential is evident from its operating profit margins in 1996, which remained around 35 per cent in Chennai and 38 per cent in Delhi. In 2010, this group has INR 2010 million turnover and comprises nearly 15% of revenue from international patients alone(Kumar, 2010).

15 The all-India estimates of the National Sample Survey Organization (NSSO) indicate that average medical and nonmedical expenditure per treatment by source of treatment has increased considerably in recent years. The estimates indicate, for instance, that between 1986–87 and 1995–96, there has been an increase of 12.42 per cent and 119 per cent respectively for government and private sources in rural India. In urban India, the corresponding increase has been respectively 60.56 per cent and 119.05 per cent (GoI 1992, 1998b). Likewise, some other studies also indicate the rising nature of medical costs in recent years (Rane 1995; VHAI 1997).

16 Some of the foreign and their Indian partners in these tie-ups include Guardian Royal Exchange and Cholamandalam group, Chubb group and Kotak Securities, Standard Life and HDFC, Royal Sun Alliance and DCM Shriram Consolidated, Prudential Insurance and ICICI, AIG and Tatas, General Accident and Bombay Dyeing, Commercial Union and the Hindustan Times group, Cigna and Ranbaxy, MetLife and

MA Chidembaran group, GIO and Sanmar group, and Canada Life and 20th-Century Finance.

17 Currently the health directorates function like any other government department. By converting them into public sector undertakings, the administrative autonomy will be increased both in terms of deployment of personnel and their pay scales, although a major portion of expenditure of these undertakings will continue to be borne by the State budgets.

18 To expedite this process a special wing has been created in the state's department of health and family welfare for the promotion of private-sector participation in public health. The emphasis is on the adoption of PHC, district and taluk (subdistrict level) hospitals and other government-run medical facilities by the private sector to improve the facilities being provided to the people. The state has sought this kind of participation in the form of new construction, maintenance and provision of equipment while the government can provide the staff, medicines and management. In fact Tamil Nadu has 1,420 PHCs, many of which are not housed in their own buildings, and there is an inadequate maintenance even at the level of taluk and district hospitals. The privatization strategy would help Tamil Nadu raise resources for maintenance. As many as 100 PHCs in the state will be maintained through various private companies and industrial houses under the PHC participation scheme

19 At one point, the state government of Andhra Pradesh wanted to privatize two PHCs in each district, which it intended to hand over to private parties or NGOs. It was thought that the government could provide 80 per cent of the required funds and that more PHCs could be entrusted to private organizations if the proposal was found feasible. However, so far the state has not implemented this idea.

20 Recently the Kerala state government has been trying to overturn the constitutional clause requiring that the funds go initially to the state treasury and then to the committee.

21 These are development bonds used as an instrument of savings.

22 For instance, in Delhi, the Apollo Hospital, which was constructed by the private company with concessional land from the government (the latter also being a partner holding a 26% share), was required to build a free OPD ward and provide 200 free beds and free diagnostic and operation theatre facilities and free meals to poor patients. Despite all this being carried out by the hospital, the government administration also insisted on giving poor patients free medicine and consumables despite the absence of such a clause in the contract (*The Hindustan Times* 1997a). Likewise, under the contract it was agreed that complicated surgeries of the heart and brain would be performed free of cost to the poor by a 'super specialist' at the hospital. However, the government has been insisting on admitting and treating all road accident victims for free at the hospital, a condition not mentioned in the clause. As a consequence of this confusion, the excellent facilities of OPD and inpatient wards, operation theatres and other diagnostic departments have remained unutilized, and the dispute remained unresolved for quite sometime before a final settlement was reached after a few years. (*The Hindustan Times* 1997b).

23 These include four categories, designated as A, B, C, and D. These cover charitable institutions willing to install at least one diagnostic or curative plant or piece of equipment on the list approved by the state government (category A), other charitable institutions not covered in this category (B), institutions willing to set up specialty hospitals approved by the state government for a particular use (C) and other hospitals and nursing homes run on commercial lines (D).

24 Because of the import liberalization on medical equipment, especially the components used to make it, companies choose to have equipment assembled in the country rather than imported as finished products, which would attract higher duties.

25 This increasing demand for high-tech treatment has also accelerated the growth in the production of health care equipment including consumables, hospital equipment

supplies and medical electronics. In fact, in 1994–95 the Indian market for medical equipment was estimated to be around Rs. 8 billion and growing at around 10 to 15 per cent in volume terms (Pal 1997).

26 In the context of a developed country, for instance in the UK, the recent reforms designed to introduce private mechanisms in the public sector have been associated with substantial transaction costs which include the cost of writing contracts, additional managerial staff deployment at various levels, monitoring implementation and thus overall higher administrative costs in the post-reform phase (Le Grand 1994). It is estimated that following the reforms, administrative and management overhead costs in the National Health Services in the UK doubled from their earlier 5–6 per cent of total health service expenditure (Health Policy Network 1995).

27 See for instance Cook and Kirkpatrick 1988; McGreevey 1990; Griffin 1990; Bennet and Mills 1993; Viveros-Long 1986; Yang 1990; Lewis and Kenney 1988; Lewis and Miller 1987; Gwynne and Zschock 1989; Arrow 1963; WHO 1991; McPake and Ngalanda Banda 1994; Bennett 1992.

28 The IRDA bill was passed by the upper and lower houses of Indian Parliament on December 2 and December 8, 1999 respectively. This controversial bill opens the insurance sector to private and foreign investors. The bill allows for an equity participation for investors up to 26 per cent of total capital. The various clauses of the bill mandate that preference may be given to companies which take up life insurance as well as provide health coverage to individuals or groups of individuals. Under the bill, (a) the insurance companies have to deploy a major portion (up to 50%) of their investible funds in the infrastructure and social sectors; (b) all new companies should provide their insurance policies for crops, rural population, workers in the unorganized sectors and economically vulnerable and backward classes and (c) in case of failure to comply with the preceding social obligations, the companies registered under IRDA will attract a penalty of Rs. 2.5 million and in the event of subsequent failure to comply they may even face deregistration.

29 See for instance Purohit 1995, 1996a, 1996b, 1996c.

30 Since these tax concessions amount to an indirect expenditure by the government, it will be useful to estimate revenues forgone through these concessions, especially to derive an exact estimate of total government expenditure on the sector. Likewise there is also a need to estimate the amount spent by the government indirectly in providing tax concessions to the health schemes of private companies.

31 Currently the hospitals themselves decide the criteria that define being poor. This is done through their public relations departments. Generally this involves an element of arbitrariness and favouring the known people. However, some of the state governments, such as in Maharashtra and Andhra Pradesh (AP), have devised a system by which poor people are given a yellow or white card. This card primarily allows the poor to purchase rice, grain and other edibles at low cost at the fair price shop. One possibility is that the same system can be used for providing free care to the poor. However, so far not all of the States have implemented such systems. Even issuance of the cards can involve corruption in the government departments, and many people may get bogus cards without satisfying the criteria laid down.

3 Conceptual framework for economic performance measurement and efficiency of the health and education systems

Generally, health system performance can be monitored with either efficiency, effectiveness or economy. Efficiency is defined as the extent to which a health agency or health system maximizes the outputs produced from a given set of inputs or minimizes the input cost of producing a given set of outputs. Effectiveness is the extent to which programs and services (outputs) of a system achieve the desired outcomes. Economy refers to buying appropriate quality resources or inputs in the most economic manner (or at least cost).

However, use of any performance measure requires defining robust measures of outputs and inputs. Public health agencies (e.g. hospitals, primary health centres and the like) which provide unpriced services outside the market mechanism bristle with the conceptual difficulty of such a precise definition of outputs and inputs. The problem becomes more acute in the absence of data pertaining to these inputs and outputs.

As such, this difficulty is partly bypassed by some performance-measurement techniques that do provide scope for 'testing' alternative input and output definitions using different combinations of inputs and outputs. Ideally, the performance measures should not be very sensitive to changes in the choice of output and input measures. It is also presumed that in assessing performance an organization's management can control certain factors. By contrast most of the factors comprising an organization's particular operating environment, such as demographics, climate and population density, are considered to be beyond the control of an organization. Some of the techniques discussed next are capable of facilitating such allowances in a consistent and robust way.

More often we discuss how well the service delivery units of general government agencies convert inputs of labour, materials and capital into outputs of services. This is captured by means of the concept of the production function. It describes the relationship between the output (number of treatments) and the input (number of labour hours). The nature of the output-input relationship depends on the particular production technology or the skills of the labour input that is used to convert the inputs into the outputs.

To illustrate the notion of production function, Figure 3.1 shows the production function for patient treatments. Points B, C and D represent the maximum number of treatments that can be produced at different input levels (or the minimum amount of labour hours required to produce a given number of treatments). The shape of the curve will depend on the hospital's particular production technology.

Given the state of technology it is possible to have different combinations of the output and input. These are depicted as different points in Figure 3.1. Adoption of a new technology may make it feasible to have different input-output combinations. For example, at Point A it is possible to produce 450 treatments using 300 hours of labour. In contrast, at Point B the hospital can produce 600 treatments using the same labour hours, which is the maximum possible number of treatments given the production technology. Thus Point B is a point of technical (or productive) efficiency. Put differently, Point A is technically inefficient compared to Point B. Points on the upper bound or 'curve' of the production function (i.e. B, C and D) are all technically efficient. These points represent the maximum output that can be produced for a given level of input. A movement from Point A to Point B by means of improved management practices denotes a productivity increase from 1.5 treatments per labour hour to 2.0, which means a 33 per cent increase in productivity. Hence improved technical efficiency could be one way for a hospital to increase its productivity.

However, higher productivity can also result from exploiting economies of scale. This can be viewed from the relationship between productivity and the hospital's scale of operations. For instance, if the hospital can readily adjust its scale or size of operations by moving from B to C, its labour hours increase from 300 to 400 hours, or 33 per cent, but the number of treatments produced increases from 600 to 1,000 units, or 67 per cent. Since the proportionate increase in labour hours is less than the proportionate increase in treatments, the productivity ratio increases from 2.0 to 2.5. This higher productivity is in effect due to exploitation of economies of scale. These could result from better management practices in the form of specialized inputs and improved inventory management. The latter could be better planned, for instance based on output growth as well as other probabilistic considerations.

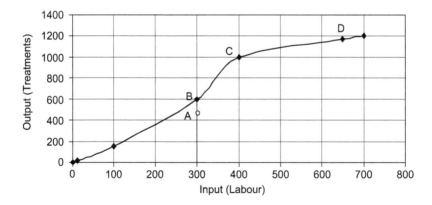

Figure 3.1 Simple production function

In contrast to the situation just discussed, if we look at the segment of the curve from C to D, we find that labour hours have increased by 250, or 63 per cent, but the number of treatments produced increased by only 170 units, or 17 per cent. This depicts that the input increases by a greater proportion than the increase in output and a reduction in the productivity ratio from 2.5 to 1.8. At this size, the hospital faces scale diseconomies.

Generally scale diseconomies arise from coordination problems which could be resolved partly by dividing a service delivery unit into two or more smaller entities. Thus as depicted in Figure 3.1, Point C represents the optimal scale for the hospital; that is the size that gives the highest possible productivity ratio. This illustration shows that the hospital could improve its productivity if it could adjust its scale of operations to reach this optimum point.

Further, if we consider the relationship between productivity and technological change, in the preceding framework a positive technological change is illustrated by an outward shift in the hospital's production function between two periods. In Figure 3.2, the production function from Figure 3.1 (i.e. Period 1) is represented as PF1.

Staff endowed with additional skills may allow the hospital to produce more treatments using the same amount of labour at every level of production. Therefore, representing this additional know-how, the production function in Period 2 (PF2) lies above the production function in Period 1. At each point on the production function in Period 2, the productivity is 2.5 times that of Period 1 – a productivity ratio of 2.5. This may be feasible, for instance, by the use of advanced skills such as the implementation of 'keyhole' surgery.

Thus we have considered three major sources of improvements in an organization's productivity ratio over time (or productivity growth), which include increases in technical efficiency, exploitation of scale economies, and technological advances. Productivity movements are intimately linked to changes in an organization's cost structure. Improvements in productivity, assuming no change in input prices, will reduce costs.[1]

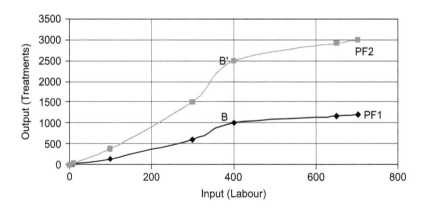

Figure 3.2 Productivity and technological improvement (single output/input)

It is also important to note that in the situation of multiple inputs the concept of technical efficiency becomes more sophisticated. It involves issues about the relationships among inputs, such as the extent to which one input can be substituted for another in the production process. Where inputs are substitutable, it may be possible to reduce the cost of production if a health care organization chooses an input mix that minimizes its total costs at prevailing input prices. When an organization chooses an appropriate mix of inputs and/or outputs that takes into account given market prices, it could attain allocative efficiency.[2]

Measuring efficiency

Three broad approaches to economic performance measurement are generally used. These are (i) index number technique, (ii) statistical programming approach, and (iii) mathematical programming approach.

Index number technique

Conceptually, technical efficiency can be assessed by comparing a set of productivity ratios across a group of health care organizations at a point in time. This would mean analysing the productivity performance of a single hospital over time (time series analysis) to compare performance across a group of hospitals at a single point in time (cross-sectional analysis). The empirical measurement of technical efficiency is generally framed in terms of a benchmark and its comparison with performance of individual units. Technical efficiency for each hospital is viewed in terms of performance relative to its peers. Technical efficiency is defined in relation to an individual firm's production technology.[3]

We can have only observable output and input data (e.g. number of FTE staff) to make benchmarks. The approach assumes that the best performers in a group are using their (common) production technology in an optimal manner; that is they are operating at best practice 'on the frontier'. However, using this approach there is no clarity, even among a small group of organizations, in assessing efficiency using partial productivity ratios because different ratios produce different performance rankings. Moreover, it is not possible to identify which organization is inefficient and the magnitude for potential improvement.[4]

Statistical programming approach

Unlike index number techniques, statistical and mathematical programming techniques do not require price information to calculate technical efficiency. These techniques, however, require data for a larger number of entities to be compared than the index numbers approach.

The statistical approach requires explicit specification of a production function (i.e. the mathematical relationship between inputs and outputs). It assumes that

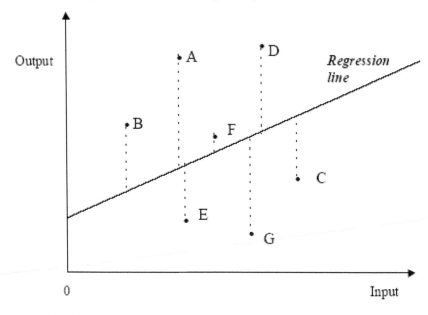

Figure 3.3 OLS regression approach to measuring efficiency

the relationship between inputs and outputs is inexact due to measurement error and other factors. This is captured by the inclusion of an error term which has well-defined probabilistic properties.

The mathematical programming approach does not presuppose a particular functional form. The shape of the efficiency frontier under the approach is determined by the output and input data. This approach also assumes an exact or deterministic relationship between inputs and outputs, which makes it sensitive to measurement error.[5]

The application of ordinary least squares (OLS) regression (Figure 3.3) to estimate an industry production function produces a measure of efficiency that is influenced by average practice rather than best practice.

The OLS technique identifies a line of best fit through a data set of output/input ratios for a group of organizations. Discrepancy between the output implied by the regression line for a given level of input (which represents average practice) and observed output at that level by assumption must be attributed entirely to systemic efficiency differences (rather than to random factors). The efficiency of organizations is ranked according to these differences. The most efficient organization, by definition, is the one with the largest positive difference (Point A in Figure 3.3).

Stochastic frontier analysis (SFA) is a more advanced statistical technique as it assumes that the gap between predicted and observed performance can be dissected into components for inefficiency and random noise (which is mainly measurement error). A simple stochastic frontier is depicted in Figure 3.4. It illustrates a group of organizations that each produce a single output using a single input.

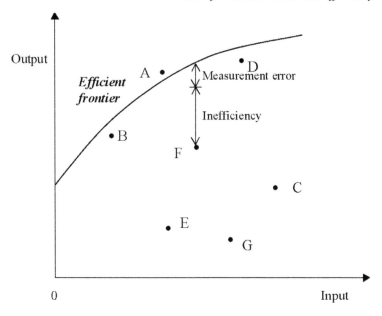

Figure 3.4 Stochastic frontier analysis

The stochastic frontier identifies the predicted performance for the best organization (A), allowing for measurement error. The other organizations (e.g. B) are below this frontier and are therefore relatively inefficient compared to the best. For these organizations SFA assumes that some of the gap between actual and predicted best performance will be measurement error. Empirical works using SFA have been reviewed by us in the later sections of this chapter.

Mathematical programming approach

Data envelopment analysis (DEA) uses mathematical programming to construct a production frontier comprising a set of linear segments. The frontier relates to best performance at a point in time. The points separating the segments are from the best-practice organizations within a sample. Figure 3.5 illustrates this approach for a group of organizations that produce a single output using a single input. As depicted in Figure 3.5, the frontier actually envelops the entities which have the best output/input ratio. Unlike DEA, as noted previously, a stochastic frontier is estimated using a regression approach from the most efficient organization within a sample.

As a nonstatistical technique, DEA is sensitive to outliers in the sample, which are often due to measurement errors and/or random events such as climate. By contrast, SFA is less susceptible to outliers as it allows for random noise in measuring inefficiency. However, a mathematical functional form (e.g. the shape of the curve for two dimensions or the shape of the plane for three dimensions) representing the underlying production technology has to be assumed before the

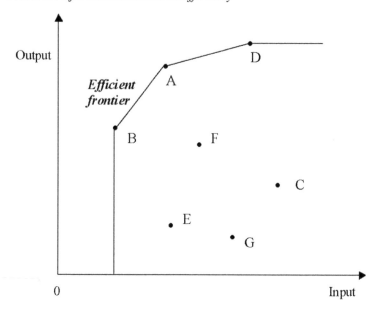

Figure 3.5 Data envelopment analysis

stochastic frontier is estimated. DEA does not presuppose a particular functional form for the frontier but allows the data to determine the shape of the frontier (e.g. in effect as a set of linear segments in two dimensions, or as flat triangles in three dimensions).

For each organization inside the frontier that is found by DEA to be inefficient, the technique identifies at least one organization on the production frontier that is a 'peer' or role model to the inefficient organization. The technique assigns a weight to each peer, reflecting the relevance of that peer to the inefficient organization. It can also determine whether an organization's technical inefficiency is primarily related to waste (i.e. the use of too many inputs to produce a given level of outputs), or to the particular scale of operations.

With the availability of input and output data for a set of similar organizations over time (panel data). the 'pure' index number approach discussed earlier can be combined with a frontier technique (DEA or SFA) using the Malmquist index number formula. This may allow a change in productivity to be dissected into the three sources: changes in technical efficiency, scale and technology.

It needs to be stressed that no single technique can provide a complete picture of performance; each technique has its own particular strengths and weaknesses. Also, trade-offs in specifying models are inevitable.

Empirical studies: a review

The growing importance of efficiency in resource utilization, particularly in the health care sector, has attracted research in the area. A number of studies have laid emphasis on the overall health system performance and its impact on health outcomes (WHO 2000; Murray and Frenk 1999). As such, these studies have focused on hospitals, nursing homes, HMOs and district health authorities (Worthington 2004; Hollingsworth and Wildman 2002a,b; Jamison, Sandbu and Wang 2001; Salomon, Mathers, Murray and Ferguson 2001; Evans, Tandon, Murray and Lauer 2001; Wang, Jamison, Bos, Preker and Peaboy 1999; Sankar and Kathuria 2004). More often, an idealized yardstick is developed which is used to evaluate the economic performance of health systems. This has been done by deploying frontier efficiency measurement techniques which involve a production possibility frontier depicting a locus of potentially technical efficient output combinations that an organization or health system is capable of producing at a point in time. An output combination below this frontier is termed as technically inefficient (Fried, Lovell and Schmidt 1993; Charnes, Cooper, Lewin and Seiford 1995; Coelli, Rao and Battese 1998). Despite the nascent nature of this application in the health care sector, an exhaustive review of studies applying these methods has been attempted, and this provides us with the details of the steps taken and empirical problems highlighted by the researchers (Hollingworths, Dawson and Maniadakis 1999; Worthington 2004). Notably, there are very few studies in the context of developing countries, and except for a few, particularly in the Indian context, the recent period is marked by the absence of such literature.

In this section, we focus on the review of studies pertaining to efficiency in health care and education sectors – for both developed and developing countries. Particularly, we highlight the studies which have empirically applied the data envelopment technique or stochastic frontier models. As noted previously, some of the papers on health care have covered an exhaustive review of studies. To avoid repetition while attempting to review all the studies, we have used reviews done by other authors and added an update of ours in this analysis. In this regard, an interesting and exhaustive review which we referred to earlier is by Worthington (Worthington 2004). This is based on some forty-seven empirical studies based on health care. The summary of the studies this paper covers is provided by the author in tabular form in Appendix 3.1 of this chapter. Two of the major conclusions from this review, presented in Appendix 3.1, are noteworthy. First, unlike in other sectors, the adoption of these quantitative methods in the health care context is still in its infancy. Measurement issues also remain pertaining to omitted outputs, unmeasured inputs and the imposition of strong and nontestable assumptions. There has been substantial misuse of frontier techniques in health services, particularly while making direct policy recommendations regarding budget controls and cuts and while using it as a marketing tool to attract contracts and factors to incorporate into the pricing models (Zuckerman, Hadley and Iezzoni 1994; Hadley and Zuckerman 1994). Second, as a consequence of the measurement-related issues, an ambiguity is also observed in terms of models set up at the first and second stages of regression analysis. Thus, health care research is yet evolving to adapt more aptly to techniques which have been primarily in the empirical domain of financial or other sectors.

Notable among the studies (applying a multicountry analysis) is the study of Evans, Tandon, Christopher, Murray and Lauer (2000). It applies a nondeterministic frontier approach to the analysis of health sector efficiency which allows us to separate random error from efficiency in the estimation procedure. The model is estimated using a panel of data from all the 191 countries that are members of the World Health Organization (WHO). In terms of output, this approach is based on an indicator of healthy life expectancy, i.e., debility adjusted life years (DALE). Three data series comprise the model: DALE, health expenditure and average educational attainment in the adult population. The panel covers the years 1993 to 1997 for all the 191 member countries of WHO; however, there is no data for some countries and years. All possible variations of the full translog model were investigated. The chosen model is reported where log of DALE was estimated as a function of log of health expenditure, log of average years of schooling and the square of log of average years of schooling. It was tested statistically by using the Hausman test to determine whether the fixed effects or random effects model was more appropriate. Based on the result of this test statistic, the fixed effects model was preferred. The resulting estimates of efficiency (i.e. performance) for each country were reported. Estimated efficiency varied from less than 0.10 to close to 1.00. In any given regression, one country has an efficiency index of 1.0 but across the 1,000 regressions, no one country was consistently the most efficient in the sample. The reported efficiency index is the average of the 1,000 scores from the individual regressions. As the researchers point out, 'Perhaps the most important conclusion of this work is that it is possible to measure and compare the efficiency of health systems across countries and over time. This is particularly important for countries introducing health system reforms, and we hope that this study encourages all countries to routinely measure the inputs and outputs of their health systems.'

Another paper by Evans and colleagues (Tandon, Murray, Lauer and Evans 2000) has introduced a new way of measuring the efficiency of health systems. Unlike previous work in this area, in addition to the more traditional goal of population health, this study defined the broad set of goals of the health system: responsiveness (level and distribution), fair financing and health care inequality. The analysis also suggests that the overall goal can be attained without increasing health expenditure; there is the possibility to increase efficiency in all countries, at all levels of health expenditure. Different functional formulations of the fixed-effect model were estimated. It estimated the full translog model as well as nested versions of the model, including the Cobb-Douglas log-linear formulation. The Cobb-Douglas log-linear was evaluated with each of the square terms and the interaction term taken separately. To measure efficiency using the production function approach, a composite index was considered to be the output of the health system. Inputs considered included total health expenditure per capita (public and private) in 1997, estimated in international dollars (using purchasing power parities, or PPPs, to convert from local currency units). As a proxy for nonhealth systems inputs, it considered educational attainment (as measured by average years of schooling in population older than 15 years). The panel covers the years from 1993 to 1997 for all 191 member countries of WHO. The resulting estimates of overall efficiency (i.e. performance) for each country are reported. The efficiency index ranges between a maximum of 0.994 for France and a minimum of 0 for Sierra Leone. In any given regression, the country with the maximum fixed effect will have a score of 1. However, the reported scores are averaged over 1,000 runs, and France was not the best-performing country in all the 1,000 runs. Furthermore, there is substantial overlap of the confidence intervals for several countries. It would not be possible to say, for instance, that the rank orders of the top three countries (France, Italy and San Marino) with respect to the overall efficiency were significantly different from each other.

The study of Spinks and Hollingsworth (2005) questions the application of data envelopment analysis (DEA) for cross-country comparisons of the technical efficiency of health production. Authors argue that theoretically such an analysis utilizes measures of the socio-economic determinants of health relevant to all social policies, not just health policy. Using OECD and WHO panel data, particularly for 2004, this paper critically analyzes a number of outstanding theoretical questions regarding the use of DEA in this setting. It concludes that unless such questions like data quality (availability and comparability), missing variables and agreement on the most indicative social determinants of health are addressed, the resultant implications for policy will be based on misleading information. Using a framework for the socio-economic determinants of health, the study concludes that policy makers should be aware of the limitations and uncertainty of using such techniques in the production of health settings.

The paper by Greene (2002) examines extensions of traditional linear fixed and random effects models that circumvent two important shortcomings of the existing fixed and random effects approaches. The author argues that measures of inefficiency in these models may be due to heterogeneity in addition to technical or cost inefficiency. This is the result of first, the strong assumption, particularly in a lengthy time span, that technical or cost inefficiency is time invariant; and second, as conventionally formulated, the fixed and random effects estimators force the invariant cross-unit heterogeneity at any time into the same term that is being used to capture the inefficiency. Thus, in this paper, a true fixed effects model is extended to the stochastic frontier model using results that specifically employ the nonlinear specifications. The random effects model is reformulated as a special case of the random parameters model. The techniques are illustrated through two applications, and one of these is a cross-country comparison of the efficiency of health care delivery. The data set used in this application is a panel observed for 191 member countries of the World Health Organization. Most countries were observed for 5 years, 1993 to 1997. This provided an unbalanced panel data set of 840 observations. This study used only the groups with five complete observations – 140 countries, or 700 observations in total.

The article by Richardson, Robertson and Wildman (2001) provides a critical opinion on the WHO methodology used in the WHO report for the year 2000. It focuses upon four issues. First, it is argued that the choice of the five objectives – maximizing population health, reducing inequalities in population health, maximizing health system responsiveness, reducing inequalities in responsiveness and financing health care – equitably gives undue prominence to the equity of financing and, more generally, inappropriately imposes a particular set of values upon all countries. There is a particularly strong case for omitting the equity of financing from this list and replacing it with an index of access, both financial and geographical. Further, the weights attached to the system objectives have not been validated. It is highly unlikely that a single set of weights or a single set of objectives can be obtained which are valid reflections of the aspirations of every country in the world. The authors suggest that subsequent analyzes may need to explore the option of using country-specific values in the models to get results that can be comparable between nations. Second, it is misleading to use the importance of weights attached to the objectives as an indication of the importance of the dimensions in the country rankings. Depending upon WHO objectives, these are also an incorrect measure of system performance. With regard to the model used to estimate the quality of life, very little consideration has been given to the validity of the underlying model. Further, it combines the scores and weights of the different objectives into a single index of performance. The authors have shown that the ranking of nations may be sensitive to the choice of the combination model. Different models have different properties, and the appropriate property for the present exercise needs to be given careful consideration. Third, the model for combining the different objectives into a single index of system performance is problematic, and alternative models are shown to alter system rankings. Fourth, the econometric model to estimate system performance does not provide a reliable basis for the evaluation of efficiency and the ranking of system performance. Finally, the authors' results suggest that the simultaneous inclusion of every country in the analysis will lead to invalid and unreliable results. This difficulty is easily overcome if there are sufficient observations to carry out sensible subanalyzes and also if adequate data availability is ensured. Also, the omitted variables may correlate with health expenditure or education to an unknown extent. Consequently, the model parameters may be distorted and country-specific effects change to an unknown extent. The authors contend that this problem may have determined many of the WHO results. The paper by Hollingsworth and Wildman (2002b) also provides a critical opinion on WHO methodology as used in the WHO report for the year 2000. This critique has focused more on the creation of a league table of health care systems based on the WHO report which highlights good and bad performers. This paper suggests that the WHO's estimation procedure is too narrow and that contextual information is hidden by the use of one method. It suggests that treating the data as a homogenous sample was incorrect since different countries have different health services. It is unlikely that OECD health services, for instance, are similar to non-OECD services. The authors emphasize that 'each health care system will have its own, reflecting its particular history, dominant ideology, and specific economic and socio-demographic circumstances', which are rather ignored by WHO methodology.

This paper by Hollingsworth and Wildman (2000b) also uses and validates a range of parametric and nonparametric empirical methods to measure efficiency using the WHO data. The rankings obtained are compared to the WHO league table, and it is demonstrated that there are trends and movements of interest within the league tables. The authors recommend that the WHO broaden its range of techniques to reveal this hidden information.

The results on the balanced panel of data in this paper demonstrate that the WHO league table is hiding valuable information on the efficiency changes in countries and of the movements of efficiency frontiers over time. It also points out that non-OECD countries show more variation in efficiency measures than OECD countries, and that the models used to estimate the efficiency of the OECD countries should be different to that used for non-OECD countries. Such evidence suggests that instead of studying the whole sample, it should be divided into countries with similar characteristics. On an empirical level, the additional techniques demonstrated in the paper show that there is more to efficiency estimates than merely ranking countries in one league table. Another paper by Hollingsworth and Wildman (2002a) makes use of cross efficiency measures as a means of validating data envelopment analysis (DEA) scores using different weighting schemes. It is a two-stage process. First, the basic DEA model is run. Cross efficiency then compares every country with all the other countries, applying the weights of the other countries (from the original DEA estimation) to the country under consideration to ascertain the effect this has on the original country's efficiency rating. An average cross efficiency score is arrived at from the re-estimation. A matrix is then used to estimate cross efficiencies (demonstrated in the paper) by using data from 30 OECD countries. Authors recommend this as a means to link the nonstochastic DEA and stochastic models to derive health (and health care) production functions, keeping in mind the features of the multiple outputs. It would be expected that average cross efficiency scores would be lower than the original scores, as a country cannot have a cross efficiency score higher than the original DEA score. The study demonstrated how a nonstochastic method (DEA) can be drawn closer to a stochastic model by introducing an element of uncertainty. Methods are available for validating the model specification, but cross efficiency takes the validation process a stage further. Once the model has been specified, cross efficiency allows validation of the actual results using peer appraisal. The study highlights cross efficiency as a useful method for post DEA analysis validation of results and the use of cross efficiency in the ranking of efficient units.

Using a worldwide panel data for the period 1990–98 and a stochastic frontier estimation method, Jayasuriya and Wodon (2002) measure the efficiency of countries in improving net primary enrolment and life expectancy; per capita expenditures in the respective social sectors and the adult literacy rate are used as inputs in the estimation of the production frontiers. These are allowed to vary by region. The determinants of the efficiency measures indicate that bureaucratic quality and urbanization have a strong positive influence on efficiency, albeit decreasing at the margin. By contrast, corruption was not found to have any statistically significant impact.

Among the country- and continent-specific studies, the study by Schmacker and McKay (2008) examines factors affecting the productive efficiency of primary care clinics in the US military health system from 1999 to 2003. The empirical analysis is based on panel data and it uses a single-stage stochastic frontier regression model. In the latter, factors affecting productive efficiency are specified as part of the inefficiency error component and estimated simultaneously with the production function. The study results indicated that primary care clinics not associated with medical centres had significantly higher levels of productive efficiency than those associated with medical centres and that having proportionately more civilian staff (and thus fewer turnovers) had a positive impact on productive efficiency. The nature of these findings also makes these applicable to the production of primary care in other settings.

The study of Jeffrey and Coppola (2004) evaluates the technical efficiency of federal hospitals in the United States using a variable returns-to-scale, input-oriented, and data envelopment analysis (DEA) methodology. The data set included 280 federal hospitals in 1998 and 245 in 2001. Results indicate that overall efficiency in federal hospitals improved from 68 per cent in 1998 to 79 per cent in 2001, which could result in a potential savings of $2.0 billion annually through more efficient management of resources. The study of Knox, Blankmeyer and Stutzman (2001) is based on data from Texas nursing facilities in 1994. It tries to demonstrate that inferences about nursing home chains by Anderson, Lewis and Webb (1999), made on the basis of the economic cost inefficiency of nursing facilities from a nationwide sample, are too fragile to support policy recommendations. Particularly, the authors question the finding of the previously mentioned study that chain facilities are more cost inefficient than independent firms and the policy assertion that mergers and subsidies to chain facilities should be discouraged. This study also uses the same data as that used by Anderson et al. and provides additional insight through some changes in methodology. It applies Nerlove's model to estimate a Cobb-Douglas cost function for Texas nursing facilities in 1994 and also apply Rousseeuw's least trimmed squares (LTS) approach. To support the cost function findings and extend their analysis, the authors also use a profit function to evaluate relative economic efficiency in Texas nursing facilities (Knox, Blankmeyer and Stutzman, 1999) which allows estimation of both technical (cost) efficiency and allocation (price) efficiency simultaneously. Their results indicate that none of the groups (profit seeking, nonprofits, chains or independents) is an absolute profit maximizer (all are inefficient because they use too much labour in relation to their fixed inputs). Further, profit seekers are between 55 per cent (OLS) and 25 per cent (LTS) more profitable than the non-profit facilities, as had been suggested by the cost function findings. However, when both cost efficiency and price efficiency are considered, chain facilities are significantly superior in efficiency to independents (between 33% [OLS] and 28% [LTS]). It is emphasized that this superior efficiency is also true for profit-seeking chains and independent facilities as well as nonprofit chains and independent facilities. This finding reverses the surprising result of the cost function and supports the 'expected' outcome for chains. Thus the study shows that estimates of cost efficiency are sensitive to the list of components included in the cost and, moreover, that a chain's cost inefficiency may be offset by allocative efficiency. Further, a need for area-specific analysis is also indicated for the region-specific population and their needs. Another paper of Knox, Blankmeyer and Stutzman (2007) examines technical efficiency in the Texas nursing home industry, which is one of the largest in the nation. Using a panel of facilities from 1999 and 2002, it estimates the production frontier using the maximum likelihood and quintile regression methodology. The study used a panel of nursing facilities participating in the Medicaid program. It defined a facility's output or the dependent variable as the number of resident days it provided in 1999 or 2002. To overcome an unduly restrictive nature of this measure of long-term care, indexes of quality and case-mix were also included as controls in some exploratory regressions. However, these were not statistically significant in any of the regressions and have not been retained in the model. The inputs to the production function or the explanatory variables in the study included the number of beds (BEDS, a proxy for the capital stock) and the annual hours worked by six groups of employees: registered nurses (RN), licensed vocational nurses (LVN), nurses' aides (AIDE), other resident care staff including social workers and activity directors (ORCS), laundry and house-keeping personnel (L&H), and food preparation staff (FOODPREP). In addition, there are dummy variables representing ownership (for-profit = 1, nonprofit = 0) and time (1999 = 1, 2002 = 0). The study results indicated that the average avoidable productivity shortfall is at least 8 per cent and perhaps as large as 20 per cent. Nonprofit facilities are notably less productive than the comparable facilities operated for profit, and the industry has constant returns to scale.

The study by Bates, Mukherjee and Santerre (2006) examines empirically the impact of various market-structure elements on the technical efficiency of the hospital services industry in various metropolitan areas of the United States in 1999. It applies data envelopment analysis and multiple regression analysis. Market-structure elements include the degree of rivalry among hospitals, extent of HMO activity and health insurer concentration. The DEA results show that the typical hospital services industry experienced 11 per cent inefficiency. Moreover, multiple regression analysis indicates that the level of technical efficiency varied directly across metropolitan hospital services industries in response to greater HMO activity and private health insurer concentration in the state. The analysis suggests that the degree of rivalry among hospitals had no marginal effect on technical efficiency at the industry level. The results also suggest that the presence of a state certificate of need law was not associated with a greater degree of inefficiency in the typical metropolitan hospital services industry.

The study of Rosko (2001) examined the impact of managed care and other environmental factors on hospital inefficiency in 1,631 US hospitals during the period 1990–1996. It used a panel stochastic frontier regression model to estimate inefficiency parameters and inefficiency scores. The study results indicated that mean estimated inefficiency decreased by about 28 per cent during the study period. It was observed that inefficiency was negatively associated with HMO penetration and industry concentration. By contrast, inefficiency was observed to be positively related with Medicare share and for-profit ownership status.

Among the studies in the European context, Kontodimopoulos, Nanos and Niakas (2003) explore the efficiency of a set of small-scale Greek hospitals known as hospital health centres (HHCs). These facilities provide primary and secondary health care and also function as health centres addressing mostly preventive medicine, hygiene and other public health issues. They are located in remote rural areas and serve the relatively small local population. Given their particular role, DEA was used to investigate their productive efficiency. The sample consisted of 17 from the 18 units existing in the Greek NHS. Variables representing production included the number of doctors, nurses and beds as inputs, and admissions, outpatient visits and preventive medical services as outputs. The DEA model was input oriented, based on constant returns to scale, and the units were ranked according to a benchmarking approach. Analyzes were performed with and without the preventive medicine variable and the results demonstrated technical inefficiencies of 26.77 and 25.13 per cent respectively. Location appeared to affect performance, with remote units, for example on small islands, being more inefficient. The results of the study raise the question of whether correcting the reduced efficiency compromises with the equity of service access for a highly dependent population. Moreover, a superior performance was observed in units which additionally offered preventive medical services, thus raising a question as to the role these facilities should play in the currently changing health care system.

The study by Gannon (2004) applies DEA and SFA to measure the technical efficiency of acute public hospitals in Ireland between 1992 and 2000 by using panel data. The author uses mainly an output measure which is not adjusted for case-mix. However, the utility of use of a measure of output adjusted with weights for diagnostic related groups to determine efficiency estimates are also discussed.

The results from the DEA and SFA approaches, to measure the production frontier and efficiency, suggest that the efficiency of hospitals may vary depending on whether a parametric approach is employed, and also on the relative weights attached to an outpatient. Focusing on regional hospitals during 1999–2000, the mean efficiency score ranges from 0.92 to 0.99. The scores for county hospitals range from 0.74 to 0.91 and for general hospitals the range is 0.84 to 0.99. In all cases, the DEA efficiency scores are higher; indicating that inefficiency (deviation from the best practice frontier) is lower than inefficiency measured by SFA. This implies that the stochastic frontier must lie above the DEA best practice frontier. The differences between the two efficiency measures calculated from DEA and SFA is quite high for county hospitals (0.15 efficiency points) and for general hospitals (0.13 efficiency points). The results from this analysis suggest that the types of hospitals with the highest level of efficiency are regional. On an average, during 1999–2000, the regional hospitals could use inputs to increase efficiency by only 1–8 per cent. However, county hospitals could increase efficiency by around 9–26 per cent during 1999–2000. Likewise, the inputs of general hospitals could be used more efficiently (by 1–16 per cent) during the same period.

The study by Hofmarcher, Paterson and Riedel (2002) investigates the evolution of efficiency and productivity in the hospital sector of an Austrian province for the period 1994–1996. Panel data has been used to design nonparametric frontier models (DEA) and to compare efficiency scores and time patterns of efficiency across medical fields. Two different approaches are used for output measurement: One approach makes use of the number of cases of mix-adjusted discharges and the inpatient days. In the second approach, credit points calculated during the course of the newly introduced diagnosis related group-type financing system have been used. The study compares individual efficiency scores for hospital wards as decision making units (DMU) in specified medical fields. Different results are reported for the two models. Model 1 (with conservative output measurement) calculates an average efficiency level of 96 per cent, while Model 2 (with credit points for output measurement) puts average efficiency at 70 per cent. Unlike in Model 1, where average efficiency hardly changes, efficiency increases modestly in the period 1994–1996 in Model 2. However, a closer look at single hospitals displays a variety of different efficiency developments over time.

Jaume Puig-Junoy (1998) measures the performance in the management of critical patients treated in intensive care units (ICUs) and evaluates the factors associated with performance, in a two-stage approach. In the first stage, this paper uses an extended version of DEA (nondiscretionary and categorical variables, and the weight constraints are used) to obtain measures of technical efficiency in the treatment of 993 critical care patients in intensive care units in Catalonia (Spain) in 1991–92. The model incorporates accurate individual measures of illness severity from mortality probability models (MPM II0), and quality outcome measures in the input-output set to obtain nonbiased efficiency measures. In the second stage, a log linear regression model is applied to test a number of hypotheses about the role of different environmental factors – ownership, market structure, dimension, internal organization, diagnostic, mortality risk and so forth – to explain differences in the efficiency scores.

St. Aubyn (2002) evaluates efficiency in the health and education sectors in Portugal. Results presented in this paper evaluating efficiency in education and health sectors are based on an estimation of efficiency frontiers. The author follows a nonparametric method of free disposal hull analysis (FDH). Some results from an alternative parametric method involving corrected least squares (CLS) to health expenditures and outcomes are also included. Two different output indicators were considered – DALE and infant mortality. Health expenditure, the input variable, is measured as total health expenditure per head in the purchasing power parities. Data is related to 1997. Results (using both indicators and both methods) show that Portugal is an inefficient country in producing health. It is almost always placed at the bottom half of the table, irrespective of whether it is viewed vertically or horizontally. Estimated inefficient expenditure varies between 9.1 and 69.8 per cent, depending on the method and indicator used.

As total expenditure was used, inefficiency may arise from either public- or private-sector performances. These inefficiencies may also be explained by variables not considered explicitly by the author, such as the different attitudes towards illness, or different levels of alcohol and drug abuse or AIDS across countries. Since the public sector is responsible for approximately two-thirds of total health expenditure, a more detailed quantitative analysis of public health expenditures is also attempted. Analysis showed that some resources are relatively scarce – general practitioners, nurses or hospital beds. Moreover, they tend to be asymmetrically distributed in geographical terms. This may well diminish efficiency in health care. On the cost side, it partly explains costs with extra remuneration for doctors and nurses. Also, using international comparisons, the authors indicate that public spending on pharmaceuticals and ancillary diagnostic services is excessively high in Portugal. This viewpoint is also supported by other studies indicating this as one of the main sources of inefficiency in the Portuguese health sector.

The study by Farsi, Filippini and Lunati (2008) examines the cost efficiency in the nursing home industry. A stochastic cost frontier model with a translog function has been applied to a balanced panel data of 1,780 observations from 356 nursing homes operating over 5 years (1998–2002) in Switzerland. It compares the estimation results from different panel data econometric techniques focusing on the various methods of specification of unobserved heterogeneity across firms. In particular, the potential effects of such unobserved factors on the estimation results and their interpretation have been discussed. This study also addresses three other empirical issues, including the measurement of economies of scale in the nursing home sector, the assessment of the economic performance of the firms by estimating their cost efficiency scores, and the role of unobserved heterogeneity in the estimation process. The findings indicate that the economies of scale are an important potential source of cost reduction in a majority of Swiss nursing homes. Taking the size as given, the efficiency performance of most individual units is practically very close to the estimated best practice. Nevertheless, the efficiency estimates suggest that some of the nursing homes can significantly reduce their costs by improving their operations.

Among the studies with a focus on the Australian region, the study by Wang, Zhao and Mahmood (2006) explores hospital-level inefficiency by applying a stochastic-frontier multi-product cost function using the 1997–98 New South Wales public hospitals comparison data. It uses a flexible translog cost function to reduce the measurement errors of the outputs of the hospital. It covers 114 acute public hospitals, and these are classified as large hospitals and small hospitals based on their size and complexity. Large hospitals include principal referral, specialist paediatric, ungrouped acute, major metropolitan and major nonmetropolitan hospitals. Small hospitals are district hospitals. The main variables included in the analysis are total variable cost, average salary of medical labour services, average salary of nonmedical labour services, inpatient service index, occasions of services, average available beds, same-day separations as a percentage of total separations, average length of stay for acute episodes and so on. The main findings of the study indicate that inefficiency accounts for 9.3 per cent of total hospital costs in large hospitals and 11.3 per cent in small hospitals (including complexity indicators). Diseconomies of scale prevail in very large hospitals, whereas scale economies appear in very small hospitals. Also the scope effects are found in both large and small hospitals. It is found that small hospitals are more labour-intensive than the larger hospitals. Yong and Harris (1999) estimate the cost frontier for large Victorian public hospitals using the econometric technique of stochastic frontier regression. The reported results use the theoretical multiproduct cost function estimated in Cobb-Douglas form. Two measures of cost – admitted inpatient expenditure (AIE; preferred if the focus is on hospital inpatient care) and total operating expenditure (TOE; a wider measure of hospital care) are used for a sample of 35 major Victorian hospitals in the analysis. A case-mix of adjusted measure of activity – the weighted inlier equivalent separations (WIES) – is used as the measure of output. The WIES is the sum of all discharges adjusted for variability (inlier equivalent separations) weighted by a Diagnosis Related Group or DRG-specific case weight based on the relative cost of the DRG for a sample of Victorian hospitals. WIES is the basic unit for variable payments which form part of the payment formula for Victorian hospitals. An estimate of the mean level of hospital cost inefficiency in 1994–95 is obtained for the period following the introduction of case-mix funding. One of the major goals of Victoria's case-mix funding system, introduced in 1993, was to promote efficiency and hence hospital efficiency. The cost frontier is estimated by the stochastic frontier regression, since it allows for data errors. Inpatient output is found to explain the majority of inter-hospital variation in total cost. By using an exponential distribution for the inefficiency component, the average level of cost inefficiency in total operating expenditure is estimated to be around 3 per cent. Where there are differences in costs between hospitals, these appear to be related to administrative, medical support and hotel labour inputs. It is concluded from the findings that Victorian hospitals do not have a high level of relative cost inefficiency, especially when compared to previous inefficiency estimates of US hospitals and other health care institutions. This is consistent with the expectation that case-mix funding is providing hospitals with appropriate incentives for cost efficiency, although there is no definite causal connection since there is no comparative data from other funding systems in Victoria or any other comparative data available prior to 1993. Mortimer and Peacock (2000) provide a critical appraisal of the methods, results and policy value of two frontier methods for hospital efficiency measurement, namely DEA and SFA. They compare the policy value of DEA- and SFA-based measures against more commonly used indicators of hospital performance. Data from a sample of 38 large Victorian public hospitals for the period 1993–94 has been used. The sample comprises all Group A and Group B hospitals operating in Victoria during 1993–94. Group A includes all Melbourne metropolitan teaching hospitals and Group B is the set of large regional and smaller suburban acute care hospitals. Possible sources of measured inefficiency are investigated via the Battese and Coelli (1995) effects model in the case of SFA-based efficiency scores and via second-stage regressions in the case of DEA-based efficiency measures. The content and consistency of DEA- and SFA-based targets and measures are then compared against simple cost/output ratios. The results of the study suggest moderate correspondence between DEA- and SFA-based efficiency scores with measured inefficiency at least partially attributable to differences between hospitals in case-mix, stay-mix, quality of care, teaching/research activity and location. More or less the same set of hospital characteristics turned out to be important in explaining 'between-hospital' variation in both DEA- and SFA-based measures of hospital efficiency. Results thus provide indications that DEA and SFA are measuring closely related variables having similar dimensions. Also, there exists a common ground between simple cost/output ratios and SFA-based measures of hospital efficiency. However, policy-ready performance measures and deliberations require that frontier-based and ratio-based options should take into account both precision and content.

Based on the concepts of marginal disutility with respect to distance, safety thresholds and 'equally distributed equivalent' distance, the paper by Mainardi

(2007) first reassesses the utility theory assumptions supporting the rationale for functional re-specifications. Partly drawing on these theoretical refinements, the analysis formulates a stochastic cost frontier hurdle model with an endogenously determined hospital distance threshold. For illustrative purposes, this model is applied to pooled biennial communal data for Chile. Health care accessibility in terms of travel cost/time is proxied by distances of administrative centres from the nearest emergency hospitals during the period 2000–03. This study suggests utility function re-specifications with implications for measurement and estimation of spatial inequality in access to health care facilities. An average safety distance threshold is also estimated in a cross-commune application for Chile. This threshold reflects health care regulators' views on individual-varying safety distance thresholds by assuming no change in utility ceteris paribus within these limits, and increasing the marginal disutility if located beyond them.

In the Nordic region, the paper by Kittelsen and Magnussen (1999) analyzes cross-sectional data on the psychiatric outpatient clinics of Norway from 79 adults (outpatient clinics for adults or VPs) and 49 children and youth (outpatient clinics for children and youth or BUPs) for 1998 using DEA. In addition to outputs, the importance of different professions or educational groups on efficiency is examined, and the results for separate samples of clinics for children and youth (BUP) and the clinics for adults (VP) are then compared. While measures of output in mental health care are even harder to find than output in other health care activities, some indicators are available. In models for determining productive efficiency, the problem is to select the output variables that best reflect the use of resources as these variables have a significant impact on measures of efficiency. For children and youth (BUP), the output data used include three types of outputs – interventions, patients and hours. For adults (VP), only one output, number of patient visits, is used. Similar input definitions for both BUP and VP include university-educated staff, college-educated staff and other staff. The main results emerging from this analysis indicate that industry efficiency is around 60 per cent in the BUP sector and 66 per cent in the VP sector. There is a constant return to scale in the BUP sector but variable returns to scale in the VP sector. Staff composition does matter in both sectors, even though marginal productivity of labour (MPLs) are quite similar.

Magnussen (1996) provides a thorough discussion of how the functioning of hospital production affects the measures of efficiency. In particular, his paper focuses on three questions that bear relevance to the policy implications of hospital efficiency analysis. The first question is whether the distribution of efficiency varies with varying output vectors. If the distribution varies, it becomes more difficult to draw conclusions about the average performance of the hospital industry and also to compare the performance of groups of hospitals. The second is whether the ranking of the hospitals varies with varying output vectors. Unstable rankings will have consequences for the monitoring of individual hospitals and the allocation of resources. The third is whether the scale properties of the technology vary with varying output vectors. If scale properties vary, so will optimal size and thereby the optimal hospital structure. The aim is not to answer how one should operationalize hospital production, but rather to illustrate the applicability of efficiency measures as instruments of monitoring and for resource allocation. Data was collected by the Central Bureau of Statistics, while the grouping of patients into DRGs was done at the Norwegian Institute for Hospital Research. Three inputs are defined: the number of physicians and nursing personnel working full-time, the number of other full-time personnel, and capital measured as the number of beds. The data used are from 46 Norwegian acute care, nonteaching hospitals for the years 1989–1991, a total sample of 138 observations. The results of the study indicate that the efficiency distributions were found to be responsive to changes in the specification of outputs. However, both the individual efficiency measures and the scale properties showed substantial variation. Thus the author concludes, 'It would, therefore, seem that the notion that resource allocation can be based on results from DEA-type models only is somewhat too optimistic. Furthermore, this analysis has shown that even the less ambitious goal of identifying the high, medium, and low performers may be difficult to reach.'

In Asia, Li and Wang's study (2008) presents an empirical analysis of the relative efficiency of the Chinese public acute hospitals. Data were obtained from the Health Information Center at the Ministry of Health for the year 2001. Public acute hospitals are categorized into level III, level II and level I hospitals in accordance with their size and complexity. In principle, a level III hospital is referred to as a hospital that provides specialist services, undertakes teaching and research and has more than 500 hospital beds. These are mainly province-affiliated hospitals, university-affiliated hospitals, and so on. A level II hospital is referred to as a hospital that provides comprehensive medical services such as surgery, partly undertakes teaching and research, serves a population size of more than 100,000 and has 100–499 hospital beds. These are mainly city district hospitals, county hospitals and some central township hospitals. A level I hospital is defined as a hospital that serves a population of less than 100,000 and has fewer than 100 hospitals beds. These are mainly distributed in towns in urban areas and communities in rural areas. The sample sizes from the three levels of hospitals are 98, 98, and 64 respectively. The study combines physical inputs and cost information to capture all the possible measures of input variables. The study applies DEA and a regression model in a multistage approach. It uses an output-oriented DEA approach. The estimation procedures include decomposition of the technical efficiency obtained as scale efficiency and 'pure' technical efficiency under the assumption of variable returns to scale. The findings indicate that on an average, the level II hospitals are the least inefficient. In addition, results of input slacks and/or output slacks show that doctor/nurse ratio and high-tech medical equipment could be further adjusted without affecting technical efficiency.

The study by Sankar and Kathuria (2004) attempts to analyze the performance of rural public health systems of sixteen major states in India using the techniques from stochastic production frontier and panel data literature. A number of data sources have been used to make a balanced panel of variables from 1986 to 1997 for the states of Andhra Pradesh, Assam, Bihar, Gujarat, Haryana, Himachal Pradesh, Karnataka, Kerala, Maharashtra, Madhya Pradesh, Orissa, Punjab,

Rajasthan, Tamil Nadu, Uttar Pradesh and West Bengal. The results show that not all states with better health indicators have efficient health systems. The study concludes that investment in the health sector alone does not result in better health indicators. Efficient management of the investment is required. Mathiyazhgan (2006) analyzed the cost efficiency of the public and private hospitals in Karnataka State in India. This is estimated through parametric and nonparametric methods by using the Hospitals Facility Survey (Government of Karnataka, 2004) in Karnataka State. The findings indicate that the choice of the econometric approach did not cause any significant difference in the results, and these are robust. The analysis indicates that hospitals (both public and private taken together in the analysis) are cost inefficient owing to the technical and allocative system of resources in the hospitals. However, the private hospitals appear relatively less inefficient than the public hospitals. Some of the main determinants of the technical and allocative inefficiencies of the public hospitals include inappropriate interventions of inpatient days care, share of medical personnel, beds capacity, quality indices and choice of location. By contrast, the factors for private hospitals relate to beds capacity and quality indices.

The paper by Suraratdechaac and Okunadeb (2006) investigated the economic relationship between medical resources and efficiency of the health care system in a developing Asian country, namely Thailand. It estimated a four-factor production system, based on 1982–1997 annual operational data comprising five cross-sectional regions per year. The translog production function and the three equations to derive demand for factor inputs were jointly estimated using the systems regression method. Results indicated that different types of medical care workers (doctors, nurses, pharmacists) influenced efficiency differently. The marginal products (MPs) of nurses and capital are the highest, and they varied across the regions. The estimates of factor substitution possibilities indicated difficult factor adjustments. The estimates differed in magnitude and significance across regions. However, the regional variations in returns-to-scale estimates in live births tended to converge with that of the Bangkok metropolis. Thus the technical changes for physicians and pharmacists were found to be labour using, but capital and nursing were found to be labour saving.

In the African region, a study by Felix Masiye (2007) using DEA in Zambian hospitals has demonstrated that inefficiency of resource use in hospitals is significant. Policy attention is drawn to the unsuitable hospital scale of operations and the low productivity of some inputs as factors that reinforce each other to make Zambian hospitals technically inefficient at producing and delivering services. It is argued that such evidence of substantial inefficiency would undermine Zambia's prospects of achieving its health goals. DEA constructs an efficiency frontier which reveals the least input requirement for obtaining a given output level, or alternatively, from an output-oriented framework, the highest output obtainable from a given input set. In this paper, the author decomposes technical efficiency into scale efficiency and efficiency due to congestion. It helps to identify the areas of action for both planners at higher levels (e.g. level of hospital staffing or capitalization) and implementers at the service delivery level.

Thus, the input-oriented measure of scale efficiency for the *j*th hospital is calculated by the following ratio:

$$SE_j = \frac{TE_j\ (Y_j, X_j\ ; CRS, S)}{TE_j\ (Y_j, X_j\ ; VRS, S)}.$$

A hospital's score will be 1 if it is scale-efficient or less than 1 if otherwise. Further, for scale-inefficient hospitals, characteristics of inefficiency are also identified by economies of scale or diseconomies of scale. An input-based measure of congestion efficiency (CE) is defined by the study, which is a ratio of the technical efficiency (TE) measure under strong disposability of inputs (TE (VRS,S)) to the TE measure under weak input disposability technology (TE (VRS,W)).

$$CE_j = \frac{TE_j\ (Y_j, X_j\ ; VRS, S)}{TE_j\ (Y_j, X_j\ ; VRS, W)}.$$

A sample size of 32 hospitals was determined based on the budget. This would encompass about 30 per cent of the first- and second-level hospitals. Further, the survey was to be conducted in five provinces (Central, Copperbelt, Eastern, Southern and Central) of the nine provinces of Zambia to ensure there was contiguity between the study sites. Two hospitals were removed due to incomplete data, leaving a sample of 30. This sample was composed of eighteen (60%) government-owned hospitals, eight (27%) church mission hospitals and four (13%) private hospitals. In terms of geographical location, 16 (53%) hospitals were based in rural areas. The four input variables included were total nonlabour cost (x_1), number of medical doctors (x_2), number of nursing and other clinical staff (x_3) and the number of nonclinical staff (x_4). It was confirmed during the field visits that there was a good degree of substitutability among clinical staff, especially in rural hospitals because of staff shortages. The input x_1 was a composite including running costs, administration, allowances, overhead costs and capital costs. To estimate x_1, all capital and equipment costs were annualized using a lifespan of 30 years for buildings and 10 years for vehicles and equipment, and a discount rate of 5 per cent. These rates have been applied in studies in Africa. Hospital service, which supposedly improves patients' health, was used as an intermediate-level output. However, quality adjustment in outputs could not be done in this study due to nonavailability of the necessary data on case-mix and quality. This implied that the case-mix and severity patterns were assumed to be constant across the sample hospitals.

According to the results, Zambian hospitals could have attained their output levels with about 30 per cent less resources, suggesting potential for better service coverage. For instance, if inefficiency is eliminated or minimized, the extra resources could be invested in a range of operational areas such as better quality patient care, new technology, expansion of service profile, staff training in needed specialties or improved staff welfare. Hospitals could also finance part of their debt stock.

Further, decomposing of technical efficiency clearly emphasized the specific role of scale and input congestion in contributing to hospital inefficiency. In particular, unsuitable hospital scale of operation or size and low productivity of some inputs reinforce each other to make Zambian hospitals technically inefficient at delivering services. In this case, strategies such as hospital mergers or downgrades may help bring down costs and improve overall efficiency in the hospital industry. It is possible that some hospitals may be using more of some resources only because they have been historically overfunded or overstaffed relative to their outputs.

The report on district hospitals in Namibia (Government of the Republic of Namibia 2004) provides information on the state of the technical efficiency of district hospitals in Namibia using DEA. It indicates the efficiency savings that are expected from all the district hospitals and the required input use if each of the inefficient hospitals functions as efficiently as its peers on the frontier. A total of 30 district hospitals were surveyed for the financial years from 1997 to 2001. The DEA analysis revealed that average efficiency scores for the 4 years 1997–98 to 2000–01, range from 62.7 to 74.3 per cent. This indicates the presence of significant amounts of inefficiency that are attributable to both pure technical and scale inefficiency. For the period under review, the constant returns to scale (CRS) technical efficiency scores show that fewer than half of the district hospitals are located on the frontier. In all the 4 years, increasing returns to scale was the most prevalent cause of scale inefficiency. The number of hospitals with decreasing returns to scale is relatively small. The study provides estimates of substantial amounts of input savings that could have been achieved had the technically inefficient hospitals operated as efficiently as their efficient peers.

Health care costs are a financial burden for developing and transition economies which have experienced a faster growing demand for their health care systems while aiming to improve efficiency. As costs become more complex, attention has shifted to the efficiency of an entire system. Data envelopment analysis is used to measure health care efficiencies and to discuss policy implications. After the collapse of the Soviet Union, the newly independent states and the Eastern European countries experienced economic chaos and instability. Although efforts were made by these countries to privatize manufacturing and commercial sectors to raise productivity, it was not the priority of these governments to drastically reduce inputs to the health care sector for improving efficiency. Also, the majority of health care workers are highly trained, and over the years, a significant amount of investment has been made on them by the governments. The study by Mirmirani (2008) uses the output-oriented CCR model (Charnes, Cooper and Rhodes 1978) to evaluate the efficiency of the health care systems of these countries. The choice of variables used in this study is guided by consistency of measurement amongst transition economies and the availability of data. The period of investigation is 1997–2001. The majority of the data is extracted from World Development Indicators, UNICEF and World Bank databases. Output variables are the average (male and female) life expectancy and infant mortality rates. The input variables include per capita health care expenditure in US dollars after adjustment for purchasing power parity, number of inpatient hospital beds per thousand of population, number of physicians per thousand of population and immunizations. During the period 1997–2001, top performers (i.e. the most efficient systems) were OECD countries (their average inputs and outputs), Albania and Armenia. The least efficient systems, over an extensive period, were Russia and Belarus followed by Latvia and Romania. In addition to the input and output variables, rates of alcohol and tobacco consumption as well as other socio-political factors also affected the efficiency rankings of transition countries. Higher efficiency in Albania and Armenia could be attributable to their policies to control the consumption of these products. Russia's inadequacy reflects the lack of restrictions on the old-command economic policies of the government as well as the degradation of the environment and high rates of alcohol and tobacco use. It is pointed out that the failure of transition economies to establish a strong health care system is due to the lack of sound policy, rising social stress and an unhealthy lifestyle. Addressing these issues requires profound changes in government policies, health education and public awareness.

The paper by Hajialiafzali, Moss and Mahmood (2007) examines the relative efficiency of hospitals owned by the Iranian Social Security Organization. It applies DEA using data for the year 2002. The results indicate that 26 of the 53 hospitals were deemed to be efficient. Inefficient hospitals had an average score of 90 per cent, implying a potential reduction in all inputs on an average by about 10 per cent with no impact on output levels. In addition to the conventional DEA measurement, efficient hospitals were ranked by calculating super-efficiency scores, by identifying unefficient hospitals and by determining the frequency of peers.

Thus, the aforesaid review of studies across different continents (Asia, Africa, Europe, Australia and America) indicates that the measurement of efficiency has been attempted in different contextual frameworks applying different quantitative techniques, with the majority of the studies having an application of either of DEA or frontier analysis. Application of the latter has covered country-specific and state-specific health systems. Different types of health units – general hospitals, specialty and super-specialty hospitals, clinics, primary health centres, nursing homes, health maintenance organizations and others – have been analyzed through these techniques. However, despite a plethora of literature and studies, the studies in the Indian context are very much limited in terms of both numbers and coverage; the latter is restricted to national- or state-level efficiency measurements only. None of the studies mentioned previously have so far focused on using quantitative techniques at the sub-state level or district level. Therefore, in the Indian context, we have attempted a sub-state-level analysis along with a state-level analysis in the next chapter.

In the education sector, previous research on the performance and efficiency of the public sector and its functions that applied nonparametric methods mostly used either FDH or DEA and find significant inefficiencies in many countries. Notable studies include Gupta and Verhoeven (2001) for education and health in Africa, Clements (2002) for education in Europe, Afonso, Schuknecht, and Tanzi (2005) for public sector performance expenditure in the OECD, Afonso and St. Aubyn (2005a, 2005b) for efficiency in providing health and education in OECD countries. De Borger, Kerstens, Moesen and Vanneste (1994), De Borger and Kerstens (1996), and Afonso and Fernandes (2006) find evidence of spending inefficiencies for the local government sector. Some studies apply both FDH and DEA methods. Afonso and St. Aubyn (2005b) undertook a two-step DEA/tobit analysis, in the context of a cross-country analysis of secondary education efficiency. Sutherland, Price, Joumard and Nicq (2007) develops performance indicators for public spending efficiency in primary and secondary education in OECD countries using both DEA and SFA. This paper assesses the potential to raise public spending efficiency in the primary and secondary education sector. To draw cross-country comparisons of the efficiency in the provision of education, the paper develops a set of comparable indicators which reflect international differences in the levels of efficiency in the primary and secondary education sector both within and among countries. The paper identifies significant scope to improve efficiency by moving towards best practice.

Using data for a sample of developing countries and transition economies, the paper by Emanuele, Guin-Siu and De Mello (2003) estimates the relationship between government spending on health care and education and selected social indicators. Unlike previous studies, where social indicators are used as proxies for the unobservable health and education status of the population, this paper estimates a latent variable model. The findings suggest that public spending is an important determinant of social outcomes, particularly in the education sector. Overall, the latent variable approach yields better estimates of a social production function than the traditional approach, with higher elasticities of social indicators with respect to income and spending, therefore providing stronger evidence that increases in public spending do have a positive impact on social outcomes.

The study by Cunha and Rocha (2012) applies DEA techniques to evaluate the comparative efficiency of public higher education institutions in Portugal. The analysis is performed for three separate groups: public universities, public polytechnics and the several faculties of the University of Porto. By using several inputs and outputs at the institutional level, the authors identify the most technically efficient institutions that may work as benchmarks in the sector. The results suggest that a great portion of institutions may be working inefficiently, contributing to a significant waste of resources. This exploratory study is considered a first step towards a deeper understanding of the efficiency determinants of higher education institutions.

Wolszczak-Derlacz and Parteka (2011) examine efficiency and its determinants in a set of higher education institutions (HEIs) from several European countries by means of nonparametric frontier techniques. The analysis is based on a sample of 259 public HEIs from seven European countries across the period of 2001–2005. They conduct a two-stage DEA analysis, first evaluating DEA scores and then regressing them on potential covariates with the use of a bootstrapped truncated regression. Results indicate a considerable variability of efficiency scores within and between countries. Unit size (economies of scale), number and composition of faculties, sources of funding and gender staff composition are found to be among the crucial determinants of these units' performance. Specifically, they found evidence that a higher share of funds from external sources and a higher number of women among academic staff improve the efficiency of the institution.

Sav (2012) provides stochastic frontier cost and (in)efficiency estimates for private for-profit colleges with comparisons to public and private nonprivate colleges. The focus is on the 2-year US higher education sector where there exists the largest and fastest-growing entry of for-profit colleges. Unbalanced panel data is employed for four academic years, 2005–2009. Translog cost frontiers are estimated with an inefficiency component that depends upon environmental factors defined by college-specific characteristics. More experienced public and private nonprofit colleges are found to be more cost efficient relative to the newer entrants. In addition, the newer for-profits exhibit greater efficiency variability but also show some evidence of efficiency gains over the academic years. There is some cursory evidence that for-profit entry is positively correlated, albeit weakly, with greater public college sector inefficiency.

The study by Ahmed (2012) investigates the public sector's efficiency in educational expenditure in the two major provinces of Pakistan. The data of Punjab and Sindh at the district level have been used and DEA has been conducted. The efficiency scores and rankings for districts in each of the provinces have been computed and analyzed.

A study of the efficiency of Uganda's public education system has been carried out by Winkler and Sondergaard (2008). This study carried out a rapid unit cost survey of 180 public and private primary schools in six districts across three regions to provide this information. This study documents the magnitude and extent of the leakage and misuse of educational resources. When possible, it identifies the principal causes of inefficiencies. However, in general, further research is needed to pinpoint causes and thus identify cost-effective solutions. For example, the study documents the problem of an inequitable and inefficient assignment of teachers across districts and schools. The internal efficiency of public secondary education is low and unit costs are high. The reasons for low efficiency include low workloads, poor teacher deployment and high teacher salaries. A significant portion of secondary school teachers are underutilized.

Appendix 3.1

Table A3.1 Studies on DEA and SFA (an overall view)

Author(s)	Methodology[a]	Sample[b]	Inputs, outputs, explanatory variables (if applicable)[c]	Analytical technique	Main findings
Banker, Conrad and Strauss (1986)	DEA	114 North Carolina hospitals, 1978	Nursing, ancillary, administrative and general services expenditure, capital expenditure. Patient days for inpatients less than 14 years, patient days for inpatients between 14 and 65 years, patient days for inpatients aged above 65 years	Comparison of returns-to-scale, marginal rates of transformation and technical efficiency	DEA identifies a richer and more diverse set of behaviour than nonfrontier techniques
Grosskopf and Valdmanis (1987)	DEA	66 Californian hospitals, 1982	Number of physicians, full-time equivalent nonphysician labour, admissions, plant and equipment assets. Acute and intensive care inpatient days, number of inpatient and outpatient surgeries, number of ambulatory and emergency care visits	Descriptive analysis across public and not-for-profit hospitals	Public hospitals have lower costs than not-for-profit hospitals
Wagstaff (1989)	DFA and SFA	49 Spanish hospitals, 1977–1981	Total costs (excluding capital expenditure), 6 case-mix categories (internal medicine, general surgery, gynaecology, paediatrics, intensive care, and others) as indexes, stock of beds, case flow, dummy variable for teaching status	Interpretation of parameter estimates	Mean level of efficiency highly dependent upon the approach employed
Ley (1991)	DEA	139 Spanish hospitals, 1984	Number of doctors, technical degree and other personnel, purchases of sanitary supplies and number of beds; patient days, discharges because of recovery (medicine, surgery, obstetrics, paediatrics and intensive care), patient days in other wards (psychiatry, tuberculosis, long-term), number of emergency cases, operations and newborns	Descriptive analysis.	Private hospitals more efficient than public, no difference in efficiency between teaching and nonteaching hospitals

Study	Method	Sample	Variables	Analysis	Findings
Fizel and Nunnikhoven (1992)	DEA	167 Michigan nursing homes, 1987.	Registered nurse hours, licensed practical nurse hours, aides and orderlies hours; skilled and intermediate-care; percentage of empty beds, number of skilled beds, assessed penalty points, Medicare patients and beds, Herfindahl index of market concentration, dummy variables for urban and profit and not-for-profit homes	Descriptive statistics across disaggregated sample; second-stage least squares regression	Second-stage regression analysis purges efficiency indices of 'confounding' factors; for-profit homes are more efficient than not-for-profit ones
Valdmanis (1992)	DEA	41 Michigan hospitals, 1982	Number of attendings, house staff, physicians, nurses, other full-time equivalent staff, admissions, beds, net plant assets; adult, paediatric, elderly, acute, intensive care inpatient days, number of surgeries, number of emergency care and ambulatory visits, total house staff	Descriptive analysis of public and private not-for-profit hospitals	Public hospitals more efficient than nonprofit hospitals; alterations in input-output model bring differences in efficiency levels and ranks
Byrnes and Valdmanis (1993)	DEA	123 California hospitals, 1983	Number of registered nurses, management and administrative personnel, number of technical services personnel, aides and orderlies, licensed practising nurses, price of labour (reported wage rate), capital (average staffed beds), price of capital (depreciation divided by number of beds). Medical-surgical acute, medical-surgical intensive and maternity discharges	Descriptive analysis	Enhances the scope of previous studies by incorporating price measures as well as physical unit measures
Chilingerian (1993)	DEA	36 US physicians, 1987	Average length of stay, total ancillary services; number of low-severity and high-severity cases; average age of patients, area of specialization, average severity, relative weight of caseload, physician's age, fraction of caseload with satisfactory outcomes, local or pre-paid practice membership	Comparison of DEA with ratio analysis, slack analysis, Mann-Whitney tests, second-stage logit regression	Key factors that influence physician efficiency include prepaid group practices vs. fee-for-service payment structure

(Continued)

Author(s)	Methodology[a]	Sample[b]	Inputs, outputs, explanatory variables (if applicable)[c]	Analytical technique	Main findings
Färe, Grosskopf, Lindgren and Roos (1993)	MI	17 Swedish hospitals, 1970–1985	Real labour input (average labour expenditure per hour), real nonlabour input (food, drugs, medical supplies and laundry excluding capital costs); short-term inpatient care (proxied by discharges), long-term chronic care (proxied by bed days), ambulatory care (proxied by doctor visits)	Descriptive analysis of relative efficiency over time	Advantages of approach over Törnqvist, Paasche and Laspeyres index-type productivity measures
Hofler and Rungeling (1994)	SFA	1,079 US nursing homes, 1985	Total variable costs, nursing staff hourly wages, hourly wage for physicians and other professional staff, hourly wage for all other staff, capital (as proxied by number of beds); skilled inpatient days, intermediate care inpatient days, other inpatient days; type of home certification, physician availability, nursing staff characteristics, geographic region, chain membership, ownership type and hospital affiliation	Second-stage OLS regression; interpretation of parameter estimates	Nursing homes appear to be cost-efficient
Kooreman (1994)	DEA	320 Dutch nursing homes, 1989	Number of medical doctors, nurses, nurse trainees, therapists, general and other staff; number of full and day-care, physical disability, and psycho-disability patients; number of beds, occupancy rate, proportion of patients older than 85 years, length of stay, hospital affiliation, regional dummies, religious affiliation, dummy variable for patients' council	Descriptive statistics, second-stage probit and tobit regressions	A number of quality indicators have a negative effect on efficiency; practical usefulness of DEA limited by the availability of data

Study	Method	Sample	Variables	Analysis	Findings
Zuckerman, Hadley and Iezzoni (1994)	SFA	4,149 US hospitals, 1986–87	Total costs, average annual salary per full-time equivalent employee, depreciation and interest expenses per bed; postadmission inpatient days, outpatient visits; percentage of beds in intensive care, non-surgery outpatient visits, long-term admissions, ratio of births to admissions, average case-mix, inpatient surgical operations per admission, index of high technology services, ratio of residents to beds, accreditation indicator, individual Medicare-specific variables	Correlation coefficients between alternative model specifications, inefficiency estimates from pooled and partitioned hospital groups	Inefficiency measures generated insensitive to functional form; large number of hospital outputs may not be treated exogenously nor homogeneously
Chattopadhyay and Ray (1996)	DEA	140 US nursing homes, 1982–93	Labour hours for dietary, housekeeping, laundry, director, registered nurse, licensed practical nurse and nurses aides staff, total expenditure on non-labour inputs; Medicare, Medicaid, private and other patient days	Descriptive analysis	For-profit home more efficient than not-for-profit homes
Lo, Shih and Chen (1996)	DEA	82 Taiwan hospitals, 1982	Number of doctors, nurses, other staff and beds; number of visits, operations and patient days, and average patient days; dummy variables for public, military, corporate, religious and university hospitals, hospital size, percentage of patients over 65 years, percentage of beds in city, dummy variable for scanning equipment	Descriptive analysis, second-stage tobit regression	Public hospitals less efficient than private hospitals

(Continued)

Table A3.1 (Continued)

Author(s)	Methodology[a]	Sample[b]	Inputs, outputs, explanatory variables (if applicable)[c]	Analytical technique	Main findings
Luoma, Järviö, Suoniemi and Hjerppe (1996)	DEA	220 Finnish health centres, 1991	Total operating costs (excluding rehabilitation), cost of purchased services, cost adjustment for remote areas; health care and medical visits to a physician, health care or medical care visits to other personnel, supervised domiciliary care visits, dental care visits, special examinations, short-term inpatients days, long-term inpatient days for heavy and non-heavy dependence categories; percentage of state subsidy, local government taxation per patient, distance to nearest hospital, proportion of population over 65 years, number of personnel posts, dummy variable for single-municipality heath centre	Descriptive analysis, second-stage Tobit regression	Inefficiency linked to larger state subsidies and higher per capita taxable income, remote centres more inefficient Efficiency also linked to increases in proportion of elderly in area
Gonzalez Lopez-Valcarcel and Barber Perez (1996)	DEA and SFA	75 Spanish hospitals 1991–93	Number of doctors, other staff and beds, total costs for cost frontier; medical, surgical, intensive care, obstetric and newborn inpatient days, number of ambulatory surgical procedures, operations with hospitalisation and total admissions, index of ambulatory/emergency visits and high-tech activity; percentage of doctors on staff, percentage of subcontracted work, rate of hospital admission per 1,000 population, dummy variables for regions	Descriptive analysis, second-stage Tobit regression	Differences in efficiency associated with size, the extent of subcontracting and the rate of capacity utilisation

Magnussen (1996)	DEA	46 Norwegian hospitals, 1989–91	Number of physicians and other personnel, number of beds; medical, surgical, simple and complex patient days, number of medical and surgical patients, number of long-term care days and outpatient visits	Descriptive analysis	Difficulty in identifying high, medium and low performers using DEA
Thanassoulis, Boussofiane and Dyson (1996)	DEA	189 UK district health authorities, 1985–86	Numbers of obstetrics/gynaecology staff, paediatricians, midwives and nurses, general practitioners' fees; number of deliveries, deliveries to resident mothers, babies less than 1 500 g birth weight and legally induced abortions, length of stay	Descriptive analysis, correlation between efficiency indexes and performance indicators	DEA and performance indicators weakly agree on unit performance; DEA as a tool for target setting
Defelice and Bradford (1997)	SFA	924 US physicians, 1984–95	Number of physician visits; weekly hours of medicine practice by physician, nursing and clerical time per physician, percentage of visits using lab tests or X-rays; years of physician experience, percentage of physicians earning in excess of $10,000 exogenous income, percentage of physicians in general or family practice, percentage of physicians working in internal medicine, paediatrics or partnerships, number of physicians in practice, percentage of physicians sharing net revenue equally and multispecialty groups; number of board-certified physicians in specialty hospitals in the county, number of HMOs and hospitals in the country, number of physicians per 1,000 county population, percentage of patients insured by Medicaid, percentage of visits provided by hospital, number of offices with lab or X-ray equipment, level of malpractice premiums	Descriptive analysis, single-stage least squares regression	No difference in efficiency between group and solo practices

(*Continued*)

Table A3.1 (Continued)

Author(s)	Methodology[a]	Sample[b]	Inputs, outputs, explanatory variables (if applicable)[c]	Analytical technique	Main findings
Parkin and Hollingsworth (1997)	DEA	75 Scottish hospitals, 1991–94	Number of staffed beds, total number of trained and learning nurses, total professional, technical, administrative and clerical staff, total non-nursing medical and dental staff, cost of drug supply, NHS capital charge on capital assets and investments; medical and surgical discharges, accident and emergency attendance, outpatient attendance, obstetrics and gynaecological discharges, other speciality discharges	Efficiency scores across different combinations of input-output and time	Large amount of difference in efficiency results depending upon specification
Rosenman, Siddharthan and Ahern (1997)	DEA	28 Florida health maintenance organizations, 1994	Total administrative expenses, total assets, total medical expenses; all enrollees, Medicare enrollees, Medicaid enrollees; plan size (total enrolment), Herfindahl index of enrolment concentration (Commercial, Medicare and Medicaid enrollees)	Descriptive analysis, second-stage OLS regressions	Efficiency is equal irrespective of organization and ownership; HMOs that accept Medicaid patients are more efficient
Chirikos (1998)	SFA	186 US hospitals, 1982–93	Total operating expenses; number of postadmission patient days with Medicare, Medicaid or other as primary payer, case weighted admission index, case-equivalent outpatient index (ratio of gross outpatient revenue to gross inpatient revenue) emergency room outpatient index (ratio of gross ambulatory revenue to gross emergency services revenue); wage	Descriptive analysis across explanatory variables	Empirical results sensitive to specification of outputs, factor prices or other covariate models; government-controlled hospitals more efficient, less-efficient

					hospitals in highly competitive, population- and physician-dense areas
			rates of three categories of personnel (inpatient and ambulatory, ancillary, and administrative), ratio of depreciation to book value of plant and equipment, ratio of interest charges to current assets.; cost per case, annual cases, control of ownership status (government, proprietary or voluntary), licensed beds, teaching status, market share, population density, and physicians per 100,000 persons		
Linna (1998)	SFA and MI, DEA	43 Finnish acute care hospitals, 1988–94	Net operating costs, total number of beds, average hourly wage rate, annual price index for local government health care expenditure; total number of emergency visits, total scheduled and follow-up visits, weighted number of total admissions, total bed days, number of residents receiving training, number of on-the-job nurse training weeks, impact weighted scientific publications; dummy variables for teaching status, readmission rate for admissions, year dummies	Descriptive analysis, rank correlation between efficiency scores, single-stage SFA incorporating efficiency effects	Choice of the modelling approach does not affect results; SFA and DEA models revealed productivity growth over period to be the result of exogenous technical change
Puig-Junoy (1998)	DEA	993 Spanish patients in 16 intensive care units (ICU), 1991–92	Patient survival probability at admission, mortality risk level, weighted ICU days, non-ICU days, available nurses and physician days per patient, technological availability; number of surviving days in hospital, surviving discharge status; dummy variable for for-profit hospitals, Herfindahl competition index, number of beds in ICU, proportion of patients in	Descriptive analysis, second-stage log-linear regression	Higher-risk patients managed less efficiently than lower-risk patients, higher technical efficiency in for-profit teaching hospitals, and those with nurse and

(Continued)

Table A3.1 (Continued)

Author(s)	Methodology[a]	Sample[b]	Inputs, outputs, explanatory variables (if applicable)[c]	Analytical technique	Main findings
			the same risk group, number of inpatient days for ICUs using clinical guidelines and nurse/physician evaluation programs, number of daily visits, dummy variable for teaching hospital, mortality risk score, age, dummy variables for respiratory failure, cardiovascular disease, trauma, urgent admission, postoperative patients with programmed admission		physician program evaluation; diagnostic variable generally unrelated
Burgess and Wilson (1998)	DEA	1,545 US hospitals, 1985–88	Number of acute-care beds, long-term hospital beds, registered nurses, practical nurses, other clinical and non-clinical labour; acute care inpatient days, case-mix adjusted acute care inpatient discharges, long-term care inpatient days, outpatient visits, ambulatory surgical procedures, inpatient surgical procedures; dummy variables for state/local government, non-profit, for-profit, Veterans Affairs and teaching hospitals, Herfindahl index of county competition, average length of stay, percentage of registered nurses, ratio of clinical to non-clinical staff, administration cost per bed day	Descriptive analysis, second-stage least squares regression	No difference in efficiency across different ownership structures or in teaching hospitals; greater expenditures on administration and nursing staff associated with higher efficiency

Source: Worthington (2004).

[a] DEA = data envelopment analysis; SFA = stochastic frontier analysis; DFA = deterministic frontier analysis; MI = Malmquist indices.
[b] Singular dates represent calendar or financial year cross-sections, intervals represent time series.
[c] In order by paragraph.

Appendix 3.2
Relationship of productivity and average cost

As indicated in the text, if input price information is available, such as the wage rate, we can analyze the relationship between productivity and average costs.

Referring to Figure 3.1 (given in the text) and assuming that the price of labour is constant at $350 per hour, consider Point B. The hospital uses 300 hours of labour. Therefore the total cost is $105,000. Since the hospital at Point B produces 600 treatments, the cost per unit (or average cost) is $175.

Similarly, at Point C the hospital uses 400 hours at $350 per hour. The total cost is $140,000 while the total output is 1,000 units. Therefore, the average cost is $140. Appendix Table A3.2 summarizes the computation of average cost for the four illustrated points.

As the hospital increases its scale of operations from B to C, *total* cost increases but *average* cost decreases due to the impact of scale economies. As the hospital moves from C to D, however, it encounters diseconomies of scale. Total costs increase at a faster rate than the increase in output.

As a result, the average cost increases from $140 to $194. Point C represents the optimal scale for the hospital, where the productivity ratio is at a maximum and average cost is at a minimum (Hughes 2002).

Table A3.2 Calculation of average cost

Point	Number of labour hours x	Labour price ($)–w	Cost ($) (x × w)	Number of treatment s–y	Average cost ($)–(x × w)/y
A	300	350	105,000	450	233
B	300	350	105,000	600	175
C	400	350	140,000	1,000	140
D	650	350	227,500	1,170	194

Appendix 3.3
Partial productivity ratios and measuring efficiency

As indicated in the text of the chapter, there is no clear way of determining technical efficiency. It is possible that the top-ranking performer for a particular ratio may not be having the requisite efficiency parameter.

With a view to demonstrating this point we present in this Appendix a case study of four hospitals (Hughes 2002).

Table A3.3 shows the inpatient output measure and full set of input data for the four hospitals, including XYZ in Year 1. Table A3.31 shows the set of partial factor productivity (PFP) ratios and their rankings across the four hospitals.

Table A3.3 Output and input data for group of hospitals

Hospital	Inpatient treatments (no. of cases) – y_1	Outpatient visits (no. of consultations) – y_2	Labour (no. of FTE staff) – x_1	Contractors (no. of hours worked) – x_2	Capital (no. of beds) – x_3	Other inputs (imputed quantity) – x_4
XYZ	800	45,000	1,300	250,000	300	200,000
ABC	900	50,000	1,400	300,000	320	220,000
LMN	700	48,000	1,200	250,000	280	160,000
HIJ	1,000	60,000	1,500	340,000	420	240,000

Table A3.31 Comparative partial factor productivity ratios and rankings (inpatient treatment output measure)

Hospital	Ratio 1 – y_1/x_1	Ratio 2 – y_1/x_2	Ratio 3 – y_1/x_3	Ratio 4 – y_1/x_4
XYZ	0.615 (3)	0.0032 (1)	2.667 (2)	0.0400 (4)
ABC	0.643 (2)	0.0030 (2)	2.813 (1)	0.0041 (3)
LMN	0.583 (4)	0.0028 (4)	2.500 (3)	0.0044 (1)
HIJ	0.667 (1)	0.0029 (3)	2.381 (4)	0.0042 (2)

Using simple PFP ratios, there is no clear way of determining technical efficiency. For example, HIJ is the top-ranking performer for Ratio 1, the third-ranking performer for Ratio 2, and the worst performer for Ratio 3. The picture would become even less clear if we considered the partial ratios incorporating the other output measure, outpatient visits.

This example illustrates that there is no clear way, even for a small group of only four organizations, to assess efficiency using partial productivity ratios because different ratios produce different performance rankings (Hughes 2002).

Notes

1 For details see Appendix 3.1.
2 The combination of allocative and technical efficiency gives a measure of cost efficiency. For a detailed discussion of allocative and cost efficiency concepts and applications see, for instance, Coelli, Rao and Battese (1998).
3 In actual practice, an organization's production technology cannot be easily observed.
4 To calculate an unambiguous measure of relative performance using an index number approach, a multilateral index can be used to facilitate a comparison of Total Factor Productivity performance across a group of organizations over time. It compares each organization in an industry to a hypothetical representative entity. The representative organization is 'constructed' from average output and input data derived from all data in a given panel. Input price (or cost) data and output price (or revenue) data are required for weighting the quantity changes of the individual entities and the representative organization (see Caves, Christensen and Diewert 1982).
5 In most practical applications measurement is inexact and therefore subject to error.

4   Our model and methodology

Notably there are very few studies in the context of developing countries, India in particular. Recent literature is nearly absent. By focusing on India in the recent period, our study thus attempts to bridge that gap.

Hypothesis and objective

We hypothesize that states differ in their technical efficiency pertaining to health and education systems due to factors which require emphasis in facility planning in these sectors (Purohit 2010e; Sankar and Kathuria 2004). It is also hypothesized that these factors differ from state to state according to their level of development. It is presumed that estimated efficiency parameters (from both types of analysis, i.e. nonparametric and parametric approaches) should help the health and education policy makers to improve state-level system performance pertaining to these sectors.

Methodology, study design and database

Nonparametric approach: free disposal hull

In this paper we use two types of techniques, namely nonparametric and parametric, that allow for a direct measurement of the relative efficiency of government spending among countries or states within a nation. In the former type we apply free disposal hull (FDH) analysis, which assesses the relative efficiency of production units in a market environment. This analysis consists of first establishing the production possibility frontier, representing a combination of best-observed production results within the sample of observations (the best practices), and second, measuring the relative inefficiency of producers inside the production possibility frontier (PPF) by the distance from the frontier. The major advantages of FDH analysis are that it imposes only weak restrictions on the production technology while allowing for a comparison of efficiency levels among producers. The only assumption made is that inputs and/or outputs can be freely disposed of, so that it is possible with the same production technology to lower outputs while maintaining the level of inputs and to increase the inputs while maintaining outputs at the same level. This assumption guarantees the existence of a continuous FDH, or PPF, for any sample of production results. Thus, FDH analysis provides an intuitive tool that can be used to identify best practices in government spending and to assess how governments are faring in comparison with these best practices.[1] In our analysis using FDH, the term 'producer' is meant to include governments. A producer is relatively inefficient if another producer uses less input to generate as much or more output. A producer is relatively efficient if no other producer uses less input to generate as much or more output. In Appendix 4.1, this is illustrated for the case of one input and one output. If a producer is engaged in the production of multiple outputs using more than one input, it becomes more difficult to establish relative efficiency. In such a situation (of multiple inputs), it is postulated that a producer is relatively inefficient if he uses as much or more of all inputs to generate as much or less of all outputs than all other producers, with at least one input being strictly higher, or one output strictly lower. Producers that are not relatively inefficient are relatively efficient.[2] Depending upon the availability of the latest and comparable information, we have applied this technique for data on major and smaller Indian states for education covering different cross sections from 2003–2011 and for health covering the period 2001–10. This analysis covers fifteen major Indian states (Andhra Pradesh [AP], Assam, Bihar, Gujarat, Harayana, Karnataka, Kerala, Madhya Pradesh [MP], Maharashtra, Orissa, Punjab, Rajasthan, Tamil Nadu [TN], Uttar Pradesh [UP], and West Bengal [WB]) and 10 smaller states (Arunachal Pradesh, Chhatisgarh, Goa, Himachal Pradesh (HP), Jammu and Kashmir (JK), Jharkhand, Manipur, Meghalaya, Mizoram and Nagaland).

Parametric technique: stochastic frontier method

In the application of parametric techniques, stochastic methods can be used to correct for measurement and other random errors in the estimation of the PPF. In any parametric techniques a functional form is postulated for the PPF, and then a set of parameters is selected that best fits the sample data.

Model specification

In the estimation of health system efficiency, our specification is based on a general stochastic frontier model that is presented as

$$\ln q_j = f(\ln x) + v_j - u_j \cdots \qquad (1)$$

where $\ln q_j$ is the health output (life expectancy or inverse of IMR) produced by a health system j;

x is a vector of factor inputs represented by per capita health facilities (including per capita availability of hospital beds, per capita primary health centres [or subcentres], per capita doctors, per capita paramedical staff, per capita skilled attention for birth);

v_j is the stochastic (white noise) error term; and

u_j is a one-sided error term representing the technical inefficiency of the health system j.

Both v_j and u_j are assumed to be independently and identically distributed (iid) with variance σ_v^2 and σ_u^2 respectively

From the estimated relationship $\ln q_j^{\wedge} = f(\ln x) - u_j$

The efficient level of health outcome (with zero technical inefficiency) is defined as

$$\ln q^* = f(\ln x).$$

This implies $\ln TE_j = \ln q_j^{\wedge} - \ln q^* = - u_j$.

Hence $TE_j = e^{-u_j}, 0 <= e^{-u_j} <= 1$.

If $u_j = 0$ it implies $e^{-u_j} = 1$.

Health system is technically efficient.

This implies that the technical efficiency of jth health system is a relative measure of its output as a proportion of the corresponding frontier output.

A health system is technically efficient if its output level is on the frontier which in turn means that q/q^* equals 1 in value.

Study design: sample and sampling technique

This study uses secondary data published in official documents of the government of India and state governments. The study makes use of a purposive sampling and therefore the focus is on fifteen major Indian states. The purpose is to carry out an analysis which reveals broadly the country's scenario at state-level disaggregation. Data used thus are presumed to be authentic and therefore reliable. The validity of the results is thus subject to the reliability of official publications and the underlying statistical techniques deployed in the study.

For the parametric approach, we cover the same fifteen major Indian states as in the nonparametric approach (AP, Assam, Bihar, Gujarat, Harayana, Karnataka, Kerala, MP, Maharashtra, Orissa, Punjab, Rajasthan, TN, UP and WB) and use panel data for 2000–2005 and 2005–2011. Use of panel data is preferred in that it does not require strong assumptions about the error term, and unlike the cross section data, the assumption of independence of technical efficiency from factor inputs is not imposed (Pitt and Lee 1981; Schmidt and Sickles 1984). We extend our estimation to the second stage, which presumes that differences in technical efficiency pertaining to health systems can be discerned at the health facility planning level from non-health-related parameters. Thus, we explain the dispersion in technical efficiency by a set of variables which includes per capita income, literacy, urbanization, per capita budgetary expenditure on health and rural water supply. Thus, our model in the second stage is:

> Dispersion in technical efficiency = f (per capita income,
> literacy, urbanization, per capita budgetary expenditure
> on health and rural water supply) + error term.... .   (2)

Thus, the main dependent variables used in the study are life expectancy (LEXP), and dispersion and independent variables include per capita income and others, namely number of primary health centres (PHCs), subcentres (SCs), community health centres (CHCs), hospitals and dispensaries, health manpower (medical and paramedical), and socio-economic parameters such as income, education and basic amenities.

Database

This study is based on secondary data. Information was collected for the years 2000–11 from various sources including *RBI Bulletin* (Reserve Bank of India 2012), Health Information of India (GoI 2000–11, various issues) and other published sources. At the all-India level, the main variables used in the study are life expectancy (LEXP), infant mortality rates (IMR), per capita income and other parameters related to health infrastructure including number of primary health centres (PHCs); subcentres (SCs); community health centres (CHCs); hospitals and dispensaries; health manpower (medical and paramedical) and other variables relevant for depicting health care facilities, their utilization, health outcomes and socio-economic parameters including income, education and basic amenities.

Statistical analysis tools used include frontier regression technique applying STATA software.

Appendix 4.1
Degree of efficiency and FDH analysis

This analysis (i.e. FDH) establishes the degree of efficiency in the following way. The first step is to identify the relatively efficient production results in the sample. In Figure A.4.1, the relatively efficient production results are A, C and D. Given that producer A's production result is feasible and there is free disposal, all production results where at least as much input is used to generate the same level of output, or less, are also feasible. These relatively inefficient production possibilities are identified by the rectangular area to the right of and below producer A, which contains producer B. Similarly, the rectangular areas to the right of and below producers C and D identify relatively inefficient production possibilities. If there is no observation in the rectangular area to the left and above an observed production result, the latter production result is among the relatively efficient production results in the sample of observations. The border of the set of production possibilities – that is, all the production results to the right of and below the relatively efficient observations – is given by the bold line connecting A, C and D in Figure A.4.1. This is the PPF, or FDH. A free disposal is required to obtain a continuous PPF. In the absence of that assumption, it could not be inferred that all output combinations on the line connecting *A, C* and *D* are feasible.

In fact a producer can be relatively efficient, even though no producer is inefficient in relation to it (i.e. there is no producer in the rectangular area to the right of and below the relatively efficient producer). Such producers are assumed to be on the PPF. Producers that are efficient by default will here be called independently efficient. Examples of independently efficient production results are producers *C* and *D* in Figure A.4.1. Producer A is not independently efficient, as producer B is inefficient in relation to A.

Using the criterion described above, a distinction can be made between relatively efficient production results (production results on the PPF) and relatively inefficient production results (production results in the interior of the production possibility set). We also use the measure of efficiency score that enables a ranking of production results. The calculation of a producer's efficiency score can be illustrated using the example in Figure A.4.1. Producer B is the only relatively inefficient producer in the figure. FDH analysis suggests two alternative ways of measuring the distance of producer B's production result from the PPF: from either the input side or the output side. In input terms, the distance is given by the line bB, that is the quotient of inputs used by producer A over inputs used by producer B, $x(A) / x(B)$. |

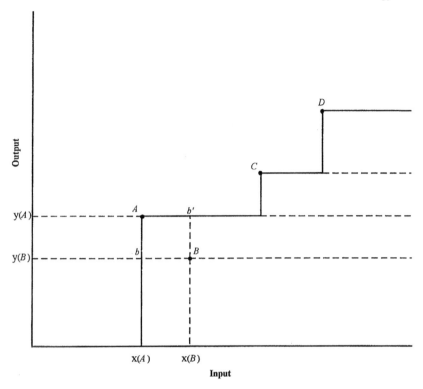

Figure A.4.1 Free disposal hull (FDH) production possibility frontier

This measure of efficiency is referred to as the input efficiency score. For all observations in the interior of the production possibility set, the input efficiency score is smaller than 1. For all observations on the PPF (producers A, C and D) the efficiency score is 1. The input efficiency score indicates the excess use of inputs by the inefficient producer, and therefore the extent to which this producer allocates its resources in an inefficient manner. On the output side, the efficiency score of producer B is given by the line b'B, that, is the output quotient y(B) / y(A). This score indicates the loss of output relative to the most efficient producer with an equal or lower level of inputs. As in the case of the input efficiency score, the output efficiency score is smaller than 1 for observations in the interior of the production possibility set (producer B) and equal to 1 for observations on the PPF (producers A, C and D). In the one-input one-output case depicted in Figure A.4.1, formulation of an efficiency score is relatively straightforward. In the case of multiple inputs and outputs, derivation of an efficiency score is more complicated.[3] Non-FDH techniques typically assume a convex PPF.[4] Consequently, the status of producer C would change; rather than being a relatively efficient unit on the PPF as under FDH, producer C would now be viewed as relatively inefficient, with a production result in the interior of the production possibility set.[5] The example in

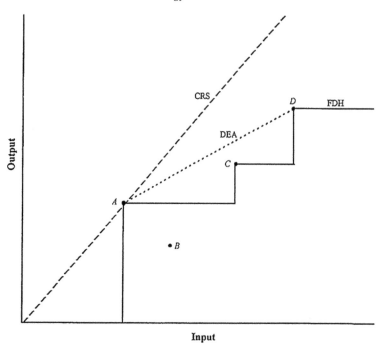

Figure A.4.2 Alternative production possibility frontiers: free disposal hull (FDH), data envelopment analysis (DEA) and constant returns to scale

Figure A.4.2 illustrates that FDH singles out more observations as relatively efficient than DEA, thereby reducing the informational value of FDH analysis.

Another drawback of FDH analysis (as well as DEA) compared with parametric techniques is that correction for random factors unrelated to efficiency is not possible and therefore statistical noise is included in the measure of inefficiency. On the other hand, both DEA and parametric techniques impose more restrictions on the production technology than FDH analysis. As noted above, DEA assumes convexity whereas parametric techniques impose a functional form for the PPF. Where these assumptions inaccurately capture the production processes underlying the observed production results, the efficiency results will be affected (Ferrier and Lovell 1990). The preceding discussion suggests that the choice between different techniques of estimating efficiency is a trade-off between imposing fewer restrictions on the production technology and obtaining relatively unambiguous results (Bauer 1990). In the case of government spending on education and health, there is little a priori justification for making certain assumptions regarding convexity and economies of scale. This argues against the use of parametric techniques and favours the use of the relatively parsimonious FDH analysis. Tulkens and Vanden Eeckaut (1995) provide a more comprehensive overview of the differences between FDH analysis and these alternative techniques.

Notes

1 Some of the studies which have employed FDH analysis include, for instance, Deprins, Simar and Tulkens (1984), Tulkens and Vanden Eeckaut (1995) and Fakin and de Crombrugghe (1997).
2 Degree of efficiency and method of FDH is explained in Figure A.4.1.
3 See, e.g. Gupta, Honjo and Verhoeven 1997.
4 For instance, the DEA technique (Charnes, Cooper and Rhodes 1978) assumes that the production possibility set is convex. With DEA, the area under the straight line connecting producers A and D would become part of the production possibility set (Figure A.4.2).
5 If the production technology is also assumed to feature constant returns to scale (i.e. if the technology can be described by a Cobb-Douglas production function), the PPF would be a straight line through the origin. In this case, producer A would be the only producer on the PPF as it would have the highest observed output-input ratio, i.e. the highest average productivity.

5 Efficiency in the health and education sectors

A macro analysis

Our results

FDH analysis: results of FDH analysis

It can be observed that for per capita public expenditure on health (in 2001–02), independently efficient states that emerged from FDH for major states are UP, Bihar, Gujarat, WB, Maharashtra and Kerala (Figure 5.1). Among the smaller states the independently efficient states are Chhatisgarh, Jharkhand, Uttarakhand, Tripura and Manipur (Figure 5.2). Likewise in Figures 5.3 and 5.4 (for 2004–05 per capita public expenditure), the situation is somewhat changed for UP, whereas other independently efficient states remain the same. Among smaller states a changed situation with lower efficiency is depicted for Tripura only (Figure 5.4). FDH for public expenditure in 2008–09 for the health sector (Figures 5.5 and 5.6) depict additional states, namely WB and Tamil Nadu, among independently efficient states (Figure 5.5), and inclusion and exclusion of Goa and Chhatisgarh respectively in the category of such (independently efficient) states (Figure 5.6). In the education sector, using literacy (2011) and public expenditure (2008–09), Bihar, UP, WB, Gujarat, Tamil Nadu, Maharashtra and Kerala (among major states) and Jharkhand, Chhattisgarh, Manipur and Himachal Pradesh (among smaller states) emerge as independently efficient states (Figures 5.7 and 5.8). By and large a similar observation can be made using net enrolment in primary schools in 2008–09 (Figures 5.9 and 5.10). Using this FDH analysis, input efficiency scores (IES) are presented in Tables 5.1–5.3. There is a range of 7–25 per cent for major states and a scope of nearly 10 per cent for smaller states to improve their input efficiency relative to the nearest independently efficient states in 2011 for the education sector (Table 5.1). In the health sector, this range is much higher for some years, such as 2004–05 (Table 5.2, last column), and it has been 1–26 per cent for major states and 6–29 per cent for smaller states for the year 2010 (Table 5.3, last column).

The results of our FDH analysis for the education and health sectors using data for Indian states, both major and smaller ones, are presented in Figures 5.1–5.10 and Tables 5.1–5.3. The description of these results follows.

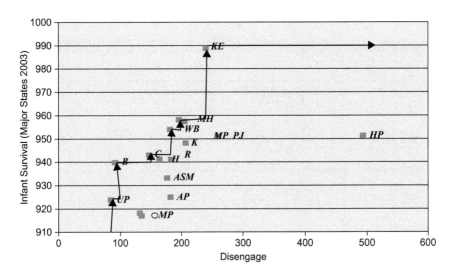

Figure 5.1 Infant survival rate (major states 2003)

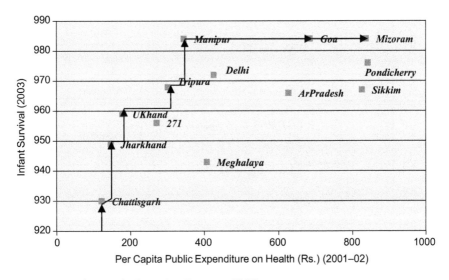

Figure 5.2 Infant survival rate (smaller states 2003)

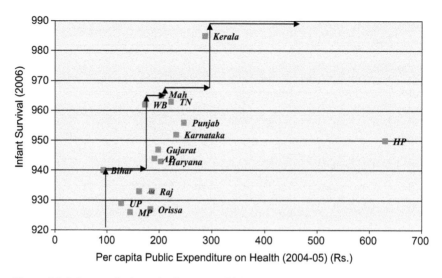

Figure 5.3 Infant survival rate (major states 2006)

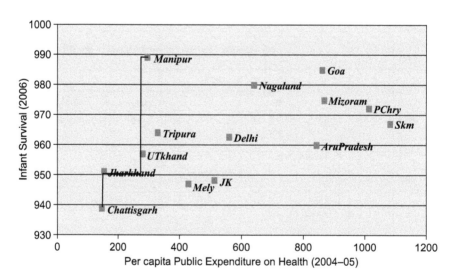

Figure 5.4 Infant survival rate (smaller states 2006)

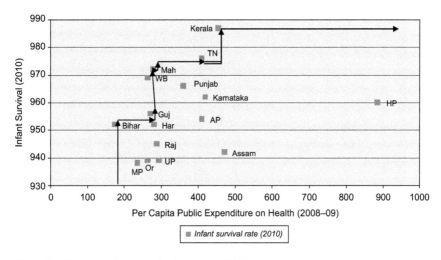

Figure 5.5 Infant survival rate (major states 2010)

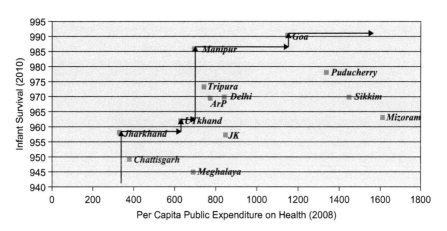

Figure 5.6 Infant survival rate (smaller states 2010)

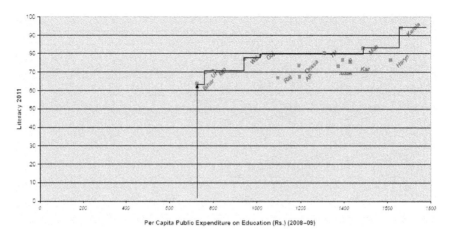

Figure 5.7 Literacy 2011 (major states)

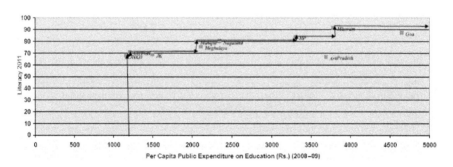

Figure 5.8 Literacy 2011 (smaller states)

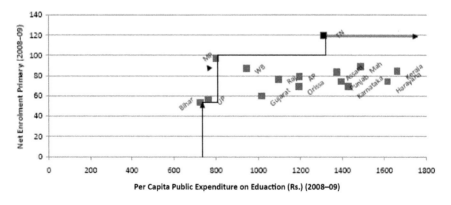

Figure 5.9 Net enrolment primary (major states, 2008–09)

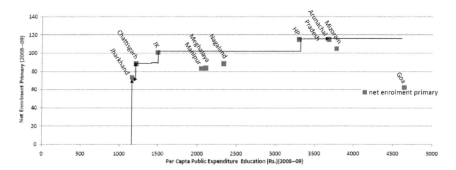

Figure 5.10 Net enrolment primary (smaller states, 2008–09)

Table 5.1 Input efficiency score (IES) (Education) (2008–11)

States	Public expenditure per capita education (in Rs.) (2008–09)	Net enrolment primary (2008–09)	IES (2008–09)	Literacy (2011)	IES (2011)
Major states					
AP	1,195.59	79.12	0.67	67.66	0.85
Assam	1,374.02	83.58	0.95	73.18	0.74
Bihar	725.89	53.38	1.00	63.82	1.00
Gujarat	1,015.67	59.75	0.79	79.31	1.00
Harayana	1,615.77	74.14	0.81	76.64	0.92
Karnataka	1,429.04	69.14	0.92	75.60	0.71
Kerala	1,661.71	84.71	0.79	93.91	1.00
MP	799.49	97.28	1.00	70.63	1.00
Maharashtra	1,487.72	88.93	0.88	82.91	1.00
Orissa	1,193.44	69.16	0.67	73.45	0.85
Punjab	1,395.89	74.15	0.94	76.68	0.73
Raj	1,096.43	76.54	0.73	67.06	0.93
TN	1,310.20	119.56	1.00	80.33	0.78
UP	763.40	56.35	1.00	69.72	1.00
WB	943.52	87.17	0.85	77.08	1.00
Smaller states					
Arunachal Pradesh	3,684.77	115.15	1.03	66.95	0.90
Chhattisgarh	1,211.87	88.30	1.00	71.04	1.00
Goa	4,648.96	62.04	0.81	87.40	0.81
HP	3,299.52	115.11	1.00	83.78	1.00
JK	1,497.35	100.69	1.00	68.74	
Jharkhand	1,162.75	73.18	1.00	67.63	1.00
Manipur	2,054.26	83.20	0.73	79.85	1.00
Meghalaya	2,110.56	83.46	0.71	75.48	0.97
Mizoram	3,780.70	104.75	1.00	91.58	1.00
Nagland	2,339.54	88.34	0.64	80.11	1.00

Source: Computed.

Table 5.2 Input efficiency score (IES) (Health) (2001–05)

States	Public expenditure per capita (in Rs.) (2001–02)	Infant survival (2003)	IES	Public expenditure per capita (in Rs.) (2004–05)	Infant survival (2006)	IES
Major states/UT						
Andhra Pradesh	182	941	0.81	191	944	0.91
Assam	176	933	0.83	162	933	1.07
Bihar	92	940	1	93	940	1.00
Gujarat	147	943	1	198	947	0.87
Haryana	163	941	0.90	203	943	1.00
Himachal Pradesh	493	951	0.49	630	950	0.46
Karnataka	206	948	0.95	233	952	0.88
Kerala	240	989	1	287	985	1.00
Madhya Pradesh	132	918	0.69	145	926	0.64
Maharashtra	196	958	1	204	965	1.00
Orissa	134	917	1.09	183	927	0.95
Punjab	258	951	0.93	247	956	0.83
Rajasthan	182	925	0.81	186	933	0.93
Tamil Nadu	202	957	1.18	223	963	0.91
Uttar Pradesh	84	924	1	128	929	0.73
West Bengal	181	954	1	173	962	1.00
Smaller states/UT						
Arunachal Pradesh	627	966	0.55	841	960	0.35
Chhattisgarh	121	930	1	146	939	1.00
Delhi	426	972	0.81	560	963	0.53
Goa	685	984	1	861	985	0.34
Jammu & Kashmir	271	956	0.66	512	948	0.57
Jharkhand	146	949	1	155	951	1.00
Manipur	345	984	1	294	989	1.00
Meghalaya	407	943	0.85	430	947	0.68
Mizoram	836	984	1	867	975	0.34
Pondicherry	841	976	0.99	1014	972	0.29
Sikkim	825	967	1.01	1082	967	0.27
Tripura	301	968	1	328	964	0.90
Uttarakhand	178	959	1	280	957	1.00
Nagaland	na	na		639	980	0.46

Source: Computed.

Table 5.3 Input efficiency score (IES) (Health) (2010)

States	Public expenditure per capita (in Rs.) (2008–09)	Infant survival rate (2010)	IES
Major states			
Andhra Pradesh	410.00	954.00	1.00
Assam	471.00	942.00	0.96
Bihar	173.00	952.00	1.00
Gujarat	270.00	956.00	1.00
Harayana	280.00	952.00	0.99
Himachal Pradesh	884.00	960.00	0.96
Karnataka	419.00	962.00	0.98
Kerala	454.00	987.00	1.00
Madhya Pradesh	235.00	938.00	0.74
Maharashtra	278.00	972.00	1.00
Orissa	263.00	939.00	1.06
Punjab	360.00	966.00	0.77
Rajasthan	287.00	945.00	0.97
Tamil Nadu	410.00	976.00	1.00
Uttar Pradesh	293.00	939.00	0.95
West Bengal	262.00	969.00	1.00
Smaller states/UT			
Arunachal Pradesh	771.00	969.00	0.90
Chhattisgarh	378.00	949.00	0.87
Delhi (UT)	840.00	970.00	0.83
Goa	1,149.00	990.00	1.00
Jammu & Kashmir	845.00	957.00	0.82
Jharkhand	328.00	958.00	1.00
Manipur	695.00	986.00	1.00
Meghalaya	690.00	945.00	0.91
Mizoram	1,611.00	963.00	0.71
Puducherry	1,333.00	978.00	0.86
Sikkim	1,446.00	970.00	0.79
Tripura	740.00	973.00	0.94
Uttarakhand	630.00	962.00	1.00

Source: Computed.

Conclusions

Results of our FDH analysis suggest a considerably better scope for improvement in efficiency of public expenditure in health relative to education. Further application of the parametric approach of stochastic frontier analysis (SFA) applied to health care and elementary education sector may indicate factors that could be isolated to improve efficiency in public expenditure in these sectors.

6   Efficiency in the health and education sectors

A state-level analysis

Parametric technique: stochastic frontier model

In the application of parametric techniques, stochastic models can be used to correct for measurement and other random errors in the estimation of the PPF. In any parametric techniques a functional form is postulated for the PPF, and then a set of parameters is selected that best fit the sample data.

Results of stochastic frontier model

In this section we present results for the health and education sectors. The former has been covered by means of two sets of data covering 2000–05 and 2005–10.

Efficiency of the health care system in India (2000–05)

To carry out our estimation of health system efficiency at the all-India level, our specification is based on a general stochastic frontier model that was presented in Chapter 3.

We cover fourteen major Indian states, and in this section we use panel data for 2000–05. The use of panel data is preferred in that it does not require strong assumptions about the error term, and unlike the cross section data, the assumption of independence of technical efficiency from factor inputs is not imposed (Pitt and Lee 1981; Schmidt and Sickles 1984). We extend our estimation to the second stage, which presumes that differences in technical efficiency pertaining to the health care system can be discerned at the district-level health facility planning stage by non-health-related parameters. Thus, we explain the dispersion in technical efficiency by a set of variables which includes per capita income, literacy, urbanization, per capita budgetary expenditure on health and rural water supply. Our model in the second stage is:

> Dispersion in technical efficiency = f (per capita income, literacy, urbanization, per capita budgetary expenditure on health and rural water supply) + error term. . . .   (A)

This study is based on secondary data. Information is collected from *Economic Survey 2007* (GoI 2007a), *Bulletin on Rural Health Services, Health Information of India* and other published sources. The main variables used in the study are life expectancy (LEXP), infant mortality rates (IMR), per capita income and other parameters related to health infrastructure, including number of primary health centers (PHCs), subcenters (SCs), community health centers (CHCs), hospitals and dispensaries; health manpower (medical and paramedical); and other variables relevant for depicting health care facilities, their utilization, health outcomes and socio-economic parameters such as income, education and basic amenities.

We hypothesize that states differ in their technical efficiency pertaining to the health care system due to factors which require emphasis in the planning of health facilities. It is also hypothesized that these factors differ among states according to their level of development. It is presumed that estimated efficiency parameters should help the makers of health policy to improve state-level health system performance.

Results and discussion

Results of our panel data estimation using the frontier model for India are presented in Table 6.1. All the independent variables to explain life expectancy (LEXP) have emerged with appropriate positive signs. Two of them representing rural specialist (SPECLISTRURAL PER LAKH) and PHCs (PHCS PER LAKH) are statistically significant. This indicates the positive impact of governmental intervention in the expansion of PHC facilities and the desirable impact on life expectancy of having rural specialists like surgeons, obstetricians and gynaecologists, physicians and paediatricians. That both the variables representing respectively nurse midwife (NURSEMW PER LAKH) and all types of beds

Table 6.1 Stochastic frontier panel data model for India (time-invariant inefficiency model) Wald chi^2(4) = 68.18; log likelihood = 290.0304; prob > chi^2 = 0.0000.

Life Expectancy (LEXP)	Coefficient	Z value
SPECLISTRURAL PER LAKH	0.002**	2.41
PHCS PER LAKH	0.004*	6.8
NURSEMW PER LAKH	0.003+	1.49
ALLBEDS PER LAKH	0.019	1.15
CONSTANT	4.184*	42.29
MU	0.117*	3.87
LNSIGMA2	−5.726*	−11.05
ILGTGAMMA	5.145*	8.91
SIGMA2	0.003	
GAMMA	0.994	
SIGMA_U2	0.003	
SIGMA_V2	0.000	

Source: Estimated.

*significance at 1% level; **significance at 2% level; +significance at 20% level.

Notes: Number of observations = 84; number of groups = 14.

(including allopathic and Indian systems of medicine) (ALLBEDS PER LAKH) have emerged with positive signs indicates the desirable role of the various inputs provided through paramedical manpower and bed facilities in various set-ups. The statistical insignificance of these inputs at the conventional level of significance indicates some inadequacy of the quantum of these inputs.

Using the results of the frontier model, actual and estimated life expectancy (LEXP) are presented for the year 2004 in Table 6.2. These depict Kerala as the most efficient state (MES), with its actual LEXP moving highest towards the estimated LEXP. This is followed by Punjab and Haryana. The lowest efficiency is depicted by Madhya Pradesh, followed by Orissa and Uttar Pradesh (Table 6.2).

Reasons for these interstate disparities could be deciphered from Tables 6.3 and 6.4, which depict major inputs for the health sector in the states. Notably, the distribution of per capita hospitals, PHCs, SCs, CHCs and beds in the states is highly inequitable. In fact, there is a considerable difference between maximum and minimum values for each of the parameters (columns 2–6, Table 6.3). Pertinently, the number of hospital beds per lakh of population is the highest (344,731) in Kerala, followed by Gujarat (175,011) and Maharashtra (140,565). Similar order holds true in regard to the number of hospitals as well (column 5, Table 6.3). The lowest number of beds (35.19) and hospitals (.115) per lakh of population remains for Madhya Pradesh. These magnitudes of highest and lowest numbers of beds and hospitals are commensurate in the same order to life expectancy and achievements of actual versus potential noted previously by our results. A similar observation cannot be made, however, pertaining to PHCs, SCs and CHCs (columns 2–4, Table 6.3). Thus a pattern of outcomes appears to have a reasonable correspondence with usage at least in regard to hospitals and beds. In terms of staff per

Table 6.2 Actual and potential life expectancy and ranks of Indian states

State	Actual life expectancy (2004)	Potential life expectancy	Actual as percentage of potential	Ranks of states according to realization of potential life expectancy
Andhra Pradesh	63.90	71.30	89.63	7
Bihar	61.20	70.76	86.49	10
Gujarat	63.70	72.84	87.45	9
Haryana	65.65	70.76	92.78	3
Karnataka	64.85	72.56	89.38	8
Kerala	73.75	74.12	99.50	1
Madhya Pradesh	57.40	70.35	81.60	14
Maharashtra	66.65	72.74	91.62	5
Orissa	58.95	71.05	82.97	13
Punjab	68.90	72.51	95.02	2
Rajasthan	61.50	72.43	84.91	11
Tamil Nadu	65.70	71.47	91.92	4
Uttar Pradesh	59.55	70.92	83.97	12
West Bengal	64.35	71.73	89.71	6

Note: Estimated.

Table 6.3 Health facilities per lakh of population

	Primary health centers	Subcenters	Community health centers	Hospitals	Beds
Andhra Pradesh	2.83	22.60	0.30	4.059	102.898
Bihar	2.22	13.91	0.14	0.316	50.667
Gujarat	3.37	22.92	0.86	5.092	175.011
Haryana	2.71	16.19	0.48	0.388	53.627
Karnataka	4.82	23.34	0.73	0.549	111.427
Kerala	3.86	21.61	0.45	6.408	344.731
Madhya Pradesh	2.69	20.00	0.52	0.115	35.191
Maharashtra	3.19	18.74	0.68	3.712	140.565
Orissa	4.10	18.94	0.74	0.749	45.713
Punjab	3.01	17.76	0.72	0.917	116.159
Rajasthan	3.96	24.28	0.75	0.204	80.042
Tamil Nadu	3.95	24.86	0.10	0.651	110.142
Uttar Pradesh	2.78	15.59	0.29	0.412	59.492
West Bengal	2.03	17.93	0.16	0.508	87.480

Source: GoI (2005d.)

lakh, Kerala does not have the highest number for any of the categories of medical or paramedical staff presented in Table 6.4. In fact, many of the poorly performing states, such as Rajasthan (highest number of nurse-midwives, female multipurpose workers and paramedical staff per lakh of population; columns 5, 7 and 8, Table 6.4), Bihar (highest number of homeopaths; column 4, Table 6.4) and Orissa (highest number of male multipurpose workers; column 6, Table 6.4), and other states such as Karnataka (highest numbers of rural specialists; column 2, Table 6.4) and Haryana (highest number of PHC doctors; column 3, Table 6.4), have much higher levels of staff inputs. These numbers point to the inadequate or ineffective utilization of staff inputs in most of the states. However, in most of the states neither the inadequate availability of health care sector inputs nor merely inefficient utilization of these inputs explains the differentials in achievements in life expectancy.

Besides the factors within the health system, as we noted in the methodology section, influences external to the system may lead to differentials in efficiency at the state level. Some of these factors could be, for instance, per capita income, per capita budgetary health expenditure, literacy, access to safe drinking water and urbanization. In general, some of these variables may significantly influence the differentials in impact on life expectancy of health system inputs. As presented in Table 6.5, the majority of poorly performing states, such as Uttar Pradesh, Rajasthan, Madhya Pradesh and Orissa, are among the low-income-category states (column 2, Table 6.5). Even the budgetary expenditure in per capita terms is lower in these states relative to better-off states such as Gujarat, Haryana and Maharashtra (column 3, Table 6.5).

Although Kerala is not the highest in terms of either per capita income or per capita budgetary expenditure on health, it has an outstanding position in terms of overall literacy, which as of the 2001 census was 90.86 per cent (column 4, Table 6.5). By contrast many of the poor and poorly performing states in terms of life expectancy

Table 6.4 Health manpower per lakh of population

State	Rural specialists	PHC doctors	Homeopaths	Nurse-midwives	Multipurpose workers (male)	Multipurpose workers (female)	Paramedical staff
Andhra Pradesh	0.215	2.768	38.926	2.659	8.196	17.799	29.21
Bihar	0.1	2.046	156.675	1.375	1.699	9.099	12.943
Gujarat	0.165	1.708	51.958	2.927	5.586	13.109	21.215
Haryana	0.191	4.231	132.551	5.694	8.56	13.831	27.198
Karnataka	1.296	3.827	43.607	5.813	8.58	16.021	30.758
Kerala	0.351	2.897	77.067	7.87	8.172	16.989	33.983
Madhya Pradesh	0.609	1.015	68.977	1.092	8.832	11.31	29.055
Maharashtra	0.483	3.402	100.896	2.774	7.536	11.525	20.95
Orissa	1.194	3.714	20.78	1.748	9.31	18.576	29.414
Punjab	0.738	1.555	139.922	2.668	6.987	10.848	20.248
Rajasthan	1.082	2.717	53.636	15.197	4.56	20.609	39.626
Tamil Nadu	1.156	3.6	60.075	0.266	5.447	16.128	22.168
Uttar Pradesh	0.232	1.269	56.217	0.45	3.214	10.176	14.863
West Bengal	0.771	1.629	55.932	1.827	6.921	11.204	20.134

Source: GoI (2005d).

Table 6.5 Income, budgetary expenditure on health, and other variables across Indian states and rural-urban areas

	Per capita GDP (in Rs.)	Per capita budgetary expenditure on health (Rs.)	Literacy	Access to safe drinking water (%)			Urbanization (%)
				Total	Rural	Urban	
Andhra Pradesh	26211	57.14	60.47	80.1	76.9	90.2	27.5
Bihar	7875	15.35	47	86.6	86.1	91.2	10.5
Gujarat	34157	85.96	69.14	84.1	76.9	95.4	38.7
Haryana	38832	48.48	67.91	86.1	81.1	97.3	31
Karnataka	27291	63.03	66.64	84.6	80.5	92.1	35.4
Kerala	30668	31.52	90.86	23.4	16.9	42.8	25.8
Madhya Pradesh	15647	34.09	63.74	68.4	61.5	88.6	27
Maharashtra	37081	80.49	76.88	79.8	68.4	95.4	44.2
Orissa	17299	39.09	63.08	64.2	62.9	72.3	15.8
Punjab	34929	11.29	69.65	97.6	96.9	98.9	36
Rajasthan	17863	32.95	60.41	68.2	60.4	93.5	23.6
Tamil Nadu	29958	43.50	73.45	85.6	85.3	85.9	48.8
Uttar Pradesh	13262	51.44	56.27	87.8	85.5	97.2	21.3
West Bengal	25223	50.12	68.64	88.5	87.0	92.3	28.2

Sources: GoI (2001a, 2001b, 2007a).

have much lower levels of literacy. On the other hand most of the states seem to be better off than Kerala in terms of access to safe drinking water in rural as well as urban areas (columns 5–7, Table 6.5). A similar mixed situation prevails in terms of level of urbanization in both poor and rich states (last column, Table 6.5). Thus, in order to explore such external factors, we used dispersion in efficiency as a dependent variable in the second stage of our regression exercise, using panel data for the district level. Among the set of explanatory variables, we included per capita income, literacy, urbanization and per capita budgetary expenditure on health and rural water supply. Our results of best fit are presented in Table 6.6.

Only two of the variables, namely literacy and rural habitat covered by safe water supply (FULCOV), have emerged as statistically significant. The results are depicted in Table 6.6. The negative sign of literacy indicates that efforts to impart literacy and thus an increased level of awareness about health-related facilities and issues have helped to reduce regional disparity in the efficiency of health systems across states. However, this has not been able to compensate for differences in public investment in different regions in rural water supply, which is indicated by a positive sign of the variable in our second stage of results (Table 6.6).

Conclusions

The results of the frontier model using panel data for fourteen major Indian states over the years 2000–05 indicate that the efficiency of public health delivery systems remains low. Considerable disparities that exist across states in terms of per capita availability and utilization of hospitals, beds and manpower inputs has adverse impact on improving the life expectancy in the states. Overcoming these factoral disparities within the health system may lead to an improvement in the state level efficiency of public health system. This may also help to improve life expectancy speedily and more equitably in poorly performing states of Bihar, Madhya Pradesh, Orissa, Rajasthan and Uttar Pradesh. However, this has to be supported with other adequate infrastructure facilities like safe drinking water supply in rural habitats to improve the outcomes in deficient states. Learning from the remarkable achievements of Kerala, an emphasis on literacy along with better utilization of health infrastructure and manpower resources could go a long way towards improving life expectancy. This may

Table 6.6 Panel data regression results for dispersion as dependent variable

R-sq: between = 0.6329; $F(2,11) = 9.48*$.

DISPERSION	Coefficient	"t" values
LITERACY	–0.003	–1.86*
FULCOV	4.83E-07	2.13*
CONSTANT	1.283	11.42*

Source: Estimated.

*Significance at 1% level.

Notes: Number of observations = 84; number of groups = 14.

require a considerable reorientation of the current health care set-up, particularly in rural areas in the poorly performing states. These could reallocate surplus manpower from within and also make the rural infrastructure more useful to the needy through adequate inputs of building, equipment and medicines. In fact there is considerable differential in budgetary expenditure per capita between better-off and poorer states. This in turn reduces the availability of basic medicines and materials in the public health system and reduces its reliability for the poor, making them depend more on the costlier private sector. Part of this problem could be tackled through funding from the National Rural Health Mission (NRHM) and also by improving rural sanitation in the poorer states. The results also suggest lack of appropriate links and coordination between economic and social sector policies, leading to suboptimal health outcomes for India's poorer states.

Efficiency of the health care sector at the substate level in India: Punjab

In this section we focus on a substate level (i.e. district-level) study of Punjab. Punjab signifies itself as one of the highest per capita income states in India, next only to Delhi, Pondicherry and Maharashtra. It has a-poverty ratio of just 6 per cent. It is the largest grain producer in the country. Economic development in Punjab is led by agriculture, and it has made the green revolution a success. However, the prosperity of Punjab has not prevented intrastate disparity. As noted in Human Development Report of Punjab,

> Amidst prosperity pockets of disparity remain. In southern, south-western Punjab, poverty rates are high. In Hoshiarpur district, the literacy level crossed 80 per cent in 2001, but in Mansa district, literacy rates are only slightly higher than of Bihar. While in India, between 1991 and 2001, the gender ratio rose from 927 to 933, in Punjab it fell from an abysmal 882 in 1991 to an even lower 874 in 2001.
>
> (Government of Punjab 2004, p. 8)

This is indicative of discrimination against women. Economic development in Punjab has been uneven and is marked by disparities between regions and communities in terms of education, health, standard of living, security and basic human rights (Government of Punjab [GoP] 2004, p. 8). Such a development pattern negates the very spirit of the Alma Ata declaration (1978), which views the health care system as a distribution mechanism. Over time both agriculture and manufacturing have also witnessed declining growth rates.

According to the sample registration system of the registrar general of India, for the year 2000, the IMR of Punjab was 52 per 1,000 live births, and life expectancy in 1996 was 67.4 years. The state ranks considerably below Kerala, which has an IMR of 14 per 1,000 live births (1999) and life expectancy of 73.1 years.

Estimates derived from census tables for life expectancy at the district level for 1981, 1991 and 2001 are presented in Table 6.7. Life expectancy in the

Table 6.7 Ranking of districts by life expectancy in Punjab, 1981, 1991 and 2001

Districts	Life expectancy in 1981	Rank in 1981	Life expectancy in 1991	Rank in 1991	Increase in the decade	Life expectancy in 2001	Rank in 2001	Increase in the decade
Amritsar	62.4	3	67.2	3	4.8	72.00	3	4.8
Bathinda	61.1	13	64.7	11	3.6	68.30	12	3.6
Faridkot	61.6	8	65.8	8	4.2	70.10	8	4.3
Fateh Garh Sahib	61.7	7	65.6	9	3.9	69.60	9	4.0
Firozpur	62.1	5	66.6	5	4.5	71.00	4	4.4
Gurdaspur	61.4	11	67.8	2	6.4	74.20	2	6.4
Hoshiarpur	60.9	15	64.5	13	3.6	68.10	14	3.6
Jalandhar	62.3	4	64.2	16	1.9	66.10	17	1.9
Kapurthala	60.4	16	64.5	13	4.1	68.70	11	4.2
Ludhiana	64.2	1	70.5	1	6.3	76.80	1	6.3
Mansa	61.1	13	64.7	11	3.6	68.30	12	3.6
Moga	61.6	8	65.9	6	4.3	70.20	6	4.3
Muktsar	61.6	8	65.9	6	4.3	70.20	6	4.3
Nawanshehar	61.8	6	64.3	15	2.5	66.70	16	2.4
Patiala	61.4	11	65.4	10	4	69.50	10	4.1
Rup Nagar	62.9	2	66.8	4	3.9	70.70	5	3.9
Sangrur	60.4	16	62.8	17	2.4	65.20	18	2.4
Punjab	61.7		65.6		3.9	67.41[1]		1.8
Highest	64.2		70.5		76.8			
Lowest	60.4		62.8		65.2			

Source: GoP (2004).

[1] For 1996.

inter-census period rose in most of the districts by 3–4 years. Generally, southern districts were worse off than northern and northeastern districts. A major decline is noticeable for Jalandhar and Nawanshahr, which fell to 16th and 15th place respectively from their earlier rankings of 4th and 6th. Other poor performers are Hoshiarpur and Kapurthala, which did not improve their comparative position in 1991. Between 1991 and 2001, the top and bottom districts in terms of life expectancy have remained unchanged.

Despite the state's high per capita income, public investment in the health care sector in Punjab is very low. It is estimated to be Rs. 204 per capita and constitutes only 0.998 per cent of net state domestic product (NSDP) (GoP 2004). More and more people in the state tend to depend on expensive and unregulated private service providers due to the poor level of public investment in primary health care. Even this meager public expenditure is biased towards tertiary and specialized care, and overall allocation is inadequate for primary and secondary health care, underprivileged areas and groups. Other notable features of the health system in Punjab include privatization and globalization of the health care system. As a reform measure, in October 1995, under a World Bank–sponsored state health system development project, an autonomous corporation, Punjab Health System Corporation (PHSC), was created. It became an overarching organization looking after 150 health care institutions which were earlier under the State Directorate of Health. With this, emphasis was laid on mobilizing resources through user fees, and the majority of patients except those below the poverty line (BPL) had to pay for services provided by the public hospitals. Even the exemptions for user fees meant for the poor did not benefit many; some case studies indicate that among the poor fewer than 0.5 per cent made use of such exemptions (Ghuman and Mehta 2006). In addition to forming the PHSC, the state encouraged private-sector investment in health. Offers of land and facilities at subsidized rates were extended to private hospitals with a clause that these institutions would treat BPL individuals (identified as holders of yellow cards), at a rate of up to 10 per cent and 5 per cent, respectively, of their outpatients and inpatients. This further deepened citizens' dependence on the private health sector.

The model used here is the previously discussed general stochastic frontier model.

At the district level only cross-sectional data are available, and a strict assumption about the distribution of the inefficiency term is required. Resulting estimates of technical efficiency will conform to the imposed distribution. It is preferable to use the standard distribution (i.e. half or truncated normal).

We presume that differences in technical efficiency pertaining to the health care system can be discerned at the district-level health facility planning stage by non-health-related parameters. Thus, we explain the dispersion in technical efficiency by a set of variables which includes per capita income (PCI), male and female income separately, literacy, rural and urban literacy separately, education deprivation, urbanization, water supply and sanitation facilities, gender development index (GDI) and persons below the poverty line (BPL). Our model in the second stage is thus:

> Dispersion in technical efficiency = f (PCI, male and female income separately, literacy, rural and urban literacy separately, female literacy, urbanization, water supply and sanitation facilities and infrastructure variables such as roads per square kilometres, BPL, GDI) + error term. . . .   (B)

Database

This study is based on secondary data. Information is collected from *Punjab Human Development Report 2004* (GoP 2004), websites of the state and other published sources. The main variables used in the study are life expectancy (LEXP); infant mortality rates (IMR); per capita income (PCI) and parameters related to human development indicators (HDI), gender development indicator (GDI) and health facilities. The information relates to the district level for the state.

Our hypothesis

It is presumed that estimated efficiency parameters should help the makers of health policy to improve district-level and thus state-level health system performance. We hypothesize that districts differ in their technical efficiency pertaining to the health care system due to factors which require emphasis in health facility planning at the district level. It is also hypothesized that these factors differ among states according to their level of development. As noted previously, we consider an affluent Indian state, namely Punjab. It is a high-income state, with per capita income of Rs. 15,800, which is above the all-India average of Rs. 11,779 in 2003–04 at constant (1993–94) prices.

Results and discussion

With regard to selection of variables representing outputs and inputs, we have followed conventionally agreed-upon indicators. As noted in the WHO report on health system performance of 191 countries (WHO 2000), we have used life expectancy at birth (LEXP) as an output indicator. It denotes that health system at the substate level (i.e. district level) should aim at improving the health of the population to achieve higher life expectancy.

The maximum likelihood estimation (MLE) results of the stochastic frontier model (SFM) for our cross section data for Punjab are presented in Table 6.8. Actual and estimated LEXP for the districts of the state are presented in Table 6.9. SFM results depict expected positive and significant signs for the population covered per medical institution (POPPERMI), population covered per doctor (POPDOC) and nurse per lakh of population (NURSEPERLAKH) (Table 6.8). A comparison of actual and estimated LEXP for the districts of Punjab (Table 6.9) depicts Ludhiana as the best performer, with its potential achieved in its actual LEXP of 76.8 years. It has achieved its potential at this level given its inputs (Figure 6.1).

Although the actual equals the potential for two other districts, namely Amritsar (72.00 years) and Gurdaspur (74.20 years), these districts rank second and third

Table 6.8 Stochastic frontier normal/half-normal model

Likelihood-ratio test of sigma_u = 0
chibar2(01) = 6.69
Prob>=chibar2 = 0.005

LEXP	Coef.	Std. Err.
POPPERMI	0.126*	9.98E-06
POPDOC	0.021*	2.92E-06
NURSEPERLAKH	0.030*	2.18E-06
Constant	2.841*	0.0001
lnsig2v	−37.829	333.2008
lnsig2u	−5.946*	0.343
sigma_v	6.10E-09	1.02E-06
sigma_u	0.051	0.009
sigma2	0.003	0.001
Lambda	8380331	0.009

Source: Estimated.

*1% level of significance.

Note: Number of observations = 17; log likelihood =38.201572; prob > chi^2 = 0.0000.

Table 6.9 Actual and expected life expectancy for the districts of Punjab

District	Actual LEXP	Estimated LEXP	Deviation from maximum efficient district	Ranks
Amritsar	72.00	72.00	−4.80	3
Bathinda	68.30	68.57	−.50	12
Faridkot	70.10	74.54	−6.70	8
Fatehgarh Sahib	69.60	72.86	−7.20	9
Firozpur	71.00	75.04	−5.80	4
Gurdaspur	74.20	74.20	−2.60	2
Hoshiarpur	68.10	70.83	−8.70	14
Jalandhar	66.10	72.54	−10.70	16
Kapurthala	68.70	69.68	−8.10	11
Ludhiana	76.80	76.80	0.00	1
Mansa	68.30	72.29	−8.50	12
Moga	70.20	75.63	−6.60	6
Muktsar	70.20	70.20	−6.60	6
Nawanshehar	66.70	72.48	−10.10	15
Patiala	69.50	71.89	−7.30	10
Rup Nagar	70.70	71.06	−6.10	5
Sangrur	65.20	71.43	−11.60	17

Source: Estimated.

respectively in relation to the most efficient district (MED), namely Ludhiana. The difference among the three districts can be seen in the relative utilization of these parameters. These are presented for all the districts in Table 6.10.

It is obvious that the better health outcome for Ludhiana is due to greater availability of nurses and better utilization of medical institutions relative to two other districts. Relative efficiency is a measure of the actual to the potential and it is with respect to MED. In this regard, Sangrur (with the lowest LEXP at 65.2 years) achieves the maximum distance or deviation (11.6%) and Firozpur (LEXP 71

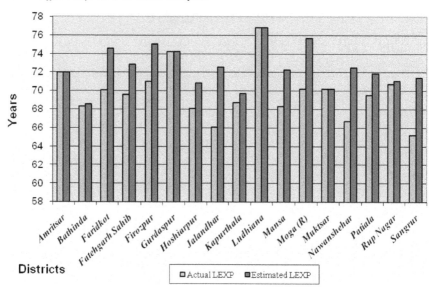

Figure 6.1 Actual and estimated life expectancy for the districts of Punjab, 2002
Source: Estimated.

years) the minimum (after Amritsar and Gurdaspur). These districts could have achieved an LEXP of 71.43 years and 75.04 years if their health systems were as efficient as that of the MED. Thus both factors count; namely lack of adequate utilization and lack of adequate resources, which is the case for some of the inputs in poorly performing districts. Table 6.10 also provides a relative view of respective Gini coefficients. Notably, a third factor is the inequitable distribution of manpower resources across these districts, which is apparent by a high value of Gini coefficients pertaining to doctors, nurses and midwife variables (Table 6.10).

Per capita availability of medical institutions is relatively not low for poorly performing districts. For instance, as compared to the population of 14,827 served per medical institution in the MED (Ludhiana), it is only 10,822 and 11,172 for Sangrur and Jallandhar respectively. However, adequate utilization of these medical institutions is affected in poorly performing districts due to lack of availability of other inputs. As depicted in Table 6.10, the availability of beds in Sangrur caters to 27 per cent more persons than in Ludhiana. In fact the availability of all three inputs in Sangrur, namely doctors, midwives and nurses, caters to 50 per cent more persons than in Ludhiana. Moreover, the availability of nurses in Sangrur results in service provided to 80 per cent more patients than in Ludhiana. Similar is the case of availability pertaining to midwives and nurses for another poorly performing district, Jallandhar. It is therefore pertinent that the requirement for more medical and paramedical personnel and more beds be included in the planning of future health facilities, and greater expenditures could be made for these purposes in the state's health budget. This may help to enhance LEXP in poorly performing districts at a faster rate to maintain pace with better-off districts.

Table 6.10 Population served per health institutions, beds, health manpower and life expectancy at Birth in Punjab's districts

District	Medical institution	Beds in medical institutions	Doctor	Midwife	Nurse	Life expectancy at birth
Amritsar	10,494	617	873	840	1,454	72
Bathinda	10,006	1,172	1,421	1,253	8,351	68.3
Faridkot	13,228	709	1,219	817	1,529	70.1
Fatehgarh Sahib	10,404	1,343	26,530	6,471	10,011	69.6
Firozpur	11,899	1,068	3,511	1,324	1,640	71
Gurdaspur	10,235	1,273	2,382	579	973	74.2
Hoshiarpur	8,842	998	1,845	669	2,057	68.1
Jalandhar	11,172	878	946	1,084	1,559	66.1
Kapurthala	9,044	971	1,867	1,463	3,910	68.7
Ludhiana	14,827	934	1,174	674	892	76.8
Mansa	10,895	1,393	27,691	7,467	16,209	68.3
Moga (R)	10,712	1,331	21,687	2,137	2,887	70.2
Muktsar	10,541	1,257	26,534	17,488	36,062	70.2
Nawanshehar	8,133	1,266	38,635	4,683	5,569	66.7
Patiala	11,102	743	724	1,532	1,696	69.5
Rup Nagar	9,455	1,141	2,468	1,198	2,983	70.7
Sangrur	10,822	1,275	2,518	1,794	4,469	65.2
Punjab	10,786	947	1,485	1,015	1,696	67.4
Gini coefficient	0.0756	0.0999	0.582	0.548	0.553	0.021

Source: GoP (2004).

However, other factors affect adequate performance of health systems at the district level. This is estimated by our second-stage exercise. It deciphers the non–health system factors that could be possible determinants of dispersion in efficiency. We have tried a set of variables including total per capita income, per capita male and female income separately, literacy, rural and urban literacy separately, urbanization, water supply and sanitation facilities, infrastructure variables such as road per square kilometre, persons below the poverty line (BPL) and gender development index (GDI). The best fit is made up of three explanatory variables – per capita female income (PCIF), GDI index and female literacy (Tables 6.11–6.14). Pertinently, unlike in state-level studies (e.g. Sankar and Kathuria 2004), PCIF, GDI and female literacy are all significant. This combination of variables indicates that the level of gender development in the state has helped to reduce disparities in health outcomes.

As presented in Table 6.15, GDI is relatively high in the districts of Punjab. It ideally should mean that men and women share equally in socio-economic development. However, factually that is not the case. At present, as calculated in the human development report of the state, GDI does not adequately represent equal opportunity in all the spheres because (a) it is not affected by gender ratio and (b) it is insensitive to low rates of female work participation prevalent in Punjab which prevent women from becoming economically empowered. Other factors such as female literacy and female income have also emerged as statistically significant in our study. Thus, lower levels of female income and female literacy act as an important deterrent to better health system performance.

Table 6.11 Descriptive statistics

	Mean	Std. deviation	N
Deviation	7.053	2.839	17
LITFM	0.625	0.093	17
PCIF	2,140.412	676.900	17
GDI	0.611	0.036	17

Source: Estimated.

Table 6.12 Model summary

Model	R	R square	Adjusted R square	Std. error of the estimate	Change statistics			
					R square change	F change	df1	df2
1	0.860	0.739	0.679	1.609	0.739	12.273	3	13

Source: Estimated.
Predictors: (Constant), GDI, LITFM, PCIF; dependent variable: DEVIATION.

Table 6.13 ANOVA

Model		Sum of squares	df	Mean square	F	Sig.
1	Regression	95.340	3	31.780	12.273	0.0004
	Residual	33.663	13	2.589		
	Total	129.003	16			

Source: Estimated.
Predictors: (Constant), GDI, LITFM, PCIF; dependent variable: DEVIATION

Table 6.14 Regression results for dispersion as dependent variable (Punjab)

Model		Unstandardised coefficients		Standardised coefficients	t
		B	Std. error	Beta	
1	(Constant)	71.541	14.050		5.092*
	LITFM	61.892	12.669	2.023	4.885*
	PCIF	0.014	0.002	3.339	5.779*
	GDI	−217.825	42.232	−2.766	−5.158*

Source: Estimated.
*Indicates statistical significance at 1% level.

Table 6.15 Gender-related development index (GDI) in Punjab – 2001

District	GDI	Rank
Amritsar	0.544	17
Bathinda	0.625	7
F. G. Sahib	0.556	16
Faridkot	0.643	4
Firozpur	0.643	4
Gurdaspur	0.565	15
Hoshiarpur	0.645	3
Jalandhar	0.632	6
Kapurthala	0.652	2
Ludhiana	0.619	9
Mansa	0.586	13
Moga	0.607	10
Muktsar	0.606	11
Nawanshehar	0.623	8
Patiala	0.6	12
Rup Nagar	0.669	1
Sangrur	0.575	14
Punjab	0.614	

Source: GoP (2004).

Conclusions

These results from our district-level analysis indicate that health sector efficiency in Punjab could be improved if disparities in performance at the district level are overcome. This would require policy initiatives to help the poorer-performing districts through adequate support. Pertinently, such districts could fare better through higher per capita public expenditure. This may improve utilization of medical institutions through the presence of essential manpower inputs. Keeping in view a relatively lower level of per capita income in these districts, oft-prescribed privatization and user fees may not be the appropriate sole remedy. It would be better to increase overall public health expenditure in these districts to deploy and make available more medical and paramedical personnel. This fact should be incorporated into health facility planning at the substate level. Further enhancement to life expectancy may be possible at a faster pace in Punjab if such efforts are coupled with steps to promote female literacy and female incomes. This could empower women, particularly in poorly performing districts, through better opportunities, leading to an increase in women's participation in the workforce. Further studies at the substate level may also be initiated and facilitated if the official information base is extended to provide public and private expenditure incurred at the district level on health and other social sectors.

Efficiency of the health care sector at the substate level in India: Maharashtra

In this section we focus on a substate-level (i.e. district-level) study of Maharashtra. According to the 2001 census, it is the second-most populous state of

India with a population of 96.7 million, of which 42.4 per cent reside in urban areas. In terms of per capita income, it is the second-richest state in India, with its per capita income 40 per cent higher than the all-India average. Its capital, Mumbai, is the country's principal financial centre and a major commercial hub. A comparison of key indicators reveals that Maharashtra's high income level has not been matched by its attainments in social development (Table 6.16).

Compared to the all-India life expectancy of 61.8 years for males and 63.5 years for females (1999–2003), the respective figures for Maharashtra are 65.2 years and 67.6 years. IMR in the state (in 2005) is also lower (at 36 per thousand) relative to the all-India IMR of 58 per thousand. However, IMR differs considerably between rural and urban areas at 58 per thousand and 31 per thousand respectively. This differential in IMR across districts of the state is also glaring. IMR varies from 31 per thousand in Mumbai to as high as 106 per thousand in Gadchiroli. According to *Human Development Report of Maharashtra* (Government of Maharashtra [GoM] 2002), 'Both qualitatively and quantitatively, there is a wide gap in health care infrastructure available in rural and urban areas.' There is a concentration of hospitals, nursing homes and qualified doctors in both the public and private sectors. In fact, in the year 2000, the number of doctors per 1,00 thousand population in urban areas was 139.8 as compared to only 23.7 in rural areas. Likewise, over 80 per cent of the beds in public hospitals are in urban areas, which cover only 42.4 per cent of the total population. This skewed distribution is also reflected at the substate level across districts and regions in Maharashtra. In general, districts such as Mumbai, Pune, Wardha and Nagpur have a better ratio of population to facilities. Rural infrastructure such as PHCs and SCs are not adequately supported by necessary inputs. Due to inadequate and declining public investment and health expenditure in the

Table 6.16 Maharashtra in a comparative framework

State	Per capita income in 2003–04 (Rs. at 1993–94 prices)	Life expectancy at birth (1999–2003)			Literacy rate (%) (2001)	Percentage of population below poverty line (30-day recall period)
		Male	*Female*	*Total*		
Maharashtra	16,479	65.2	67.6	66.4	76.88	25.02
Karnataka	13,141	62.9	66.4	64.6	66.64	20.04
Punjab	15,800	67.6	69.6	68.6	69.65	6.1
Gujarat	16,779	62.5	64.6	63.5	69.14	14.07
Madhya Pradesh	8,284	57.2	56.9	57.1	63.74	37.43
Tamil Nadu	12,976	64.3	66.5	65.4	73.4	21.12
All India	11,799	61.8	63.5	62.7	64.84	26.1

Sources: GoA (2007a); *The Economic Times* (2005); GoM (2002).

Table 6.17 Number of hospitals, beds and dispensaries per lakh population across states and by rural and urban areas

States	Hospitals			Beds			Dispensaries		
	Rural	Urban	Total	Rural	Urban	Total	Rural	Urban	Total
Andhra Pradesh	1.7	10.6	4.2	19.8	189.8	65.5	0.4	0.4	0.4
Gujarat	0.6	15.1	5.6	24.3	422.5	161.7	8.2	31.2	16.1
Haryana	0.1	1.5	0.4	4	152.8	40.6	0.3	4.1	1.2
Karnataka	0.1	1.7	0.6	10.4	233.5	79.4	1.8	1.6	1.7
Kerala	6.5	7.5	6.7	198	414.2	255.1	6.4	6.4	6.4
Maharashtra	0.9	8.3	3.8	20.7	219.7	97.7	0.7	24.4	9.9
Punjab	1.8	2.2	1.9	62.9	156.2	90.4	7.7	3.6	6.5
Tamil Nadu	0.2	1.7	0.7	11.8	232.9	87.5	0.4	1.9	0.9
West Bengal	0.2	1.4	0.5	11.7	237	73.7	0.8	0.7	0.7
All India	0.7	4.3	1.6	19.4	212.7	69.1	1.7	6.7	3

Source: GoM (2002).

1990s, Maharashtra's position in comparison to some major Indian states has worsened (Table 6.17).

Partly this worsening could be due to population growth and in-migration which has increased the density of population between 1961 and 2001 by two and half times to the current level of 314 persons per square kilometre.

To carry out our estimation of health system efficiency at the all-India level, our specification is based on the general stochastic frontier model presented earlier. In the second stage of estimation, we presume that differences in technical efficiency pertaining to the health care system can be discerned at the district-level health facility planning stage by non-health-related parameters. Thus, we explain the dispersion in technical efficiency by a set of variables which includes per capita income (PCI), male and female income separately, literacy, rural and urban literacy separately, urbanization, water supply and sanitation facilities, gender development index (GDI) and persons below poverty line (BPL). Our model in the second stage is thus:

Dispersion in technical efficiency = f (PCI, male and female income separately, literacy, rural and urban literacy separately, urbanization, water supply and sanitation facilities, infrastructure variables such as road per square kilometre, BPL, GDI) + error term. . . .   (C)

Database

This study is based on secondary data. Information is collected from *Human Development Report of Maharashtra, 2002* (GoM 2002), websites of the state and other published sources. Main variables used in the study are life expectancy (LEXP), infant mortality rates (IMR), per capita income (PCI) and parameters related to human development indicators (HDI), gender development indicator (GDI) and health facilities. The information relates to the district level for the state.

Our hypothesis

It is presumed that estimated efficiency parameters should help the makers of health policy to improve district-level and thus state-level health system performance. We hypothesize that districts differ in their technical efficiency pertaining to the health care system due to factors which require emphasis in health facility planning at the district level. It is also hypothesized that these factors differ among states according to their level of development. As noted previously, we consider an affluent Indian state, Maharashtra. It is a high-income state, with its per capita income above the all-India average (Table 6.16).

Results and discussion

Results of our frontier model for Maharashtra are presented in Table 6.18. All the independent variables to explain the inverse of IMR have emerged with appropriate signs and are statistically significant. Notably immunization coverage (THREE DOSES) has the highest magnitude (.626), followed by percentage of institutional delivery (.173) (INSTDELPERCENT) and urban availability of health facilities (.057) (URBANBEDS).

Using the results of the frontier model, actual and estimated IMR are presented in Table 6.19. These depict that Mumbai is the most efficient district

Table 6.18 Stochastic frontier normal/half-normal model for Maharashtra

Wald chi^2(3) = 4.722e+10; log likelihood = .45024468; prob > chi^2 = 0.0000; dependent variable: Inverse IMR; likelihood-ratio test of sigma u = 0; chibar2(01) = 7.06; prob>= chibar2 = 0.004.

Explanatory variable	Coefficient	Standard error
URBANBEDS	0.057*	.000011
INSTDELPERCENT	0.173*	4.30e–06
THREE DOSES	0.626*	.0000201
Constant	–7.514*	.0000623
Other statistics		
lnsig2v	–42.193	1654.818
lnsig2u	–1.481*	.2581989
sigma_v	6.89e–10	5.70e–07
sigma_u	.4767326	.0615459
sigma2	.227274	.0586819
lambda	6.92e+08	.0615459

Source: Estimated.

*Indicates 1% level of significance.

Note: Number of observations = 30.

Table 6.19 Actual and estimated IMR in Maharashtra's districts

District	Actual IMR	Estimated IMR	Excess of actual IMR over estimated (%)
Mumbai	37	37	0
Thane	46.00	42.30	8.75
Raigad	63.00	39.81	58.25
Ratnagiri	75.00	41.18	82.14
Sindhudurg	70.00	37.63	86.02
Nashik	79.00	45.91	72.09
Dhule	73.00	55.01	32.69
Jalgaon	71.00	46.73	51.95
Ahmednagar	47.00	47.00	0
Pune	52.00	46.25	12.43
Satara	51.00	38.75	31.61
Sangli	41	41	0
Solapur	68.00	50.46	34.76
Kolhapur	55.00	40.35	36.32
Aurangabad	56.00	46.63	20.09
Jalna	76.00	46.79	62.42
Parbhani	50	50	0
Beed	52.00	44.05	18.05
Nanded	68.00	42.64	59.48
Osmanabad	70.00	46.33	51.08
Latur	57.00	50.59	12.68
Buldhana	82.00	46.15	77.68
Akola	101.00	39.19	157.73
Amaravati	94.00	42.63	120.50
Yavatmal	124.00	47.54	160.86
Wardha	88.00	40.25	118.64
Nagpur	75.00	50.13	49.61
Bhandara	81.00	47.76	69.60
Chandrapur	96.00	50.19	91.26
Gadchiroli	106.00	78.78	34.55

Source: GoM (2002) and our estimates.

(MED) with its lowest actual IMR (32 per thousand) coinciding with estimated IMR. Three other districts, Ahmednagar, Sangli and Parbhani, with their actual IMR at 47, 41 and 50 respectively, depict their actual coinciding with potential. However, owing to their overall higher level of IMR relative to Mumbai, these districts cannot be considered as MED. Thus in terms of actual IMR being higher than potential IMR, except for districts with zero deviations, Thane district is the fourth-most efficient district (with deviations at 8.75% from its potential) and Yavatmal is the least-efficient district with actual nearly 2.6 times higher than potential (Table 6.19)

Performance of these districts relative to MED is presented in terms of their deviation from MED in Table 6.20. Pertinently, ranks computed based on these deviations depict that next to Mumbai, the second- and third-most efficient districts are Sangali and Thane. The lowest rank denoting the lowest performance is depicted for Yavatmal (Table 6.20).

Table 6.20 Deviations from maximum efficient district in Maharashtra

	Deviation from maximum efficient district	Rank
Mumbai	0	1
Thane	9.00	3
Raigad	26.00	12
Ratnagiri	38.00	19
Sindhudurg	33.00	15
Nashik	42.00	22
Dhule	36.00	18
Jalgaon	34.00	17
Ahmednagar	10.00	4
Pune	15.00	7
Satara	14.00	6
Sangli	4.00	2
Solapur	31.00	13
Kolhapur	18.00	9
Aurangabad	19.00	10
Jalna	39.00	21
Parbhani	13.00	5
Beed	15.00	7
Nanded	31.00	13
Osmanabad	33.00	15
Latur	20.00	11
Buldhana	45.00	24
Akola	64.00	28
Amaravati	57.00	26
Yavatmal	87.00	30
Wardha	51.00	25
Nagpur	38.00	19
Bhandara	44.00	23
Chandrapur	59.00	27
Gadchiroli	69.00	29

Source: GoM (2002) and our estimates.

Reasons for these interdistrict disparities can be deciphered from Table 6.21, which depicts major inputs for the health sector in the state. Notably, the distribution of dispensaries and Indian system of medicines (ISM) institutions in the state is highly inequitable. This is obvious from high values of Gini coefficients for these parameters, .716 and .502 respectively. Moreover, there is a considerable difference between maximum and minimum values for each of the parameters (last two rows, Table 6.21).

Notable features that emerge for the highest efficiency of Mumbai are the highest number of ANMs per lakh of population in Mumbai (352 per lakh); a very low percentage of public-sector hospitals in the district (8%) and the urban nature of the district, depicted by 100 per cent of the beds, hospitals and dispensaries being located in urban areas. By contrast, the least efficient district of Yavatmal has fewer than half (compared to Mumbai) per lakh availability of ANMs (108 per lakh), the highest percentage of public-sector hospitals (nearly 65%) and nearly 53 per cent of the beds in urban areas. This outcome suggests better utilization of

Table 6.21 Health facilities, manpower and public sector–urban percentage in Maharashtra's districts

	Population served per				All medical institutions	ANM per lakh	Percentage in public sector		Percentage in urban areas		
	Bed	Hospital	Dispensary	ISM institutions			Hospitals	Dispensaries	Hospitals	Dispensaries	Beds
Mumbai	3,000	13,764	5,251	65,617	3,593	351.67	8	100	100	100	100
Thane	1,420	21,468	3,720	73,562	3,040	205.56	42.9	47.2	97.1	50.8	90.9
Raigad	2,615	20,192	12,296	200,000	7,378	143.03	18.1	5.9	96.5	96.4	99.2
Ratnagiri	1,017	34,529	324,577	300,000	28,472	127.52	15.7	10.7	88.4	95.5	66
Sindhudurg	2,569	20,337	7,110	9,016	3,325	155.02	22	47.5	79.3	100	81.8
Nashik	1,715	21,192	8,144	44,975	5,203	107.78	18.3	13.2	87.8	100	69.3
Dhule	2,004	14,809	12,227	63,466	6,058	103.68	15.9	2.9	95	100	69
Jalgaon	2,256	6,742	17,453	63,224	4,516	92.29	7.9	6.3	71.7	95.3	76.8
Ahmednagar	1,987	25,691	12,892	31,940	6,766	94.61	7.8	7.8	87.7	99.6	60.7
Pune	539	11,163	17,257	300,000	6,631	218.51	19.7	100	90.4	100	67.9
Satara	2,758	13,703	184,016	100,000	11,710	120.95	33.7	11.6	95.1	99.5	83.4
Sangli	1,536	11,438	12,093	22,542	4,662	178.05	10	17.6	74.5	100	68.5
Solapur	1,540	1,9631	26,124	200,000	10,514	124.26	8.6	100	14	3.3	35.8
Kolhapur	2,504	36,544	14,755	42,470	8,426	139.82	24.4	3.8	84.9	3.8	39.7
Aurangabad	1,374	21,350	2,502	200,000	2,212	121.2	27.7	100	72.5	26.5	73.1
Jalna	2,351	25,152	477,897	89,606	18,864	82.16	19.7	13.8	82.5	66.7	75.3
Parbhani	2,710	23,672	21,192	42,792	8,865	86.25	25.7	10.7	80	100	55.3
Beed	2,130	26,973	36,134	23,355	9,297	104.94	18.6	11.4	88.7	100	56.7

(Continued)

Table 6.21 (Continued)

	Population served per					ANM per lakh	Percentage in public sector		Percentage in urban areas		
	Bed	Hospital	Dispensary	ISM institutions	All medical institutions		Hospitals	Dispensaries	Hospitals	Dispensaries	Beds
Nanded	1,840	27,212	17,876	44,528	8,685	98.44	16	5.7	98.1	61.9	93.4
Osmanabad	1,564	38,320	47,900	41,912	14,118	104.44	17.8	12.4	92.1	99.4	76.8
Latur	3,005	28,896	440,670	62,953	18,954	122.15	12.8	2.5	93.4	100	73.5
Buldhana	2,349	27,533	12,957	17,089	5,813	135.45	16.1	7.8	93.1	94.8	76.3
Akola	948	22,815	8,619	47,492	5,528	156.03	11.7	2.4	92.2	92.2	76.8
Amaravati	761	11,064	7,557	7,812	2,851	122.59	16.8	10.3	94.7	87.9	71.9
Yavatmal	1,795	26,303	19,492	41,191	8,803	107.98	64.7	43.2	85.4	52.5	53.4
Wardha	483	27,354	19,009	86,270	9,925	124.98	19.4	7.3	96.9	99.5	91.8
Nagpur	715	9,624	41,130	29,279	6,159	181.95	22.8	100	44.7	84.3	69.9
Bhandara	2,164	52,755	79,132	29,154	15,176	120.09	22.5	5.5	61.9	47.2	51.4
Chandrapur	972	20,027	9,701	16,630	4,692	134.26	7.6	4.2	81.7	67.2	64.7
Gadchiroli	3,422	48,659	22,357	22,357	9,090	147.39	11.3	23.1	47.1	56.8	14.8
Gini coefficient	0.238	0.242	0.716	0.502	0.329	0.174	0.281	0.638	0.108	0.200	0.143
Maximum value	3,422	52,755	477,897	300,000	28,472	351.67	64.7	100	100	100	100
Minimum value	483	6,742	2,502	7,812	2,212	82.16	7.6	2.4	14	3.3	14.8

Source: GoM (2002); Sharma (n.d.).

private-sector facilities with urbanization and better efficiency in health outcomes and reduced IMR. It also indicates the importance of per capita availability of paramedical staff. Looking from the parameters of population served per bed, Mumbai's high efficiency may be due to its very high utilization of beds, 3,000 population served per bed, which is behind only Gadchiroli (3,422 population served per bed) and Latur (3,005 population served per bed).

Besides the factors within the health system, influences external to the system may lead to differentials in efficiency at the district level. To explore such external factors, we used dispersion in efficiency as a dependent variable in the second stage of our regression exercise. Among the set of variables we used as explanatory variables were per capita income, number of families below poverty line (BPL), total literacy, male and female literacy separately, number of primary and secondary educational institutions separately, dropout rate, gender development index (GDI), rural habitat fully covered by water supply and percentage coverage through safe drinking water, toilet facilities (TOILETS) and human development indicator (HDI). The results of best fit are presented in Tables 6.22–6.25.

Table 6.22 Descriptive statistics

	Mean	Std. deviation	N
Dispersion	3E+32	2E+33	30
BPL	1E+05	6E+04	30
Toilets	2E+01	1E+01	30

Source: Estimated.

Table 6.23 Model summary

R	R square	Adjusted R square	Std. error of the estimate	df1	df2	Sig. F change	Durbin-Watson
0.800	0.639	0.613	1.02E+33	2	27	1.05E-06	2.025

Source: Estimated.
Predictors: (Constant), Toilets, BPL; Dependent variable: Dispersion.

Table 6.24 ANOVA

	Sum of squares	Df	Mean square	F	Sig.
Regression	4.98E+67	2	2.49E+67	23.93*	1.05E–06
Residual	2.81E+67	27	1.04E+66		
Total	7.79E+67	29			

Source: Estimated.
Predictors: (Constant), Toilets, BPL; Dependent variable: Dispersion.

Table 6.25 Coefficients

	Unstandardised coefficients		Standardised coefficients	t	Sig.
	B	Std. error	Beta		
Constant	−2.1E+32	5.46E+32		−0.390	0.700
BPL	−8.7E+27	3.43E+27	−0.298	−2.548**	0.017
Toilets	7.75E+31	1.29E+31	0.699	5.986*	2.19E–06

Source: Estimated.

*Denotes significance at 1% level; **denotes significance at 2% level.

Note: Dependent variable: Dispersion.

Two variables, BPL and TOILETS, have emerged as statistically significant. The negative sign of BPL indicates that efforts to reduce poverty have helped to reduce regional disparities in efficiency of health systems across districts. However, the lack of sanitation facilities as depicted by the positive sign of TOILETS indicates that insufficient effort and public investment in the development of rural sanitation has hampered the outcome of direct intervention through the health delivery system in the state. It may be useful if this inadequacy is overcome through appropriate efforts.

Conclusions

The results of the frontier model using district-level information in Maharashtra indicate that despite urbanization and direct health sector intervention in the state, the efficiency of the public health delivery system remains low. Considerable deficiency of public health manpower inputs and prevailing disparities across districts has an adverse impact on improving life expectancy in the state. The main factors within the health system contributing to the discrepancies in interdistrict performance are inequitable distribution of beds and dispensaries, availability of skilled attention at birth and inadequate staffing relative to patient load in less urbanized districts of the state. Overcoming these factors may lead to an improvement in the district-level efficiency of the public health system. This may also help the state to reduce IMR in deficient districts such as Yavatmal and improve life expectancy speedily and more equitably. Achieving this may require a considerable increase in medical and public health expenditure, which has not kept pace in the state relative to other better-off states in the country. It will call for resource mobilization for the sector through innovative steps and more effective use of funds. Besides the direct inputs from the health sector, a more concerted effort to improve rural sanitation in poorer-performing districts may add to overall reduction in IMR and improved life expectancy in the state.

Efficiency of the health care system at the substate level in Karnataka

We extend our analysis in this section to focus on the efficiency of the health care system at the substate level (i.e. district level) in India using Karnataka state and its district-level panel data. We explore the reasons for the relative performance of different districts using panel data for the state with the frontier estimation technique. The overall income average of Karnataka state makes it representative of a middle-income category in the country, with substate-level variations in its health system parameters. Situated in the southern region of India, the state constitutes 5.83 per cent of the total geographical area of the country (191,791 sq km), and it has a population of 53 million, which according to the 2001 census accounts for 5.13 per cent of India's population. It is the ninth-largest state among India's twenty-eight major states and seven Union Territories, with a population density (in 2001) of 275 (as compared to 324 at the all-India level), and about 66 per cent of population live in rural areas.

A comparison of key social development indicators for Karnataka with those of some major states is presented in Table 6.26. As mentioned previously, it is a middle-income state, with a per capita income of Rs. 13,141 that is higher than the all-India average (Table 6.26). Its life expectancy and literacy rates are slightly above the country's average (Table 6.26).

Compared to the all-India life expectancy of 61.8 years and 63.5 years for males and females (1999–2003), the respective figures for Karnataka are 62.9 years and 66.4 years. According to the Karnataka Human Development Report of the State (Government of Karnataka [GoK] 2006, p. 66), there exist 'significant interdistrict variations in human development and the skewed distribution of historically given expenditures, in favour of districts with higher

Table 6.26 Karnataka in a comparative framework with some major states in different income categories

State	Per capita income in 2003–04 (Rs. at 1993–94 prices)	Life expectancy at birth (1999–2003)			Literacy rate (%) (2001)
		Male	Female	Total	
Karnatatka	13,141	62.9	66.4	64.6	66.64
West Bengal	11,612	63.5	65	62.7	68.64
Maharashtra	16,479	65.2	67.6	66.4	76.88
Punjab	15,800	67.6	69.6	68.6	69.65
Gujarat	16,779	62.5	64.6	63.5	69.14
Madhya Pradesh	8,284	57.2	56.9	57.1	63.74
Tamil Nadu	12,976	64.3	66.5	65.4	73.4
All India	11,799	61.8	63.5	62.7	64.84

Sources: GoI (2007a); *The Economic Times* (2005, p. 9).

human development indicators' which 'makes it necessary to introduce strategic changes in resource allocation'. Considerable disparity also exists between rural and urban areas in health care infrastructure. There is a concentration of hospitals, beds and dispensaries in urban areas, resulting in higher per capita availability in these areas relative to their rural counterparts (Table 6.27). This skewed distribution is also reflected in sub-state level across districts and regions in Karnataka. Due to inadequacy of public investment and health care expenditure, Karnataka's position in comparison to all India average and some major Indian states remains at a lower level (Table 6.27).

Model specification and methodology for this substate-level analysis also remains the same as those adopted for earlier states. This study is based on secondary data. Information is collected from human development reports of Karnataka (GoK 2006) and other states, websites of the states, *Economic Survey 2007* (GoI 2007a), *Reproductive and Child Health Survey* (GoI 2006c) and other published sources. The main variables used in the study are life expectancy (LEXP), infant mortality rates (IMR), per capita income (PCI) and other parameters related to human development, gender development and health care facilities. The information relates to district level for the state.

We hypothesize that districts differ in their technical efficiency pertaining to the health care system due to factors which require emphasis in planning health facilities at the district level. It is also hypothesized that these factors differ among states according to their level of development. It is presumed that estimated efficiency parameters should help the makers of health policy to improve district-level and thus state-level health system performance. As noted earlier, we consider a middle-income Indian state, Karnataka, which has a per capita income slightly above the all-India average (Table 6.26).

Table 6.27 Number of hospitals, beds and dispensaries per lakh population across states and by rural and urban areas (Karnataka and some major Indian states in different income categories)

States	Hospitals			Beds			Dispensaries		
	Rural	*Urban*	*Total*	*Rural*	*Urban*	*Total*	*Rural*	*Urban*	*Total*
Andhra Pradesh	1.7	10.6	4.2	19.8	189.8	65.5	0.4	0.4	0.4
Gujarat	0.6	15.1	5.6	24.3	422.5	161.7	8.2	31.2	16.1
Haryana	0.1	1.5	0.4	4	152.8	40.6	0.3	4.1	1.2
Karnataka	**0.1**	**1.7**	**0.6**	**10.4**	**233.5**	**79.4**	**1.8**	**1.6**	**1.7**
Kerala	6.5	7.5	6.7	198	414.2	255.1	6.4	6.4	6.4
Maharashtra	0.9	8.3	3.8	20.7	219.7	97.7	0.7	24.4	9.9
Punjab	1.8	2.2	1.9	62.9	156.2	90.4	7.7	3.6	6.5
Tamil Nadu	0.2	1.7	0.7	11.8	232.9	87.5	0.4	1.9	0.9
West Bengal	0.2	1.4	0.5	11.7	237	73.7	0.8	0.7	0.7
All India	0.7	4.3	1.6	19.4	212.7	69.1	1.7	6.7	3

Source: GoM (2002).

Results and discussion

Results of our panel data estimation using the frontier model for Karnataka are presented in Table 6.28. All the independent variables to explain life expectancy (LEXP) have emerged with appropriate signs and are statistically significant. Notably the variables representing total delivery in institutional set-up (TOT-DELINST), number of medical institutions in the state (MEDINST) and rural population served per subcentre (PERSC) have emerged with positive signs. This indicates the positive impact of governmental intervention in the expansion of hospital facilities and the desirable impact of institutional delivery coverage in enhancing life expectancy. That both the variables representing respectively rural population coverage per subcentre and total number of medical institutions have emerged with positive signs indicates adequacy of the various inputs provided through medical institutions and rural health subcentres.

Using the results of frontier model, actual and estimated life expectancy (LEXP) are presented for the years 1991 and 2004 in Tables 6.29 and 6.30. These depict Koppal and Dakshina Kannada as the most efficient districts (MED), with their actual LEXP moving highest towards their estimated LEXP in the respective 2 years. However, in terms of highest percentage increase in actual life expectancy we find Hassan the best performer in the duration 1991–2004.

Reasons for these interdistrict disparities can be deciphered from Table 6.31, which depicts major inputs for the health sector in the state. Notably, the distribution of per capita hospitals, primary health centers (PHCs), beds and ANMs

Table 6.28 Stochastic frontier panel data model for Karnataka (time-invariant inefficiency model)

Wald chi^2(3) = 112.24; log likelihood = 127.6591; prob > chi^2 = 0.0000.

LEXP	Coefficient	Std. err.
TOTDELINST	0.040*	0.009
MEDINST	0.044*	0.014
PERSC	0.054**	0.019
CONSTANT	3.413*	0.150
MU	0.065**	0.023
LNSIGMA2	−7.025*	0.300
ILGTGAMMA	1.406**	0.553
SIGMA2	0.001	0.000
GAMMA	0.803	0.087
SIGMA_U2	0.001	0.000
SIGMA_V2	0.000	0.000

Source: Estimated.

*Denotes significance at 1% level; **denotes significance at 5% level.

Notes: Number of observations = 54; number of groups = 27.

Table 6.29 Actual and estimated (potential) life expectancy for districts in Karnataka

		Actual life expectancy (2004)	Potential life expectancy (2004)	Actual as % of potential (2004)
1	Bagalkot	60.80	68.30	89.02
2	Bangalore rural	66.50	70.56	94.25
3	Bangalore urban	67.30	73.05	92.13
4	Belgaum	67.70	71.72	94.40
5	Bellary	66.10	68.01	97.19
6	Bidar	63.30	67.64	93.58
7	Bijapur	62.60	67.43	92.84
8	Chamarajnagar	63.50	67.07	94.67
9	Chikmaglur	63.20	67.87	93.12
10	Chitradurga	64.60	69.43	93.05
11	**Dakshina Kannada**	**67.40**	**67.82**	**99.38**
12	Davangere	65.80	69.25	95.01
13	Dharwad	61.90	66.69	92.82
14	Gadag	62.70	66.38	94.46
15	Gulbarga	62.90	68.71	91.54
16	Hassan	65.20	68.99	94.50
17	Haveri	62.20	66.56	93.44
18	Kodagu	63.30	66.04	95.86
19	Kolar	64.20	70.32	91.30
20	Koppal	63.50	65.19	97.41
21	Mandya	62.90	69.86	90.03
22	Mysore	64.80	69.90	92.70
23	Raichur	63.90	67.10	95.22
24	Shimoga	67.40	68.41	98.52
25	Tumkur	65.30	70.34	92.84
26	Udupi	67.80	68.72	98.66
27	Uttara Kannada	62.90	68.51	91.81

Source: Estimated.

in the state is highly inequitable. In fact, there is a considerable difference between maximum and minimum values for each of the parameters (columns 2–4, Table 6.31). Pertinently, the number of hospital beds per lakh of population is the highest (234) in Kodagu, followed by Mysore (137), Bangalore Urban (123), Chikmaglur (113) and Dharwar (112). In terms of staff per lakh, it is again Kodagu (83.67), followed by Chikmaglur (57.67) and Uttar Kannada (53.04). In terms of population served per PHC, the maximum and minimum are for Bidar (28,760) and Udupi (14,550). In terms of population served per subcentre, the corresponding maximum and minimum are for Raichur (6,250) and Dakshina Kannada (2,660). These values of inputs do not indicate that the low workload on subcentre in Dakshina Kannada is helping to produce the district's better life expectancy. By contrast, Kodagu district, with the lowest population served per medical institution (10.17 thousand) and the maximum number of hospital beds (234) and staff per lakh (83.67), ranked 6th and 10th respectively in 2004 and 1991 in terms of its distance of potential, and unlike Hassan, where the highest actual increase in LEXP took place (9.58%) between 1991 and 2004, Kodagu has shown

Table 6.30 Ranks of districts in Karnataka according to realization of potential life expectancy

	District/Year	Ranks of districts according to realization of potential life expectancy		% increase in actual LEXP, 1991–2004
		1991	2004	
1	Bagalkot	26	**27**	3.05
2	Bangalore rural	9	13	3.26
3	Bangalore urban	24	22	3.86
4	Belgaum	16	12	5.12
5	Bellary	8	5	5.25
6	Bidar	6	14	3.77
7	Bijapur	15	18	5.74
8	Chamarajnagar	5	9	1.60
9	Chikmaglur	21	16	5.16
10	Chitradurga	12	17	2.87
11	**Dakshina Kannada**	**2**	**1**	2.12
12	Davangere	13	8	4.44
13	Dharwad	22	20	4.74
14	Gadag	14	11	4.50
15	Gulbarga	19	24	5.71
16	**Hassan**	**27**	10	**9.58**
17	Haveri	11	15	4.36
18	Kodagu	10	6	3.77
19	Kolar	20	25	3.55
20	**Koppal**	**1**	4	5.83
21	Mandya	25	26	3.28
22	Mysore	18	21	3.02
23	Raichur	7	7	5.79
24	Shimoga	3	3	2.43
25	Tumkur	17	19	3.65
26	Udupi	4	2	2.57
27	Uttara Kannada	23	23	3.28

Sources: Estimated; GoK (2006).

Note: Figures in bold denote changes between 1991 and 2004 in rankings.

only a 3.77 per cent increase in LEXP in that time. Thus in most of the districts neither the adequate availability of health care sector inputs nor merely efficient utilization of these inputs can explain the differentials in LEXP. However, to some extent, among other inputs, this differential pattern in efficiency is explained by percentage of the population not having the facilities of safe drinking water, toilets and electricity in rural and urban areas separately (Table 6.32). In fact, the highest-achieving district, Hassan, has a much lower nonavailability in rural areas (17.06%) relative to either Kodagu (30.35%), Bidar (28.96%), Koppal (33.24%), Udupi (29.69%), Raichur (39.32%) or Dakshina Kannada (32.18%). This clearly suggests that the availability of safe drinking water, toilets and electricity for the rural population has played a strong, supportive role in enhancing the overall

Table 6.31 Health facilities and immunization status in Karnataka's districts

District	Population served per medical institution (in thousands)	Number of hospital beds per lakh population	Staff per lakh	Population served per PHC (in thousands)	Population served per SC (in thousands)	Children aged 1 year received complete immunization (%)
Bagalkot	26.32	47	26.58	26.81	7.66	64.4
Bangalore Rural	15.46	51	36.73	20.74	5.29	92.7
Bangalore Urban	37.19	123	14.23	27.46	6.08	72.1
Belgaum	23.14	50	24.04	24.54	5.58	74.3
Bellary	20.36	91	25.31	25.32	5.28	77.3
Bidar	23.39	67	34.35	28.76	5.23	89
Bijapur	22.15	67	28.11	22.63	4.99	77.6
Chamarajnagar	14.63	86	40.08	15.96	4.11	84.8
Chikmaglur	10.94	113	57.67	18.29	2.84	95.9
Chitradurga	14.45	88	51.19	22.41	6.23	80.8
Dakshina Kannada	**20.97**	**96**	**37.62**	**18.68**	**2.66**	**93.3**
Davangere	15.34	99	31.71	18.33	5.07	93.4
Dharwad	34.12	112	24.75	25.95	4.33	86.3
Gadag	19.69	57	29.94	22.45	5.17	86.9
Gulbarga	19.06	66	26.16	22.66	4.69	81
Hassan	**11.02**	**110**	**45.13**	**17.58**	**3.11**	**84.4**
Haveri	16.39	54	33.01	23.37	3.95	81.2
Kodagu	10.17	234	83.67	16.63	2.96	109.7
Kolar	17.41	99	35.57	23.68	5.24	79.3
Koppal	**21.18**	51	22.16	24.08	6.16	72.8
Mandya	13.58	91	40.09	20.46	3.97	81.5
Mysore	14.90	137	44.15	17.36	3.49	90.2
Raichur	25.38	58	19.76	26.82	6.25	88.8
Shimoga	13.88	110	44.63	19.38	2.91	109.5
Tumkur	17.40	61	34.01	21.69	5.09	78.4
Udupi	13.10	89	38.75	14.55	3.64	93.8
Uttara Kannada	12.51	105	53.04	15.72	3.14	80
Karnataka	18.56	88	26.58	21.42	4.46	81.94

Source: GoK (2006).

Table 6.32 Population having none of the three facilities of safe drinking water, toilets and electricity (%) (2001)

District	Total	Rural	Urban
Bagalkot	29.03	33.42	18.24
Bangalore Rural	12.04	13.99	4.72
Bangalore Urban	3.07	9.18	2.28
Belgaum	21.52	25.66	8.5
Bellary	24.61	30.95	13.17
Bidar	24.73	28.96	8.6
Bijapur	33.36	38.84	13.61
Chamarajnagar	32.93	36.14	14.29
Chikmaglur	19.82	22.65	8.26
Chitradurga	20.28	22.67	9.65
Dakshina Kannada	21.67	32.18	5.51
Davangere	16.73	20.38	8.44
Dharwad	14.97	18.97	11.74
Gadag	19.97	20.84	18.32
Gulbarga	30.78	38.18	9.6
Hassan	14.94	17.06	5.1
Haveri	22.29	24.58	13.09
Kodagu	27.03	30.35	5.8
Kolar	12.32	14.88	4.49
Koppal	31.24	33.24	21.51
Mandya	19.2	20.77	10.87
Mysore	18.7	27.67	3.78
Raichur	34.06	39.32	18.68
Shimoga	18.63	24.79	7.42
Tumkur	18.32	21.15	6.61
Udupi	25.25	29.69	6.13
Uttara Kannada	18.34	22.53	8.14
Karnataka (state average)	19.13	25.66	6.88

Source: GoK (2006).

efficiency of the health system, in addition to the adequate utilization of basic health inputs of hospitals, PHCs, SCs and medical and paramedical staff. Our analysis thus suggests that improvement in LEXP in the less-efficient districts may be feasible expeditiously if these facilities are made available to reduce rural-urban disparities in the state.

Besides the factors within the health system, as we noted in the methodology section, influences external to the system may lead to differentials in efficiency at the district level. To explore such external factors, we used dispersion in efficiency as a dependent variable in the second stage of our regression exercise using panel data for the district level. Among the set of variables we used as explanatory variables we included per capita income (PCI), gross domestic product per worker, total literacy, male and female literacy separately, total enrolment, proportion of out-of-school children, population density and gender development index. The results of best fit are presented in Table 6.33.

Only three of the variables, namely gender development index (GDI), population density (POPDENS) and proportion of out-of-school children (OUTSCLPER),

Table 6.33 Panel data regression results for dispersion as dependent variable
R-sq: between = 0.3559; $F(3,23) = 4.24$**

DISPERSION	Coefficient	Standard error
GDI	–0.397*	0.120
POPDENS	1.980E-05**	1.040E–05
OUTSCLPER	–0.003**	0.001
Constant	1.312*	0.074

Source: Estimated.

*Denotes significance at 1% level; **denotes significance at 5% level.

Notes: Number of observations = 54; number of groups = 27.

have emerged as statistically significant. The negative sign of GDI as well as OUTSCLPER indicates that efforts to impart female literacy and increased level of retention in the schools have helped to reduce regional disparities in efficiency of the health system across districts (Table 6.33). However, this has not been able to compensate for deficiencies in public investment and health sector investment policies in the state which have not taken into account changing population densities in different regions and districts of the state (Table 6.34, column 3) and the impact of which is indicated by a positive sign of the variable in our second stage of results (Table 6.34).

In fact, for some of these districts increase in population density has constrained their achievements. Besides Bangalore Urban, for instance, examples of these districts also include Bellary, Koppal, Gulberga and Raichur (Table 6.34, column 3). Pertinently, the high level of rural poverty (ranging above 40%) in some of the districts, such as Gulberga, Kolar, Bellary, Chitradurga and Raichur, has also played a constraining role in overcoming district-level disparities in life expectancy. A number of these districts (Bellary, Chitradurga, Kolar and Koppal) with high rural poverty have shown a high increase in NDDP in 1991–2002. However, a further break-up of this income growth across sectors indicates that this growth in NDDP has been achieved due to higher growth in their secondary and tertiary sectoral incomes. Consequently, rural poverty and disparities in income have influenced their health outcomes and life expectancy, for which the direct health sector inputs have not been able to compensate. Besides these constraining factors, a positive aspect of the development in the state is observed through a positive impact of improvement in GDI. In fact, better-performing districts, such as Hassan, Koppal, Raichur and Gulberga in terms of achievements in their life expectancy, have depicted greater improvement in GDI in 1991–2001 (Table 6.34, column 1).

Overall, it is evident from the results that in addition to differentials in availability and efficient utilization of health system inputs, inequitable distribution of income across rural and urban sectors, changing population densities in respective districts as well as lack of a gender-specific focus of public-sector intervention in terms of education and other opportunities has led to disparities in health

Table 6.34 Changes in GDI, population density and growth rates of NDDP (Karnataka's districts)

District/Sectors	Improvement in GDI (1991–2001) (%)	Increase in population density (1991–2001) (%)	No. of rural families below poverty line (2001)	Growth rate of NDDP (1991–2002) (at constant prices)			
				Primary sector	Secondary sector	Tertiary sector	All Sectors
Bagalkot	18.22	18.96	23.5	6.8	4.3	7.6	6.4
Bangalore Rural	22.14	12.15	35.75	8.9	7.6	11.9	9.7
Bangalore Urban	23.48	34.80	15.67	2	6.2	11.3	9.1
Belgaum	20.95	17.60	23.7	4.2	4.5	7.2	5.4
Bellary	21.44	22.45	44.57	4	6.2	7.5	5.8
Bidar	19.92	19.48	39.6	2.5	5.5	6.9	4.9
Bijapur	17.90	17.01	42	1.6	5.9	6.7	4.3
Chamarajnagar	18.01	9.25	36	4.4	2.6	6.7	4.8
Chikmaglur	15.64	12.06	27	2.6	4.2	5.5	3.8
Chitradurga	20.23	14.74	41.5	3.9	4.7	6.8	5.1
Dakshina Kannada	10.70	14.60	15.4	4.2	-1	9.7	5.1
Davangere	17.17	14.83	20	4	3.1	6.8	4.8
Dharwad	17.89	12.91	39	3.9	5.2	5.9	5.3
Gadag	24.70	13.59	46.4	5.1	3.6	9.8	6.7
Gulbarga	25.69	21.38	33.7	2.6	6.6	7.4	5.3
Hassan	24.26	10.00	27.13	3.6	6.2	6.9	5.2
Haveri	24.17	13.31	32	5.3	5.4	8.2	6.4
Kodagu	11.83	11.76	19	1.3	5.1	4.9	2.8
Kolar	21.39	13.70	40.27	5.4	3	6.3	5.3
Koppal	31.07	24.81	42.5	3.2	10	9.7	7.1
Mandya	20.77	7.25	29.86	3.5	4.8	6.6	4.9
Mysore	21.98	15.02	28.14	5.4	5.9	8.3	6.9
Raichur	25.59	21.72	43.2	1.5	6.7	4.9	3.5
Shimoga	15.56	12.87	36	3.8	3.9	7.6	5.4
Tumkur	17.05	11.47	31.4	3.9	4.1	7.1	5.1
Udupi	9.32	6.72	24.67	4.2	0.4	7	5.1
Uttara Kannada	16.61	10.92	30.45	1.5	7.7	6.3	4.6

Source: GoK (2006).

outcomes (or life expectancy). This also suggests a need for appropriate links and coordination between economic and social sector policies, particularly at the district level, that could avoid suboptimal health outcomes for the poorer districts in the middle-income states in the country.

Conclusions

The results of the frontier model using district-level information in Karnataka indicate that the efficiency of the public health delivery system remains low. Considerable disparities across districts in terms of per capita availability of hospitals, beds and manpower inputs have an adverse impact on improving life expectancy in the state. Overcoming these factoral disparities within the health system may lead to an improvement in the district-level efficiency of the public health system. This may also help the state to improve life expectancy speedily and more equitably in deficient districts. However, this has to combine with adequate infrastructure facilities like a safe drinking water supply, toilets and electricity to improve the outcomes in the deficient districts of Bagalkot, Kolar, Kodagu and Uttar Kannada. This may also require a considerable increase in medical and public health expenditure in rural areas in the state. This could be attempted partly through funds from the National Rural Health Mission (NRHM) and also by improving rural sanitation in poorer districts. In addition, rural poverty and disparities in income, overall skewed distribution of income across rural and urban sectors, changing population densities in respective districts as well as lack of a gender-specific focus of public sector intervention in terms of education and other opportunities have influenced health outcomes and life expectancy, for which the direct health sector inputs have not been able to compensate. The results also suggest a need for strengthening links and coordination between economic and social sector policies, particularly at the district level, the absence of which has led to suboptimal health outcomes for the poorer districts in India's middle-income states.

Efficiency of the health care system at the substate level in Madhya Pradesh

In this section we focus on a substate-level (i.e. district-level) study of a poorer state in India known as Madhya Pradesh (MP). Despite being a poorer state, in the past decade MP has made rapid strides. Its per capita income has been growing consistently from 1993–94 to the present. In 1993–93, the per capita income in MP was Rs. 6,577. It grew to Rs. 7,088 in 1996–97 and Rs. 8,284 in 2003–04 (Government of Madhya Pradesh [GoMP] 2002, *The Economic Times* 2005). This growth has led to a decline in rural and urban poverty (GoI 2001a). The former, in the period from 1993–94 to 1999–2000, declined from 40.6 to 37.1 per cent. Urban poverty in this duration declined from 44.4 to 38.4 per cent. Simultaneously, human development indicators have shown better performance relative to other poorer states such as Uttar Pradesh and Bihar (GoI 2002c). Yet most of the major indicators in the state are below the national average and stand amongst the lowest in the country.

Despite the fact that the state government is the single largest provider in preventive care and public health, government's direct role as service provider is declining with greater dependence of the rural population on private health providers. According to NSSO data, in the mid-1990s nearly 70 per cent of those who were seeking outpatient care in rural and urban areas availed it from the private sector. Between the mid-1980s and 1990s, there was a nearly 30 per cent increase in inpatient care utilization from the private sector, and at present nearly 50 per cent of those requiring health care are receiving inpatient care in the private sector. Some studies attribute this to a nonoptimal mix of inputs, inadequate focus on the Indian system of medicine, nonavailability of drugs and indifferent behaviour and irregular availability of staff, all factors which have made overall delivery of services less effective and led to uneven benefits across social classes and genders (Gopalakrishnan and Agnani 2001). These factors indeed raise our concern regarding the issue of efficiency of the public health system in the state of MP, and we explore this question of health system performance further at the substate level.

Objective of the study and our hypothesis

The objective of our study is to establish efficiency parameters that could help the makers of health policy to improve district-level and thus state-level health system performance. In line with other state-level case studies, we hypothesize that districts differ in their technical efficiency pertaining to the health care system due to factors which require emphasis in planning health facilities at the district level. It is also hypothesized that these factors differ among states according to their level of development. As noted previously, we consider a poorer Indian state, Madhya Pradesh, which was below the all-India average of Rs. 11,779 in 2003–04 at constant (1993–94) prices. Geographically it is the second-largest state, with 9.4 per cent of the country's area. It also belongs to the category of BIMARU[1] states where health indicators are poor. These characteristics of the state we presume will also influence district-level efficiency relative to a better-off state in the country.

At the district level only cross sectional data are available, and a strict assumption about the distribution of the inefficiency term is required. Resulting estimates of technical efficiency will conform to the imposed distribution. It is preferable to use the standard distribution (i.e. half or truncated normal).

We presume that differences in technical efficiency pertaining to the health care system can be discerned at the district-level health facility planning stage by non-health-related parameters. Thus, we explain the dispersion in technical efficiency by a set of variables which represent income, poverty, literacy and related variables, gender development index (GDI), rural water supply, and human development indicator (HDI). Our model in the second stage is thus:

> Dispersion in technical efficiency = f (per capita income, number of families below poverty line (BPL), literacy, male and female literacy separately, number of primary and secondary educational institutions separately, dropout

rate, gender development index (GDI), rural habitat fully covered by water supply, percentage coverage through safe drinking water and human development indicator (HDI)) + error term. . . .   (D)

This study is based on secondary data. Information was collected from *The Madhya Pradesh Human Development Report 2002* (GoMP 2002), the Reproductive and Child Health survey of India (GoI 2006c), websites of the state and other published sources. The main variables used in the study are life expectancy (LEXP), per capita income (PCI) and parameters related to human development indicators (HDI), gender development indicator (GDI) and health facilities. The information relates to the district level for the state.

Results and discussion

The results of our frontier model are presented in Table 6.35. All the variables, namely population per primary health centers (POPPERPHC), primary health centers (PHC) with adequate staff (ADQSTAFF) and subcenters per lakh of population (SHCPERLAKH), have emerged significant with expected positive signs. The actual and estimated life expectancy at birth (LEXP) for the districts (substate-level units) of MP is presented in Table 6.36. It can be observed that Indore with its actual LEXP and estimated LEXP coinciding at 69.7 years has emerged as the most efficient district (MED), although actual and estimated LEXP with the given level of inputs also coincide for two other districts, Dewas (LEXP 63.3 years) and Mandsaur (LEXP 58.5 years). Despite this

Table 6.35 Stochastic frontier normal/half-normal model for Madhya Pradesh

Log likelihood = 70.548
Number of observations = 45
Wald chi^2(3) = 8.214e+09
Prob > chi^2 = 0.0000

LEXP	Coefficient	Std. err.
POPERPHC	0.174*	2.60E-06
SHCPERLAKH	0.325*	9.65E-06
ADQSTAFF	0.016*	2.53E-06
Constant	1.600*	5.24E-05
lnsig2v	−37.408	242.9984
lnsig2u	−4.587*	0.210819
sigma_v	7.53E-09	9.15E-07
sigma_u	0.101	0.011
sigma2	0.0102	0.002
Lambda	1.34E+07	0.011

Source: Estimated.

*Indicates 1% level of significance.

Notes: Likelihood–Ratio test of sigma_u = 0: chibar2 (01) = 10.19; prob>=chibar2 = 0.001.

Table 6.36 Actual and estimated life expectancy in Madhya Pradesh's districts

District	Actual life expectancy	Estimated life expectancy	Actual life expectancy (as % of potential)
Balaghat	58.50	61.82	94.63
Barwani	59.60	63.71	93.55
Betul	54.70	63.22	86.52
Bhind	59.90	60.75	98.61
Bhopal	64.90	76.13	85.24
Chhatarpur	50.40	59.82	84.26
Chhindwara	60.40	63.21	95.56
Damoh	54.00	62.00	87.10
Datia	55.20	61.11	90.33
Dewas	63.30	63.30	100.00
Dhar	63.40	64.65	98.07
Dindori	62.60	62.60	100.00
EastNimar	57.70	62.47	92.36
Guna	53.50	60.52	88.40
Gwalior	65.30	67.59	96.62
Harda	55.60	60.26	92.27
Hoshangabad	55.60	62.39	89.11
Indore	69.70	69.70	100.00
Jabalpur	57.50	70.51	81.55
Jhabua	55.80	63.71	87.58
Katni	57.50	61.05	94.18
Mandla	62.60	63.32	98.86
Mandsaur	58.50	58.50	100.00
Morena	57.40	60.51	94.87
Narsimhapur	56.90	60.41	94.20
Neemuch	58.50	62.77	93.20
Panna	53.00	59.02	89.79
Raisen	55.30	60.36	91.61
Rajgarh	54.20	58.94	91.96
Ratlam	58.10	63.14	92.02
Rewa	53.60	58.04	92.35
Sagar	54.00	61.93	87.19
Satna	49.60	59.97	82.71
Sehore	54.50	60.80	89.63
Seoni	59.90	64.23	93.26
Shahdol	57.10	67.40	84.71
Shajapur	58.30	58.50	99.66
Sheopur	57.40	61.31	93.62
Shivpuri	47.30	59.60	79.36
Sidhi	58.00	59.74	97.09
Tikamgarh	52.80	59.24	89.13
Ujjain	59.80	62.55	95.60
Umaria	57.10	61.14	93.39
Vidisha	54.70	59.43	92.04
West Nimar	59.60	62.33	95.63

Source: GoMP (2002) and our estimates.

matching of actual and estimated LEXP, these districts cannot be considered as MED due to their lower LEXP relative to Indore. The lowest-performing district is Shivpuri with low actual LEXP (47.3 years), which remains only 79.36 per cent of its potential LEXP (54.6 years) (Table 6.36). The ranks of these districts according to their deviation from the MED are presented in Table 6.37.

Two of the districts, Bhopal and Jabalpur, have a potential for increasing LEXP even higher than the MED. However, unlike in Indore, shortfall of actual realization of the potential LEXP for these districts does not indicate them as efficient. Therefore, the rank for these two districts (Bhopal and Jabalpur) using deviations from MED are not computed because it may not give an appropriate picture of their efficiency. Thus, except for these districts, the second-most efficient district is Gwalior (with deviation at 2.11 years from MED), and the least efficient district is Rewa, with deviation at 11.66 years from MED.

The reasons for this difference in district-level efficiency can partly be traced in Table 6.38, which presents input levels for each of the districts in MP. Pertinently, Table 6.38 shows that Gwalior has a higher load of rural population at PHC (43,103 patients) relative to Indore (28,270 patients), but it is lower compared to Rewa (55,062 patients). Further, the number of adequately staffed PHCs (76.7%) and PHCs with adequate supplies (76.7%) makes this district more efficient in performance relative to Rewa. The latter has merely one-twelfth of the input levels of Gwalior for both these parameters. In the case of Indore, lower rural population load per PHC makes up for the lower number of adequately staffed and adequately supplied PHCs. Notably, the skilled attention at birth is much higher in Indore (72%) relative to Gwalior (61.8%) and Rewa (20.8%). Also, in most of the inputs, the difference between the lowest and highest values is very high. The distance between these values is 10 times for population per PHC, more than 2 times for rural population served per SHC, nearly 9 times for skilled attention at birth, 15 times for number of adequately staffed PHC and 25 times for adequately supplied PHC (Table 6.38). Inequity as depicted by the Gini coefficient is notably high (.409) for the inputs of supplies (Table 6.38).

Thus the main factors within the health care system responsible for discrepancies in the performance of individual districts include inequitable distribution of supplies, availability of skilled attention at birth and inadequate staffing relative to patient load of rural population at PHCs. This is also corroborated by other studies which indicate that (i) there is a shortage of doctors in the state, which is 28 per cent and 19 per cent respectively for class I and class II doctors; (ii) attendance by staff in rural health centers is poor (Bajpai, Dholkia and Sach 2005) and (iii) some of the districts – Bhopal, Gwalior, Datia, Morena, Damoh and Tikamgarh – have no vacancies, particularly for main doctors and health officers. By contrast, eight districts – Katni, Ratlam, Barwani, Jhabua, Shajapur, Shadol, Dindori and Sidhi – have over 30 per cent vacancies (GoMP 2002).

Table 6.37 Deviation from maximum efficient district in Madhya Pradesh

District	Deviation from maximum efficient district (MED)	Rank
Balaghat	–7.88	21
Barwani	–5.99	7
Betul	–6.48	10
Bhind	–8.95	27
Bhopal	6.43	n.c.
Chhatarpur	–9.88	34
Chhindwara	–6.49	11
Damoh	–7.70	19
Datia	–8.59	24
Dewas	–6.40	9
Dhar	–5.05	4
Dindori	–7.10	14
EastNimar	–7.23	16
Guna	–9.18	28
Gwalior	–2.11	2
Harda	–9.44	32
Hoshangabad	–7.31	17
Indore	0.00	1
Jabalpur	0.81	n.c.
Jhabua	–5.99	6
Katni	–8.65	25
Mandla	–6.38	8
Mandsaur	–11.20	41
Morena	–9.19	29
Narsimhapur	–9.29	30
Neemuch	–6.93	13
Panna	–10.68	39
Raisen	–9.34	31
Rajgarh	–10.76	40
Ratlam	–6.56	12
Rewa	–11.66	43
Sagar	–7.77	20
Satna	–9.73	33
Sehore	–8.90	26
Seoni	–5.47	5
Shahdol	–2.30	3
Shajapur	–11.20	42
Sheopur	–8.39	22
Shivpuri	–10.10	36
Sidhi	–9.96	35
Tikamgarh	–10.46	38
Ujjain	–7.15	15
Umaria	–8.56	23
Vidisha	–10.27	37
West Nimar	–7.37	18

Source: Estimated.

n.c. = not computed.

Table 6.38 Health facilities, rural distribution and the adequacy of inputs in Madhya Pradesh

District	Population per health centre	Rural population per PHC	Rural population served per SHC	Deliveries attended by skilled staff (%)	Percentage of PHCs with adequate		
					Staff	Infrastructure	Supply
Balaghat	4,394	35,767	4,377	29.4	21.115	6.110	3.004
Barwani	3,889	29,776	3,846	34.5	37.713	13.736	13.736
Betul	4,469	33,398	4,190	34.2	29.371	5.871	26.576
Bhind	6,795	57,305	5,950	18.9	31.500	15.800	5.312
Bhopal	23,549	35,767	5,677	69.7	22.198	n.a.	11.134
Chhatarpur	6,275	28,057	6,087	24.4	45.150	5.003	17.462
Chhindwara	4,645	20,845	4,406	43.3	52.457	2.509	47.465
Damoh	6,044	58,506	5,417	29.1	59.740	33.448	6.686
Datia	6,155	44,570	5,635	32.9	44.256	n.a.	22.198
Dewas	5,886	37,970	4,944	99.9	45.604	18.174	59.145
Dhar	3,776	29,047	3,631	35.7	40.045	13.330	66.686
Dindori	2,694	23,019	3,019	17.6	5.003	n.a.	9.974
EastNimar	5,240	27,127	4,605	42.8	16.777	9.974	6.686
Guna	6,716	54,615	6,068	36.3	42.098	5.312	15.800
Gwalior	13,251	43,103	6,401	61.8	76.708	7.691	76.708
Harda	6,679	53,298	6,116	42.6	40.045	n.a.	59.740
Hoshangabad	6,497	46,828	5,240	42.6	20.697	16.777	29.079
Indore	17,830	28,270	6,622	72	41.679	16.777	37.338
Jabalpur	9,988	57,560	4,772	44.4	59.740	13.330	13.330
Jhabua	3,581	39,864	3,687	22.4	39.252	21.328	46.525
Katni	5,688	44,144	5,177	44.4	17.637	n.a.	11.822
Mandla	3,561	28,639	3,730	17.6	35.874	3.597	10.697
Mandsaur	5,858	20,929	6,292	46.4	46.525	13.330	56.826
Morena	7,182	65,477	6,347	33	49.899	n.a.	37.338
Narsimhapur	5,632	42,331	5,585	27.8	46.993	11.822	n.a.

Neemuch	5,712	29,067	4,983	46.4	43.816	18.728	56.261
Panna	5,339	49,739	5,329	13.5	7.691	n.a.	15.333
Raisen	5,491	39,710	5,219	29.4	15.029	20.086	49.899
Rajgarh	6,143	33,422	6,242	34.2	37.713	13.736	30.877
Ratlam	6,103	32,582	5,103	60.4	49.899	13.599	31.817
Rewa	6,425	55,062	6,164	20.8	6.890	3.387	6.890
Sagar	7,094	49,325	5,838	43	44.701	3.387	27.660
Satna	6,009	32,957	5,748	16.9	26.576	6.686	20.086
Sehore	6,129	52,020	5,818	38.5	64.715	17.637	76.708
Seoni	3,621	36,041	3,680	42.6	55.147	3.387	41.264
Shahdol	3,339	24,992	2,844	51.7	14.585	n.a.	20.697
Shajapur	6,294	50,042	6,075	39.7	10.486	10.486	n.a.
Sheopur	5,597	58,892	5,294	33	42.948	14.296	56.826
Shivpuri	6,578	92,384	6,035	47.3	18.174	9.116	27.385
Sidhi	5,186	37,361	5,196	10.4	13.330	3.287	3.287
Tikamgarh	6,684	55,044	6,351	29.5	29.371	n.a	41.264
Ujjain	8,592	49,884	6,162	68.2	31.187	18.728	37.338
Umaria	5,159	39,358	4,976	51.7	25.028	n.a.	12.554
Vidisha	7,104	47,724	6,628	27.8	44.256	16.777	55.701
West Nimar	4,262	24,388	4,352	34.5	43.380	9.974	16.777
Gini Coefficient	0.223	0.182	0.105	0.235	0.264	0.396	0.409
Minimum Value	2,694	20,845	2,844	10.4	5.003	2.51	3.004
Maximum Value	23,549	92,384	6,628	99.9	76.708	33.448	76.708

Sources: GoMP (2002) and GoI (2006a).

Further, as presented in Table 6.39, considerable vacancies exist in the entire state relative to various categories of doctors. The proportion varies between 100 per cent (for civil surgeons) and 56 per cent (for Chief Medical and health officer [CMO&H]) and 28.2 per cent (for specialists). This scarcity in rural areas is glaring even relative to the all-India average. In contrast to all-India figures for shortfalls/in position, it is considerably higher for the state as a whole (Table 6.40).

In addition to the factors within the health system, influences external to the system may lead to differentials in efficiency at the district level. To explore such external factors, we used dispersion in efficiency as a dependent variable in the second stage of our regression exercise. Among the set of variables

Table 6.39 State of doctors in government medical centres, 2001

Post	Sanctioned	Filled	Vacant	Vacancy %
Class I (July 2001)				
Specialist	739	530	209	28.2
Class II (June 2001)				
Chief Medical and Health Officer (CMO&H)	45	20	25	56
Civil Surgeon	45	Nil	45	100

Source: GoMP (2002).

Table 6.40 Health manpower in rural areas in Madhya Pradesh

Type of health personnel	Required number	Shortfall since not sanctioned (nos.)	Shortfall as % of sanctioned strength	% vacant even with the sanctioned strength
Total specialists (surgeon, OB&GY, physicians, pediatricians)				
MP	1,368	968	70.76	42.8
India	11,652	7,332	62.92	43.1
Doctors at primary health centres				
MP	1,760	291	16.53	13.1
India	23,179	2,186	9.43	14.4
Pharmacists				
MP	2,032	0	0.00	25.3
India	26,092	6,790	26.02	10.8
Laboratory technicians				
MP	2,032	685	33.71	14.4
India	26,092	13,133	50.33	19
Nurse Midwife				
MP	4,084	3,118	76.35	0
India	43,573	20,419	46.86	22.1

Source: GoMP (2004).

Table 6.41 Regression results for deviations for Madhya Pradesh
Adjusted R square = 0.227; df2 = 41; F = 5.298*

Dependent variable: DEVIATIONS	Unstandardised coefficients		Standardised coefficients		
	B	Std. error	Beta	t	Sig.
Constant	12.701	4.814		2.638**	0.012
GDI	29.140	12.740	0.444	2.287**	0.027
SAFWATER	−0.040	0.022	−0.253	−1.821+	0.076
HDI	−32.344	10.222	−0.621	−3.164*	0.003

Source: Estimated.

*Denotes significance at 1% level; **denotes significance at 5% level; +denotes significance at 10% level.

we used as explanatory variables were per capita income, number of families below poverty line (BPL), total literacy, male and female literacy separately, number of primary and secondary educational institutions separately, dropout rate, gender development index (GDI), rural habitat fully covered by water supply, percentage coverage through safe drinking water and human development indicators (HDI). The results of best fit are presented in Table 6.41. Three variables – GDI, safe water supply coverage and HDI – have emerged as statistically significant (Table 6.41). Among these, other variables except GDI have a negative sign which depicts that efforts to improve HDI and proper water facilities have helped the state reduce disparities in efficiency at the district level.

However, the negative sign of GDI suggests that the level of gender development among districts has not helped to reduce district-level disparities in health care system performance. This phenomenon of diverse impact of GDI and HDI can be explained if we look at Table 6.42. Despite high HDI and GDI, movements of GDI and HDI are not commensurate with the MED. For instance, Indore, the MED, is ranked first in HDI but in GDI it is 13th. Dewas district, which has a lower efficiency ranking, has the first rank in GDI. In fact, as per some reports, despite various measures such as reservations for women in Panchayats, advocacy for women's rights and promotion of institutional deliveries, women lag behind men in health, education and liberty to rights.[2] This explains the negative sign of GDI, indicating that gender development in the state has been moving away from supporting the trend in HDI. This may be due to factors other than LEXP that influence GDI. Thus to overcome the adverse impact of GDI on LEXP and increase the efficiency of the health system, more efforts to overcome disparities at the district level may prove useful.

Conclusions

The results of our frontier model using district-level information in MP indicate that despite decentralization and health sector reforms in the state, the efficiency

Table 6.42 Comparative profile of HDI and GDI for the districts of Madhya Pradesh

District	HDI	Rank	Gender-related development index (GDI)	Rank
Balaghat	0.58	15	0.598	7
Barwani	0.422	44	0.488	37
Betul	0.537	30	0.558	20
Bhind	0.566	19	0.512	32
Bhopal	0.663	2	0.547	24
Chhatarpur	0.449	43	0.447	44
Chhindwara	0.586	13	0.575	15
Damoh	0.568	18	0.586	11
Datia	0.543	28	0.549	22
Dewas	0.61	10	0.634	1
Dhar	0.559	23	0.533	28
Dindori	0.557	24	0.617	5
EastNimar	0.563	21	0.517	31
Guna	0.493	36	0.476	40
Gwalior	0.624	8	0.527	30
Harda	0.588	12	0.579	14
Hoshangabad	0.584	14	0.53	29
Indore	0.694	1	0.581	13
Jabalpur	0.572	17	0.508	34
Jhabua	0.372	45	0.45	43
Katni	0.542	29	0.558	20
Mandla	0.578	16	0.563	18
Mandsaur	0.632	4	0.622	4
Morena	0.52	32	0.436	45
Narsimhapur	0.61	10	0.588	10
Neemuch	0.626	7	0.591	8
Panna	0.47	41	0.462	42
Raisen	0.645	3	0.584	12
Rajgarh	0.504	34	0.548	23
Ratlam	0.63	6	0.633	2
Rewa	0.478	39	0.5	36
Sagar	0.565	20	0.545	25
Satna	0.483	38	0.476	40
Sehore	0.56	22	0.59	9
Seoni	0.55	26	0.563	18
Shahdol	0.525	31	0.535	27
Shajapur	0.617	9	0.627	3
Sheopur	0.514	33	0.569	17
Shivpuri	0.473	40	0.512	32
Sidhi	0.555	25	0.57	16
Tikamgarh	0.468	42	0.486	38
Ujjain	0.632	4	0.615	6
Umaria	0.492	37	0.508	34
Vidisha	0.549	27	0.482	39
West Nimar	0.498	35	0.543	26
Gini coefficient		0.067	0.054	
Minimum value		0.372	0.436	
Maximum value		0.694	0.634	

Source: GoMP (2002) and our estimates.

of the public health delivery system remains low. Considerable deficiency of public health manpower inputs and prevailing disparities across districts has an adverse impact on improving life expectancy in the state. The main factors within the health system for discrepancies in interdistrict performance are inequitable distribution of supplies, availability of skilled attention at birth and inadequate staffing relative to patient load of the rural population at primary health centers. Overcoming these factors may lead to an improvement in the district-level efficiency of the public health system. This may also help the state improve life expectancy speedily and more equitably. This may require a considerable increase in medical and public health expenditure from the current level of Rs. 164 per capita (in 2004–05), which is much lower than the all-India average of Rs. 304 per capita (GoI 2005a). This calls for resource mobilization for and within the sector. This may be coming forth in part with the recommendations of the Twelfth Finance Commission from a grant in aid of Rs. 1.8 billion over the period 2006–10. The remaining gap may require innovative steps and more effective use of funds from patient welfare committees. In addition to the direct inputs from the health sector, a more conducive environment for gender development, including improvements in equal opportunities for women in health, education and other rights, may provide the necessary impetus towards reducing maternal morbidity and mortality and add to overall life expectancy in the state.

Efficiency of the health care system: a substate-level analysis for West Bengal

In this section we focus on a substate-level (i.e. district-level) analysis of the health care system performance of West Bengal. According to the 2001 census, with a population of about 82 million, West Bengal is the fourth-most populous state in India. Situated in the eastern region of the country, it accounts for about 2.7 per cent of India's area (88,752 square km) and with about 7.8 per cent of the country's population, this state ranks first in terms of density, with 904 per square kilometer. About 72 per cent of the people in the state live in rural areas, and nearly 31.85 per cent of its population is below the poverty line (Government of West Bengal [GoWB] 2004).

A comparison of key social development indicators for West Bengal is presented in Table 6.43. It is a low-income state with its per capita income of Rs. 11,612,which is lower than the all-India average (Table 6.43). Despite being a low-income state, its life expectancy and literacy rates are slightly above the country's average (Table 6.43).

Compared to the all-India life expectancy of 61.8 years for males and 63.5 years for females (1999–2003), the respective figures for West Bengal are 63.5 years and 65 years. However, considerable disparity exists between rural and urban areas in health care infrastructure. There is a concentration of hospitals, beds and dispensaries in urban areas, resulting in higher per capita availability in these areas relative to their rural counterparts (Table 6.44). This skewed distribution is

Table 6.43 West Bengal in a comparative framework

State	Per capita income in 2003–04 (Rs. at 1993–94 prices)	Life expectancy at birth (1999–2003)			Literacy rate (%) (2001)
		Male	Female	Total	
West Bengal	11,612	63.5	65	62.7	68.64
Maharashtra	16,479	65.2	67.6	66.4	76.88
Karnataka	13,141	62.9	66.4	64.6	66.64
Punjab	15,800	67.6	69.6	68.6	69.65
Gujarat	16,779	62.5	64.6	63.5	69.14
Madhya Pradesh	8,284	57.2	56.9	57.1	63.74
Tamil Nadu	12,976	64.3	66.5	65.4	73.4
All India	11,799	61.8	63.5	62.7	64.84

Sources: GoI (2007a); *The Economic Times* (2005, p. 9); GoWB (2004).

also reflected at the substate level across districts and regions in West Bengal. In general, districts like Kolkata and Haora have a better availability of per capita health care facilities. Rural infrastructure like primary health centers (PHCs) and subcenters (SCs) are not adequately supported by necessary inputs. Due to the inadequacy of public investment and health care expenditure, West Bengal's position in comparison to the all-India average and some major Indian states remains at a lower level (Table 6.44).

Our hypothesis

In line with our other case studies, here also we hypothesize that districts differ in their technical efficiency pertaining to the health care system due to factors which require emphasis in planning health facilities at the district level. It is also hypothesized that these factors differ among states according to their level of development. It is presumed that estimated efficiency parameters should help the makers of health policy to improve district-level and thus state-level health care system performance. Since we focus on a low-income Indian state, West Bengal, which has a per capita income slightly below the all-India average, it is presumed that these factors in the particular state in general differ from any other state which may have a per capita income above the country's average (Table 6.43).

Keeping in view a general applicability of stochastic frontier estimation in establishing a norm for health system efficiency, we base our specification on a general stochastic frontier model that has been discussed earlier.

We extend our estimation to the second stage, which presumes that differences in technical efficiency pertaining to the health care system can be discerned at the district-level health facility planning stage by non-health-related parameters. Thus, we explain the dispersion in technical efficiency by a set of variables which includes per capita income (PCI); male and female literacy separately; total enrolment; teacher-pupil ratios in primary, middle and secondary educational

Table 6.44 Number of hospitals, beds and dispensaries per lakh population across states and by rural and urban areas

States	Hospitals			Beds			Dispensaries		
	Rural	Urban	Total	Rural	Urban	Total	Rural	Urban	Total
Andhra Pradesh	1.7	10.6	4.2	19.8	189.8	65.5	0.4	0.4	0.4
Gujarat	0.6	15.1	5.6	24.3	422.5	161.7	8.2	31.2	16.1
Haryana	0.1	1.5	0.4	4	152.8	40.6	0.3	4.1	1.2
Karnataka	0.1	1.7	0.6	10.4	233.5	79.4	1.8	1.6	1.7
Kerala	6.5	7.5	6.7	198	414.2	255.1	6.4	6.4	6.4
Maharashtra	0.9	8.3	3.8	20.7	219.7	97.7	0.7	24.4	9.9
Punjab	1.8	2.2	1.9	62.9	156.2	90.4	7.7	3.6	6.5
Tamil Nadu	0.2	1.7	0.7	11.8	232.9	87.5	0.4	1.9	0.9
West Bengal	**0.2**	**1.4**	**0.5**	**11.7**	**237**	**73.7**	**0.8**	**0.7**	**0.7**
All India	0.7	4.3	1.6	19.4	212.7	69.1	1.7	6.7	3

Source: GoM (2002).

institutions separately; population growth; population density; urban population; percentage of male and female labour force; rural habitat fully covered by water supply and percentage coverage through safe drinking water and sanitation facilities. Our model in the second stage is thus:

> Dispersion in technical efficiency = f (PCI, male and female income respectively, literacy, rural and urban literacy separately, teacher-pupil ratio in primary and secondary level institutions, urbanization and other infrastructure variables such as water supply and sanitation facilities) + error term. . . . (E)

To estimate these models, we have used secondary data. Information was collected from the human development reports of West Bengal (GoWB 2004) and Maharashtra (GoM 2002), websites of the states, *Economic Survey 2007* (GoI 2007a), *Reproductive and Child Health Survey, 2006* (GoI 2006c) and other published sources. The main variables used in the study are life expectancy (LEXP), infant mortality rates (IMR), per capita income (PCI) and other parameters related to human development, gender development and health care facilities. The information relates to the district level for the state.

Results and discussion

Results of our frontier model for West Bengal are presented in Table 6.45. All the independent variables to explain life expectancy (LEXP) have emerged with appropriate signs and are statistically significant. Notably, the variables representing hospitals per ten thousand population (HOSPITENTH) and full immunization (FULL) have emerged with positive signs. This indicates the positive impact of governmental intervention in the expansion of hospital facilities and

Table 6.45 Stochastic frontier model for West Bengal

Number of observations = 18; Wald chi^2(4) = 1.491e + 09
Log likelihood = 27.289313; prob > chi^2 = 0.0000

LEXP	Coefficient	Std. err.
HOSPITENTH	0.0533*	1.59E–06
FULL	0.1005*	6.46E–06
ADQINFRA	–0.0008*	5.18E–06
ADQSUPPLY	–0.0021**	5.44E–06
Constant	3.8974*	4.16E–05
lnsig2v	–37.4982	407.4233
lnsig2u	–4.48373*	0.3333
sigma_v	7.20E–09	1.47E–06
sigma_u	0.1062	0.0177
sigma2	0.0113	0.0037
Lambda	1.48E+07	0.0177

Source: Estimated.

*Significance at 1% level.

the desirable impact of full immunization coverage in enhancing life expectancy. The fact that both the variables representing, respectively, percentage of PHCs with adequate infrastructure (ADQINFRA) and adequate supply (ADQSUPPLY) have emerged with negative signs indicates inadequacy of the various inputs provided through PHCs. This could be clearly observed from a cursory glance at the figures for these two variables (Table 6.46). In most of the districts, the percentage of PHCs with adequate infrastructure is very low, ranging from 5 per cent to 52 per cent. Likewise, the corresponding percentage for district PHCs with adequate supplies of medicines and materials is abysmally low, from 3.8 per cent to 36.7 per cent. Also, the districts with higher LEXP are those with a higher percentage of PHCs having adequate infrastructure facilities and supplies.

Using the results of our frontier model, actual and estimated LEXP are presented in Table 6.47. These depict that Kolkata (the state capital) is the most efficient district (MED), with its highest actual LEXP (74.5 years) coinciding with estimated LEXP. Four other districts, Uttar Dinajapur, North 24 Paraganas, Haora and South 24 Parganas, depict their actual LEXP (respectively at 62 years, 68.4 years, 71.4 years and 67.4 years) coinciding with their potential LEXP. However, owing to their overall lower level of LEXP relative to Kolkata, these

Table 6.46 Life expectancy (LEXP), adequacy of Infrastructure (ADQINFRA) and adequacy of water supply in West Bengal's districts with their ranks

	LEXP	Rank	ADQINFRA	Rank	ADQSUPPLY	Rank
Darjiling	68.9	5	51.7	1	24.1	5
Jalpaiguri	62	12	16.7	5	36.7	1
Koch Bihar	54.9	17	17.9	4	25.6	3
Uttar Dinajpur	62	12	20	3	25	4
Dakshin Dinajpur	63.4	11	5.3	17	21.1	10
Maldah	54.5	18	10	15	23.3	7
Murshidabad	59	15	15	6	17.5	13
Birbhum	57	16	13.9	8	16.7	14
Barddhaman	69.4	4	15	6	21.8	9
Nadia	64	10	12	10	24	6
North TFP	68.4	6	13.3	9	20	11
Hugli	70.9	3	11.4	12	12.9	17
Bankura	64.9	9	24.7	2	14.1	16
Puruliya	61.5	14	7.1	16	14.3	15
Medinipur	66	8	10.5	14	27.3	2
Haora	71.4	2	11.3	13	3.8	18
Kolkata	74.5	1	12	10	23	8
South TFP	67.4	7	5	18	20	11
Maximum value	74.5		51.7		36.7	
Minimium value	54.5		5		3.8	

Source: Estimated; GoI (2006c).

Table 6.47 Actual and potential life expectancy in West Bengal's districts

District	Actual life expectancy	Potential life expectancy	Actual Life expectancy (as % of potential)
Darjiling	68.90	72.08	95.59
Jalpaiguri	62.00	69.95	88.64
Koch Bihar	54.90	69.70	78.76
Uttar Dinajpur	62.00	62.00	100.00
Dakshin Dinajpur	63.40	68.83	92.12
Maldah	54.50	67.07	81.25
Murshidabad	59.00	63.68	92.65
Birbhum	57.00	66.93	85.17
Barddhaman	69.40	71.49	97.07
Nadia	64.00	72.78	87.94
North 24 Parganas	68.40	68.40	100.00
Hugli	70.90	73.25	96.79
Bankura	64.90	69.72	93.09
Puruliya	61.50	71.54	85.97
Medinipur	66.00	68.84	95.88
Haora	71.40	71.40	100.00
Kolkata	74.50	74.50	100.00
South 24 Parganas	67.40	67.40	100.00

Sources: GoWB (2004) and our estimates.

districts cannot be considered as MED. Thus in terms of actual LEXP being lower than potential LEXP, except for districts with zero deviations, Barddhaman is the second-most efficient district and Koch Bihar is the least efficient district with actual at nearly 78.76 per cent of its potential (Table 6.47).

Performance of these districts in terms of their deviation from MED is presented in Table 6.48. Pertinently, ranks computed based on these deviations depict that next to Kolkata, the second- and third-most efficient districts are Haora and Hooghli. The lowest rank denoting the lowest performance is depicted for Maldah (Table 6.48).

Some of the reasons for these interdistrict disparities can be deciphered from Table 6.49, which depicts major inputs for the health sector in the state. Notably, the distribution of per capita hospitals, PHCs, beds and ANMs in the state is highly inequitable. In fact, there is a considerable difference between maximum and minimum values for each of the parameters (columns 2–4, Table 6.49). Pertinently, most of the facilities and inputs are concentrated in Kolkata, making it the most efficient district in the state (Table 6.49). Thus, in most of the districts adequate availability of health care sector inputs is the constraining factor rather than merely efficient utilization of these inputs. Among other inputs, except for improved water facilities, a similar pattern of disparities prevails with regard to availability of rural family welfare centers, sanitation facilities and immunization coverage. Impact of this inequitable distribution of health care sector inputs is pertinently reflected in the population density and urban poverty ratios, the former being the highest for the state capital, Kolkata, which also is the MED (Table 6.50, columns 2–4).

Table 6.48 Deviations from the maximum efficient district in West Bengal

	Deviations from the maximum efficient district	Rank
Darjiling	5.60	5.00
Jalpaiguri	12.50	12.00
Koch Bihar	19.60	17.00
Uttar Dinajpur	12.50	12.00
Dakshin Dinajpur	11.10	11.00
Maldah	20.00	18.00
Murshidabad	15.50	15.00
Birbhum	17.50	16.00
Barddhaman	5.10	4.00
Nadia	10.50	10.00
North 24 Parganas	6.10	6.00
Hugli	3.60	3.00
Bankura	9.60	9.00
Puruliya	13.00	14.00
Medinipur	8.50	8.00
Haora	3.10	2.00
Kolkata	0.00	1.00
South 24 Parganas	7.10	7.00

Source: Our estimates.

This inequitable pattern of regional development in the state is associated with the urban population's getting a larger chunk of available resources, and it is evident from the ratio of urban to rural consumption which exceeds 1 in all the districts (Table 6.50, column 5). Consequently, the rural poverty ratios are high in poorly performing districts (Table 6.50, column 6). Our analysis thus suggests that improvement in the LEXP in the less efficient districts may be feasible expeditiously if health sector resources are reallocated to reduce rural-urban disparities in the state.

In addition to the factors within the health system, influences external to the system may lead to differentials in efficiency at the district level. To explore such external factors, we used dispersion in efficiency as a dependent variable in the second stage of our regression exercise. Among the set of variables we used as explanatory variables we included per capita income; total literacy; male and female literacy separately; total enrolment; teacher-pupil ratios in primary, middle and secondary educational institutions separately; population growth; population density; urban population; percentage of male and female labour force; rural habitat fully covered by water supply and percentage coverage through safe drinking water and sanitation facilities. The results of best fit are presented in Tables 6.51–6.54.

Only two of the variables, female literacy (LITFEM) and total literacy, have emerged as statistically significant. However, the former had a higher value of adjusted R square, and the results are depicted in Table 6.51. The negative sign of LITFEM indicates that efforts to impart female literacy have helped to reduce

Table 6.49 Health facilities, sanitation and immunization status in West Bengal

District	Number of hospitals per ten thousand population	Number of PHCs per ten thousand population	Number of hospital beds per lakh population	ANM per lakh	Number of rural family welfare centres	Population using adequate sanitation facilities (%)	Population using improved water resources (%)	Children aged 1 year received complete immunisation (%)
Darjiling	0.74	1.93	151	250.94	73	28.4	75.6	60.8
Jalpaiguri	0.29	1.34	39	112.01	527	17.7	98.1	62
Koch Bihar	0.44	15.99	60	71.02	25	8.6	98.6	49.8
Uttar Dinajpur	0.17	1.12	30	n.a.	293	9.3	99.5	28.5
Dakshin Dinajpur	0.27	1.68	54	n.a.	237	11	99.6	40.5
Maldah	0.27	1.36	35	69.28	16	10.6	99.4	38.9
Murshidabad	0.27	1.54	48	94.05	30	13.5	99.4	39.4
Birbhum	0.3	2.57	75	85.07	428	13.9	99.3	34.9
Barddhaman	0.56	1.94	100	113.33	768	32.4	99.3	51.8
Nadia	0.56	1.28	113	130.37	28	25.4	99.2	68.9
North Twenty Four Pargana	0.23	0.82	29	132.19	779	39.4	99	65.6
Hugli	0.59	1.38	73	122.54	45	32.7	99.3	67.8
Bankura	0.28	2.73	87	113.58	514	10	98.2	67.3
Puruliya	0.47	2.83	89	106.95	471	8.1	93.8	38
Medinipur	0.35	1.8	48	121.87	70	9.1	99	46
Haora	0.54	1.33	80	98.32	97	29.4	99.1	56
Kolkata	1.75	NA	434	244.67	92	75.2	99.5	82.9
South Twenty Four Parganas	0.22	1.22	22	73.3	34	11.3	99.2	59.4
Minimum value	0.17	0.82	22	69.28	16	8.1	75.6	28.5
Maximum value	1.75	15.99	434	250.94	779	75.2	99.6	82.9
Gini coefficient	-0.318	-0.423	-0.408	-0.205	-0.542	-0.368	-0.018	-0.152

Sources: GoWB (2004); Sharma (n.d.).

Table 6.50 Population density and rural-urban characteristics in West Bengal

Districts	Population density (per sq. km)	Urban population / urbanization (%)	Urban poverty ratio (%)	Ratio of urban to rural consumption	Rural poverty ratio (%)
Darjiling	510	32.44	15.21	1.6	19.66
Jalpaiguri	547	17.74	61.53	1.12	35.73
Koch Bihar	732	9.1	15.44	1.71	25.62
Uttar Dinajpur	778	12.06	19.29*	1.74*	27.61*
Dakshin Dinajpur	677	13.09			
Maldah	881	7.32	6.6	1.53	35.4
Murshidabad	1,101	12.49	49.56	1.35	46.12
Birbhum	663	8.58	21.83	1.75	49.37
Barddhaman	985	37.18	17	1.41	18.99
Nadia	1,172	21.27	15.51	1.69	28.35
North Twenty Four Pargana	2,181	54.3	9.99	1.52	14.41
Hugli	1,601	33.48	11.43	1.48	20.43
Bankura	464	7.37	52.38	1.42	59.62
Puruliya	405	10.07	6.47	2.15	78.72
Medinipur	685	10.49	19.25	1.76	19.83
Haora	2,913	50.39	1.33	1.42	7.63
Kolkata	24,760	100	11.17		
South 24 Parganas	694	15.77	8.5	1.83	26.86

Sources: GoWB (2004) and Sharma (n.d.).

*For combined Uttar and Dakshin Dinajapur.

Table 6.51 Dependent variable: DISPERSION

Adjusted R square = 0.203
F=5.326**
df2=16.00

Explanatory variable	Unstandardised coefficients (B)	Standardised coefficients (beta)
Constant	1.288*	
LITFEM	–0.004	–0.500**

Source: Estimated.

*Denotes significance at 1% level; **denotes significance at 5% level.

regional disparities in efficiency of the health care system across districts. However, these have not been able to compensate for public investment policies in the health sector in the state which are skewed towards urban areas.

Conclusions

The results of our frontier model using district-level information in West Bengal indicate that the efficiency of the public health care delivery system remains low. Considerable disparities across districts in terms of per capita availability of

Table 6.52 Stochastic frontier panel data model for India (life expectancy male) (2005–11) (time-invariant inefficiency model)

Time-invariant inefficiency model: Number of obs = 105; obs per group: min = 7
Wald chi²(3) = 29.19; log likelihood = 275.66912; prob > chi² = 0.0000

Lexpmale	Coef.	z
Totalspecialists	0.004	1.83**
Anm	0.014	2.12*
Totalnobloodbank	0.043	3.25©
Constant	3.929	52.360©
Mu	0.081	3.520©
Lnsigma2	−5.802	−10.910©
Ilgtgamma	2.879	4.890©
Sigma2	0.003	
Gamma	0.947	
Sigma_U2	0.003	
Sigma_V2	0.000	

*5% level of significance; **10% level of significance; ©1% level of significance.

Table 6.53 Stochastic frontier panel data model for India (life expectancy female) (2005–11) (time-invariant inefficiency model)

Time-invariant inefficiency model: Number of groups = 15; number of obs = 105; obs per group: min = 7; Wald chi²(3) = 30.54; log likelihood = 272.69235; prob > chi² = 0.0000

Lexpfemale	Coef.	z
Totalspecialists	0.004	1.8*
Anm	0.017	2.57**
Totalnobloodbank	0.048	3.21**
Constant	3.942	46.21**
Mu	0.112	4.59**
Lnsigma2	−5.546	−11.810**
Ilgtgamma	3.144	6.09**
Sigma2	0.004	
Gamma	0.959	
Sigma_u2	0.004	
Sigma_v2	0.000	

*10% level of significance; **1% level of significance.

Note: We also tried the alternative model using random effects. However, the results of Hausman test indicated fixed effect model.

hospitals, beds and manpower inputs have an adverse impact on improving the life expectancy in the state. Overcoming these factoral disparities may lead to an improvement in the district-level efficiency of the public health care system. This may also help the state improve life expectancy speedily and more equitably in deficient districts like Maldah, Puriliya and Koch Bihar. This may require a

Table 6.54 Actual and estimated life expectancies (males) in selected Indian states

State	Actual life expectancy	Potential life expectancy	Actual as % of potential	Ranks of states according to realization of potential life expectancy (males)
Andhra Pradesh	65.40	76.17	85.86	14
Assam	61.60	70.12	87.85	11
Bihar	67.10	70.24	95.52	4
Gujarat	67.20	72.33	92.90	6
Haryana	67.90	69.61	97.54	2
Karnataka	66.50	73.57	90.39	8
Kerala	72.00	73.10	98.49	1
Madhya Pradesh	62.50	72.91	85.72	15
Maharashtra	67.90	75.99	89.35	10
Odisha	62.30	70.99	87.76	12
Punjab	68.70	70.83	96.99	3
Rajasthan	66.10	72.06	91.73	7
Tamilnadu	67.60	75.17	89.92	9
Uttar Pradesh	64.00	74.48	85.93	13
West Bengal	68.20	72.34	94.28	5

Source: Estimated.

considerable increase in medical and public health expenditure in rural areas in the state. It especially calls for resource mobilization for improving infrastructure facilities and maintenance of essential supplies at PHCs. This could be attempted partly through funds from the NRHM and also by improving rural sanitation in poorer districts.

Efficiency of the health care system in India (2005–11)

Results of our panel data estimation using the frontier model for India (males and females) are presented in Tables 6.52 and 6.53. All the independent variables to explain life expectancy (LEXP) have emerged with appropriate positive signs. Three of these variables, rural specialists (Total specialists), auxiliary nurse midwives (ANM)/female health workers and total number of blood banks (blood banks) are statistically significant.

Discussion

The results of our FDH analysis (in Chapter 5) suggest considerably more scope for improvement in efficiency of public expenditure in health relative to education. A further parametric approach of stochastic frontier analysis (SFA) presented here indicates factors that could be isolated to suggest ways to improve efficiency in public expenditure in the sector.

As mentioned earlier, we hypothesize that states differ in their technical efficiency pertaining to the health care system due to factors which require emphasis in the planning of health facilities. It is also hypothesized that these factors differ

among states according to their level of development. It is presumed that estimated efficiency parameters should help the makers of health policy to improve
state-level health system performance.

As presented in the results, our findings indicate the positive impact of governmental intervention in the expansion of PHC facilities and the desirable impact of
having rural specialists such as surgeons, obstetricians and gynaecologists, physicians and paediatricians for enhancing life expectancy. The fact that the ANM
variable has emerged with positive signs indicates the desirable role of the various
inputs provided through paramedical manpower. Statistical significance of these
inputs at the conventional level of significance and the blood bank variable suggest that the system has indeed worked towards providing some of the desirable
inputs. However, whether these have been utilized as efficiently as to be considered optimum is revealed through our comparison of actual and estimated life
expectancy for males (LEXP) for the year 2010 in Table 6.54. These depict Kerala
as the most efficient state (MES), with its actual LEXP the highest in reaching
nearer to the estimated LEXP. Kerala is followed by Punjab and Haryana. Further,
the least efficiency for males is depicted by Madhya Pradesh, followed by Andhra
Pradesh and Uttar Pradesh. For female life expectancy, these rankings for the latter type (i. e. moving from the lowest-ranking state) are depicted by Uttar Pradesh
followed by Madhya Pradesh and Assam (Table 6.55).

Reasons for these interstate disparities can be deciphered from Tables 6.56 and
6.57, which depict major inputs for the health sector in the states. Notably, the distributions of per capita hospitals, primary health centers (PHCs), subcentres (SCs),
community health centers (CHCs) and beds in the states are highly inequitable.
In fact, there is a considerable difference between maximum and minimum values for each of the parameters (columns 2–6, Table 6.56). Pertinently, population

Table 6.55 Actual and estimated life expectancies (females) in selected Indian states

State	Actual life expectancy	Potential life expectancy	Actual as % of potential	Ranks of states according to realization of potential life expectancy (females)
Andhra Pradesh	69.40	82.01	84.62	12
Assam	62.80	74.67	84.10	13
Bihar	66.70	74.84	89.13	9
Gujarat	71.00	77.33	91.82	5
Haryana	69.80	74.03	94.29	3
Karnataka	71.10	78.74	90.29	7
Kerala	76.80	78.13	98.29	1
Madhya Pradesh	63.30	78.04	81.11	14
Maharashtra	81.78	87.19	93.79	4
Odisha	64.80	75.65	85.65	11
Punjab	71.60	75.45	94.90	2
Rajashthan	69.20	77.00	89.87	8
Tamilnadu	70.60	80.70	87.49	10
Uttar Pradesh	64.40	79.95	80.55	15
West Bengal	70.90	77.37	91.64	6

Source: Estimated.

Table 6.56 Health facilities per thousand population and population served per government hospital and beds (2011)

State	Population served per government hospital	Population served per government hospital bed	Subcentres (per thousand)	PHCs (per thousand)	CHCs (per thousand)
Assam	194,863	3,912	4.604	0.938	0.108
Bihar	451,325	5,606	9.696	1.863	0.07
Gujarat	135,694	313	7.274	1.123	0.305
Haryana	159,721	3,122	2.508	0.444	0.107
Karnataka	63,309	913	8.87	2.31	0.18
Kerala	74,861	1,045	4.575	0.809	0.224
Madhya Pr	155,470	2,490	8.869	1.156	0.333
Maharashtra	82,264	1,654	10.58	1.809	0.365
Odisha	23,970	2,653	6.688	1.228	0.377
Punjab	130,066	2,658	2.95	0.446	0.129
Rajashthan	83,076	2,640	11.487	1.517	0.376
Tamilnadu	112,959	1,391	8.706	1.204	0.385
Uttar Pr	229,118	3,499	20.521	3.692	0.515
West Bengal	139,676	1,283	10.356	0.909	0.348

Source: GoI (2012b).

served per government hospital bed is the highest (5,606) in Bihar, followed by Assam (3,912) and Uttar Pradesh (3,499). Similar order holds true with regard to population served per government hospital, with the highest figure for Bihar (451,325) followed by Uttar Pradesh (229,118) and Assam (194,863) (column 1, Table 6.56). The magnitude of the highest and the lowest number for population served per government hospital bed and hospitals in the states is ranked slightly differently from the order of life expectancy and its achievements (i.e. actual vs. potential life expectancy) in our results. Similar observations, however, cannot be made pertaining to other facilities such as PHCs, SCs and CHCs (Table 6.56, columns 4–6). There appears to be a pattern of these facilities depicting higher numbers per thousand population in Uttar Pradesh, which is in contrast to its lowest ranking of life expectancy outcomes, thus depicting inadequate utilization of these facilities. Kerala does not have the highest number for any of the categories of these facilities, as shown in Table 6.56. In fact, in terms of manpower, again Uttar Pradesh seems to have the highest per thousand specialists at CHC (1.89), health assistants (4.52) and female ANMs (22.46) (Table 6.57, columns 3, 4 and 7). It has the second-highest number of doctors at PHCs (2.86) and female Lady Health Visitor (LHV) or Lady Health Worker (2.04) (Table 6.57, columns 2 and 5). This pattern also reinforces the lower utilization of manpower in the state and points to the inadequate or ineffective utilization of staff inputs in poorly performing states. However, in most of the states, neither the inadequate availability of health care sector inputs nor merely inefficient utilization of these inputs explains the differentials in achievements in life expectancy.

In addition to the factors within the health system, as we noted earlier, influences external to the system may lead to differentials in efficiency at the state

Table 6.57 Health manpower per thousand population (2011)

	Number of doctors at PHCs	Specialists at CHCs	Health assistants (male)	Female (LHV)	Health workers (male)	Female/ANM
Andhra Pradesh	2.35	0.41	1.92	1.15	5.08	21.65
Assam	1.56	0.22	0.00	0.45	2.39	8.72
Bihar	3.53	0.15	0.56	0.36	1.07	16.94
Gujarat	0.78	0.08	0.76	0.88	4.87	6.43
Haryana	0.53	0.05	0.13	0.40	1.82	5.03
Karnataka	2.09	0.58	0.82	1.04	3.15	11.43
Kerala	1.12	0.77	0.63	0.80	1.29	4.17
Madhya Pradesh	0.81	0.23	0.14	0.55	3.70	12.52
Maharashtra	2.29	0.60	2.36	2.96	8.16	21.73
Orissa	0.53	0.44	0.00	0.92	2.21	7.93
Punjab	0.49	0.30	0.24	0.39	1.83	4.10
Raj	1.47	0.57	0.20	1.42	1.59	17.64
Tamil Nadu	1.70	0.00	1.90	1.02	1.22	9.77
Uttar Pradesh	2.86	1.89	4.52	2.04	1.73	22.46
West Bengal	1.01	0.18	0.00	0.00	4.48	12.97

Source: GoI (2012b).

level. Some of these factors could be per capita income, per capita budgetary health expenditure, literacy, access to safe drinking water and urbanization. In general, the differential impacts on life expectancy of health system inputs may be due to significant influence of some of these variables. As presented in Table 6.58, the majority of poorly performing states such as Uttar Pradesh, Madhya Pradesh and Bihar are among the low-income-category states (column 5, Table 6.58). Even the budgetary expenditure (as percentage of total state budget) is lower in some of these states, such as Madhya Pradesh, but this also holds for some of the relatively better-off States such as Punjab, Haryana and Maharashtra (column 5, Table 6.58).

Although Kerala does not have the highest figures in terms of either per capita income or budgetary expenditure on health, it has an outstanding position in terms of overall literacy, which is 90.91 per cent, according to the 2011 census (column 2, Table 6.58). In contrast, many of the poor and poorly performing states, in terms of life expectancy, have much lower levels of literacy. A similar situation prevails in terms of level of urbanization in poorer states relative to their counterparts in better-off states (column 3, Table 6.58). Thus, to explore such external factors, we used dispersion in efficiency as a dependent variable in the second stage of our regression exercise, using panel data for the state level. Among the set of explanatory variables, we included per capita income, male and female enrolment, budgetary expenditure on health (in per capita as well as percentage of total state budget separately), and total rural habitats covered fully by water supply schemes. The results using panel data for the states between 2005 and 2011 indicated two of these variables, per capita income (Pc income) and gross primary enrolment (boys and girls separately), as statistically significant in the males and females dispersion results (Tables 6.59 and 6.60).

Table 6.58 Literacy, urbanization and budgetary expenditure on health and per capita income (2011)

State	Literacy (2011)	Urbanization	Expenditure on medical and public health as % of total state budget	Per capita net state domestic product at constant (2004–05) prices
Andhra Pradesh	67.66	33.49	3.8	40,366
Assam	73.18	14.08	4.8	21,406
Bihar	63.82	11.3	3.9	13,632
Gujarat	79.31	42.58	4.3	52,708
Haryana	76.64	34.79	3.2	59,221
Karnataka	75.6	38.57	4	39,301
Kerala	93.91	47.72	5	49,873
Madhya Pradesh	70.63	27.63	3.5	22,382
Maharashtra	82.91	45.23	3.5	62,729
Orissa	73.45	16.68	4.1	25,708
Punjab	76.68	37.49	3.5	44,752
Rajasthan	67.06	24.89	5.4	26,436
Tamil Nadu	80.33	48.45	4.8	51,928
Uttar Pradesh	69.72	22.28	4.8	17,349
West Bengal	77.08	31.89	4.5	32,228

Table 6.59 Results for dispersion as dependent variable (males)

Fixed-effects (within) regression; number of obs = 90
Number of groups = 15
R square: within = 0.2249; obs per group: mi = 6
  between = 0.0000
    overall = 0.0026; F(3,72) = 6.96
corr (u_i, Xb) = –0.1194; prob > F = 0.0004

Dispersionmale	Coef.	t
Pcincome	0.0000*	–1.9200
Rural habitat covered fully by water supply	–0.0004	–0.1200
Gross primary enrolment boys	–0.0272**	–3.3600
Constant	0.2371**	4.1500
Sigma_U	0.0503	
Sigma_E	0.0095	
Rho	0.9657	

*10% level of significance; **1% level of significance.

F test that all u_i = 0: F(14, 72) = 67.59; prob > F = 0.0000

Note: We also tried the alternative model using random effects. However, the results of the Hausman test indicated a fixed effect model.

The positive sign of per capita income indicates the impact of inequality in income across states on the disparities in health outcomes. The negative sign of gross enrolment indicates that an increased level of awareness about health-related facilities and issues has helped to reduce regional disparities in the efficiency of the health care system across states. However, this has not been able

Table 6.60 Results for dispersion as dependent variable (females)

Fixed-effects (within) regression; number of obs = 90
Number of groups = 15
R square within = 0.1147; obs per group: min = 6
      between = 0.0920
      overall = 0.0854
F(3,72) = 3.11
corr (u_i, Xb) = 0.1750; prob > F = 0.0316

Dispersionfemale	Coef.	t
Pcincome	0.0000	−1.45
Rural habitat covered fully by water supply	0.0004	0.11
Gross primary enrolment girls	−0.0264*	−2.10
Constant	0.2496**	3.28
Sigma_U	0.0579	
Sigma_E	0.0102	
Rho	0.9698	

*5% level of significance; **1% level of significance.

F test that all u_i = 0: F(14, 72) = 60.47; prob > F = 0.0000

Note: We also tried the alternative model using random effects. However, the results of the Hausman test indicated a fixed effect model.

to compensate for other deficiencies of low investments and poor utilization of existing heath care facilities.

Conclusions

The results of the frontier model, using panel data for fifteen major Indian states in the years 2005–11, indicate that the efficiency of the public health care delivery system remains low. Considerable disparities across states in terms of per capita availability and utilization of hospitals, beds and manpower inputs have had an adverse impact on life expectancy in the poorer states. Overcoming these factoral disparities may lead to an improvement in state-level efficiency of the public health care system. This may also help improve life expectancy speedily and more equitably in the poorly performing states of Madhya Pradesh and Uttar Pradesh, possibly by as much as by 20 per cent. However, this has to be supported with other factors such as greater budgetary expenditure to improve availability of medicines and materials at rural facilities and better management of health personnel in the rural areas to ensure their adequate utilization. Learning from the remarkable achievements of Kerala, an emphasis on literacy by reducing dropout rates along with better utilization of health infrastructure and manpower resources could go a long way in improving life expectancy. This may require a considerable reorientation of the current health care set-up, particularly in the rural areas in the poorly performing states. These could reallocate surplus manpower from within and also make the rural infrastructure more useful to the needy through adequate inputs of building, equipment and medicines. In fact, there is a considerable differential in budgetary expenditure per capita between the better-off and the poorer states. This in turn reduces the availability of basic medicines and materials in the public health care system and reduces its reliability for the poor, making them more dependent on the costlier private sector. Part of this problem could be tackled through funds from NRHM and also by improving rural sanitation in the poorer states. The results also suggest a lack of appropriate links and coordination between economic and social sector policies, leading to suboptimal health outcomes for the poorer states in the country. Our results of SFA for 2005–11 corroborate the analysis for earlier periods from other studies (Sankar and Kathuria 2004; Purohit 2010c).

Efficiency of elementary education in India (2000–11)

The frontier estimation for education is carried out using a set of explanatory variables which include facilities such as common toilets, girls' toilets, drinking water and student classroom ratio; manpower variables such as pupil-teacher ratio, availability of female teachers, age of the schools in terms of older schools established since 1994; and other policy inputs such as utilization of school development grants or teaching learning material grants or enrolment of students from the categories of scheduled castes and scheduled tribes. These variables are used to explain enrolment at the primary and upper primary levels, enrolment of girls at the primary and upper primary levels and enrolment in the government schools. The explanatory variables corresponding to primary or upper primary level are used to explain the primary or upper primary level enrolments respectively.

The results of primary and upper primary enrolment are presented in Tables 6.61 and 6.62. Three variables, drinking water facility in primary schools (P1 dw), enrolment of SC (SCP) and age of the school (P1 sage), have emerged as statistically significant with positive signs. Among these, two variables indicate that basic facilities such as drinking water and older established schools have been helpful in encouraging primary enrolments. At the same time, the positive impact of SC category reservation is visible with the positive and significant SC variables.

However, the results of upper primary enrolment indicate that the major determinant is the entry into the primary level. Further, Tables 6.63 and 6.64 depict the primary enrolment in government schools (EGS) and primary enrolment of girls (GE). The primary enrolment in government schools is also mainly influenced by availability of basic facilities such as drinking water supply in the schools. There is a positive and significant coefficient for this variable (coefficient of P1dw is .492). The other significant factors to determine primary enrolment in government schools include SC girls' enrolment in primary (coefficient is .214) and school development grant (coefficient is .180). The positive impact of SC girls' enrolment and that of school development grant indicate that budgetary expenditure on these items has helped to increase primary enrolment in government schools. The results pertaining to girls' enrolment in primary level (P1ge)depict the significant role of basic amenities such as girls' toilets (coefficient .082) as well as the pupil-teacher ratio (.395), number of female teachers (.338) and school development grant (.385) (Table 6.64). These results seem to

Table 6.61 Time-invariant inefficiency model for primary schools

Time-invariant inefficiency model
Number of obs = 160; Group variable: state; Number of groups = 16
Obs per group: min = 10; avg = 10; max = 10; Wald chi^2(4) = 162.00
Log likelihood = −308.81329; prob > chi^2 = 0.0000

primary	Coef. (z values)
p1dw	2.033*
	(8.550)
scp	1.117*
	(4.600)
inpgr	0.791**
	(2.500)
p1sage	0.405**
	(2.360)
constant	1.445
	(1.160)
mu	−0.623
	(−0.120)
lnsigma2	1.587
	(1.550)
ilgtgamma	−0.003
	(0.000)
sigma2	4.890
gamma	0.499
sigma_u2	2.442
sigma_v2	2.448

Source: Estimated.

*Significant at 1% level; **significant at 5% level.

reinforce complementarity of government budgetary inputs since enrolment in government schools is determined by other items, such as pattern of expenditure favoring deployment of teachers, female teachers and grants given for school development.

However, Table 6.65 relating to upper primary enrolment of girls depicts four of the variables, girls' toilets (Up1gt), student classroom ratio (of upper primary), percentage of female teachers (Up1ft) and school development grants (sdg) as significant variables. These indicate that many factors, such as girls' toilets, student classroom ratio and female teachers, contribute to girls' enrolments at the upper primary level. At the same time, government expenditure to provide school development grants has also helped to increase the upper primary enrolment of girls.

The relative performance of states using the parameters of enrolment at primary level and upper primary level, enrolment in government schools and girls' enrolment is presented in Tables 6.66 to 6.69. The highest achievement in terms of primary enrolment relative to a norm estimated by frontier analysis indicates the top achiever as Maharashtra (85%) and the lowest as Orissa (1%) (Table 6.66 and Figure 6.2).

Table 6.62 Time-invariant inefficiency model for
upper-primary schools

Time-invariant inefficiency model
Number of obs = 159
Group variable: state; number of groups = 1
Obs per group: min = 9; avg = 9.9; max = 10
Wald chi^2(2) = 17,398.89
Log likelihood = 10.612172; prob > chi^2 = 0.0000

uprimary	Coef. (z values)
primary	0.963*
	(119.440)
up1dw	0.008
	(0.400)
constant	0.188
	(1.210)
mu	0.176
	(0.290)
lnsigma2	−1.338
	(−1.500)
ilgtgamma	1.796**
	(1.730)
sigma2	0.262
gamma	0.858
sigma_u2	0.225
sigma_v2	0.037

Source: Estimated.

*Significant at 1% level; **significant at 5% level.

The reasons for this gap in performance can be deciphered from a look at the values of various variables depicting the number of schools and teachers for these states (Table 6.67). The major difference between Maharashtra and Orissa is the numbers of private schools and enrolment in private schools (per 1,000 population), which are very low for the latter (.02 and 1.984 respectively) relative to Maharashtra (at .05 and 14.69) (Tables 6.67 and 6.68).

The relative performance in terms of upper primary enrolment is depicted in Table 6.69 and Figure 6.3. In this case, Kerala is first in achievement relative to the frontier norm with 92 per cent, followed by Tamil Nadu and Maharashtra. The lowest performer is Orissa. The notable difference between Kerala and Orissa at the upper primary level can partly be deciphered from facilities (schools) and manpower variables (teachers) in these two states. In particular, the extent of private schools and private teachers per capita is much higher in Kerala (.02 and .19) relative to Orissa (with .04 and .08 respectively for private schools and private teachers) (Tables 6.70 and 6.71).

Likewise, the relative performance of girls' enrolment at the primary level depicts Karnataka as the highest achiever (92%), followed by Rajasthan (88%) and Orissa (87%) (Table 6.72 and Figure 6.4). The lowest performer in this regard seems to be Punjab, with 62.85 per cent achievement of the norm. This

Table 6.63 Time-invariant inefficiency model for the primary enrolment in government schools

Time-invariant inefficiency model
Number of obs = 160; group variable: state; number of groups = 16 Obs. per group: min = 10; avg = 10; max = 10 Wald chi²(3) = 122.75; log likelihood = –135.24662; prob > chi² = 0.0000

plegs	Coef. (z)
p1dw	0.492*
	(3.380)
scgp	0.214***
	(1.670)
sdg	0.180***
	(1.660)
constant	0.775**
	(2.140)
mu	–3.273
	(–0.130)
lnsigma2	0.318
	(0.060)
lgtgamma	1.349
	(0.220)
sigma2	1.375
gamma	0.794
sigma_u2	1.091
sigma_v2	0.283

Source: Estimated.

*Significant at 1% level; **significant at 5% level; ***significant at 10% level.

difference partly can be due to different values of determining variables in these states which include girls' toilets, pupil-teacher ratio, number of female teachers and age of the schools (percentage schools established in 1994) (Tables 6.74 and 6.75). Except for age of the school denoting percentage of schools established since 1994 Punjab has a better position. It probably implies that the role of older, established schools has been crucial in Karnataka to produce higher female enrolment.

In terms of upper primary, the highest achiever for girls' enrolment emerges as Rajasthan (65%), followed by Karnataka (46.42%), and with lowest being Bihar (23%) (Table 6.73 and Figure 6.5). The reasons for this difference in performance between Rajasthan and Bihar seem to be lower magnitudes of four variables in the latter. The girls' toilets, student classroom ratio, pupil teacher ratio and established older schools since 1994 in Bihar remain 82.4, 72, 52 and 1.7 (Tables 6.74 and 6.75). These values are appreciably lower than the corresponding values for Rajasthan, which remain as 96.8, 21, 17 and 65.5.

In terms of enrolment in government schools at the primary level, Bihar tops the list with 97 per cent achievement. This is followed by West Bengal (92%) and Orissa (91%) (Table 6.76).

Table 6.64 Time-invariant inefficiency model for primary enrolment of girls (GE)

Time-invariant inefficiency model: Number of obs = 160
Group variable: state; number of groups = 16
Obs per group: min = 10; avg = 10; max = 10
Wald chi^2(4) = 206.99; log likelihood = –70.61260; prob >
chi^2 = 0.0000

p1ge	Coef. (z)
p1gt	0.082***
	(1.880)
p1ptr	0.395*
	(3.550)
p1ft	0.338*
	(2.980)
sdg	0.385*
	(5.960)
constant	–0.576
	(–1.170)
mu	–0.093
	(–0.080)
lnsigma2	–1.383
	(–1.430)
ilgtgamma	0.026
	(0.010)
sigma2	0.251
gamma	0.506
sigma_u2	0.127
sigma_v2	0.124

Source: Estimated.

*Significant at 1% level; **significant at 5% level; ***significant at
10% level.

Conclusions

There are notable interstate variations in terms of achieved efficiency relative to the norm established by frontier estimation. For instance, in primary
level enrolment a high-income state, Maharashtra, ranks first, followed by
Uttar Pradesh and Rajasthan. The lowest performer appears to be Orissa. The
major difference between Maharashtra and Orissa is in the numbers of private schools and enrolment in private schools (per 1,000 population), which
are very low for the latter (.02 and 1.984 respectively) relative to Maharashtra (at .05 and 14.69). In upper primary enrolments Kerala ranks at the top,
with Orissa at the bottom. The reasons are traced back in the availability of
facilities (schools) and manpower variables (teachers) in these two states. In
particular, the extent of private teachers per capita is much higher in Kerala
(.19) relative to Orissa (.08). In primary-level enrolments of girls, Karnataka
is the highest achiever, with Punjab at the lowest point. This difference can
be due in part to different values of determining variables in these states,

Table 6.65 Time-invariant inefficiency model relating to upper primary enrolment of girls

Time-invariant inefficiency model: Number of ob = 159
Group variable: state; number of groups = 16
Obs per group: min = 9; avg = 9.9; max = 10
Wald chi^2(4) = 446.01
Log likelihood = –97.961234; prob > chi^2 = 0.0000

up1ge	Coef. (z)
up1gt	0.753
	(17.46*)
up1scr	0.395
	(2.51**)
up1ft	–0.196
	(–1.95***)
sdg	0.165
	(2.67*)
constant	0.145
	(0.14)
mu	0.783
	(0.98)
lnsigma2	–1.449
	(–9.75*)
ilgtgamma	–1.016
	(–2**)
sigma2	0.234
gamma	0.265
sigma_u2	0.062
sigma_v2	0.172

Source: Estimated.

*Significant at 1% level; **significant at 5% level; ***significant at 10% level.

Table 6.66 Actual and estimated primary school enrolments in India

State	Primary actual	Primary estimated	% achieved	Ranks
Andhra Pradesh	7,439,990	15,732,670	47	8
Assam	3,927,800	5,724,581	69	5
Bihar	15,881,096	20,729,119	77	2
Goa	114,236	533,674	21	13
Gujrat	5,858,007	8,084,587	72	3
Harayana	2,443,617	24,576,469	10	15
Karnataka	5,417,852	24,321,469	22	12
Kerla	2,286,196	3,388,643	67	6
Madhya Pradesh	10,396,606	21,319,442	49	7
Maharashtra	10,337,204	12,210,539	85	1
Orissa	132,758	25,367,008	1	16
Punjab	2,587,700	25,929,192	10	14
Rajasthan	8,657,184	32,249,078	27	11
Tamil Nadu	6040,033	20,649,466	29	9
Uttar Pradesh	26,188,737	37,872,280	69	4
West Bengal	10,086,011	35,390,713	28	10

Source: Estimated and National University of Educational Planning and Administration 2002–03 to 2011–12.

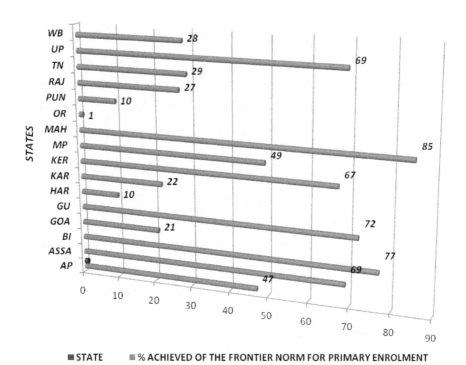

Figure 6.2 Achieved efficiency as percentage of frontier norm in primary enrolment
Sources: Estimated and National University of Educational Planning and Administration 2002–03 to 2011–12.

Table 6.67 Primary schools by government and other types (per 1,000 population)

Primary only	Total schools (current year)	Total schools (previous year)	Government schools	Private schools	Madrasas & unrecgonised schools
Andhra Pradesh	0.83	0.84	0.69	0.12	0.02
Assam	1.47	1.47	1.14	0.02	0.30
Bihar	0.39	0.40	0.39	0.00	0.00
Goa	0.70	0.69	0.60	0.10	0.00
Gujarat	0.18	0.18	0.17	0.01	0.00
Harayana	0.41	0.41	0.37	0.03	0.01
Karnataka	0.43	0.43	0.38	0.05	0.00
Kerala	0.24	0.20	0.09	0.13	0.01
Madhya Pradesh	1.27	1.26	1.15	0.10	0.02
Maharashtra	0.44	0.44	0.39	0.05	0.00
Orissa	0.89	0.88	0.85	0.02	0.01
Punjab	0.57	0.58	0.49	0.02	0.06
Rajasthan	0.72	0.72	0.64	0.07	0.02
Tamil Nadu	0.48	0.47	0.32	0.16	0.00
Uttar Pradesh	0.73	0.67	0.54	0.19	0.00
West Bengal	0.83	0.82	0.74	0.07	0.02

Source: Estimated and National University of Educational Planning and Administration 2002–03 to 2011–12.

Table 6.68 Primary enrolment in government and private schools (per 1,000 population)

Primary only	Total enrolment (previous year)	Enrolment in government school	Enrolment in private school	Enrolment in Madrasas and unrecognised schools	Enrolment in government school, rural	Enrolment in private school, rural
Andhra Pradesh	64.30	37.71	25.18	1.59	43.09	14.54
Assam	101.93	9.54	1.53	19.84	100.07	1.58
Bihar	72.36	69.69	0.01	0.01	72.28	0.01
Goa	37.50	19.87	20.25	0.00	28.08	15.13
Gujarat	12.71	11.54	1.70	0.00	13.92	1.22
Harayana	57.17	55.32	2.91	0.81	62.53	2.10
Karnataka	17.05	12.50	4.25	0.04	15.55	3.23
Kerala	27.02	8.10	18.01	1.09	9.46	19.66
Madhya Pradesh	114.25	93.97	10.79	1.25	110.24	7.34
Maharashtra	35.73	20.26	14.69	0.12	28.60	3.97
Orissa	57.63	52.76	1.98	1.18	56.33	1.69
Punjab	49.19	44.22	1.58	3.36	54.09	0.83
Rajasthan	43.39	35.57	5.36	1.32	41.61	4.79
Tamil Nadu	44.72	20.39	23.53	0.16	28.00	18.45
Uttar Pradesh	109.93	74.42	42.33	0.76	86.06	39.12
West Bengal	89.97	78.77	7.61	1.62	91.23	6.78

Source: Estimated and National University of Educational Planning and Administration 2002–03 to 2011–12.

Table 6.69 Actual and estimated upper primary enrolments in India

	Upper primary actual	Upper primary estimated	% achieved	Ranks
Andra Pradesh	3,811,106	4,968,010	76.71292	6
Assam	1,833,175	2,782,304	65.88694	11
Bihar	4,969,501	10,700,489	46.44181	15
Goa	71,769.15	92,570.89	77.52885	5
Gujarat	2,518,943	4,097,182	61.47989	13
Harayana	1,280,870	1,765,775	72.5387	8
Karnataka	3,007,020	3,800,260	79.12669	4
Kerala	1,533,679	1,656,206	92.60195	1
Madhya Pradesh	4,921,235	7,115,741	69.15983	9
Maharashtra	5,848,700	7,077,349	82.6397	3
Orissa	29,745.11	106,908.6	27.82292	16
Punjab	1,401,369	1,866,004	75.09997	7
Rajasthan	3,740,014	5,966,613	62.68237	12
Tamil Nadu	3,736,201	4,219,681	88.54228	2
Uttar Pradesh	9,215,985	17,314,070	53.2283	14
West Bengal	4,741,907	6,907,373	68.64994	10

Source: Estimated and National University of Educational Planning and Administration 2002–03 to 2011–12.

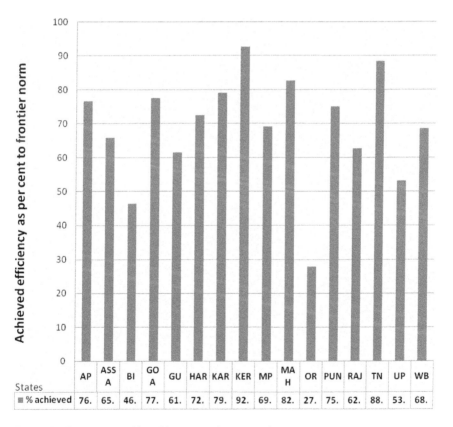

Figure 6.3 Percentage achieved in upper primary enrolment

Sources: Estimated and National University of Educational Planning and Administration 2002–03 to 2011–12.

Table 6.70 Per capita availability of schools

Upper primary only	Total schools (current year)	Total schools (previous year)	Government schools	Private schools	Madrasas and unrecognised schools
Andhra Pradesh	0.00	0.00	0.00	0.00	0.00
Assam	0.35	0.35	0.16	0.18	0.02
Bihar	0.00	0.00	0.00	0.00	0.00
Goa	0.06	0.04	0.02	0.03	0.00
Gujarat	0.01	0.01	0.00	0.00	0.00
Harayana	0.10	0.09	0.10	0.00	0.00
Karnataka	0.01	0.01	0.00	0.00	0.00
Kerala	0.02	0.02	0.00	0.02	0.00
Madhya Pradesh	0.41	0.41	0.39	0.02	0.00
Maharashtra	0.00	0.00	0.00	0.00	0.00
Orissa	0.10	0.10	0.06	0.04	0.00
Punjab	0.11	0.11	0.11	0.00	0.00
Rajasthan	0.00	0.00	0.00	0.00	0.00
Tamil Nadu	0.00	0.00	0.00	0.00	0.00
Uttar Pradesh	0.31	0.28	0.23	0.08	0.00
West Bengal	0.06	0.05	0.06	0.00	0.00

Source: Estimated and National University of Educational Planning and Administration 2002–03 to 2011–12.

Table 6.71 Per capita availability of teachers

Upper primary only	Total teachers (previous year)	Government teachers	Private teachers	Teaching in Madrasas and unrecognised schools	Govt. schools, rural	Private schools, rural
Andhra Pradesh	0.00	0.00	0.00	0.00	0.00	0.00
Assam	2.35	1.04	1.19	0.12	0.16	0.19
Bihar	0.02	0.02	0.00	0.00	0.00	0.00
Goa	0.49	0.17	0.45	0.00	0.04	0.04
Gujarat	0.03	0.01	0.01	0.00	0.00	0.00
Harayana	0.36	0.38	0.01	0.00	0.12	0.00
Karnataka	0.03	0.02	0.01	0.00	0.00	0.00
Kerala	0.23	0.05	0.19	0.00	0.00	0.02
Madhya Pradesh	1.14	1.04	0.08	0.00	0.47	0.01
Maharashtra	0.01	0.00	0.00	0.00	0.00	0.00
Orissa	0.24	0.18	0.08	0.00	0.06	0.04
Punjab	0.49	0.50	0.00	0.00	0.15	0.00
Rajasthan	0.02	0.02	0.00	0.00	0.00	0.00
Tamil Nadu	0.00	0.00	0.00	0.00	0.00	0.00
Uttar Pradesh	0.82	0.60	0.35	0.00	0.27	0.08
West Bengal	0.23	0.24	0.01	0.01	0.07	0.00

Source: Estimated and National University of Educational Planning and Administration 2002–03 to 2011–12.

Table 6.72 Girls' enrolment at the primary level (actual and estimated values)

State	Primary GE actual	Primary GE estimated	% achieved	Ranks
Andhra Pradesh	49.10	60.82	80.72	7
Assam	50.00	60.53	82.61	5
Bihar	49.60	77.97	63.61	15
Goa	47.40	73.02	64.91	13
Gujarat	47.80	61.18	78.13	8
Harayana	49.30	69.53	70.90	11
Karnataka	48.80	53.12	91.86	1
Kerala	49.90	66.99	74.49	10
Madhya Pradesh	50.50	61.11	82.64	4
Maharashtra	47.50	62.01	76.60	9
Orissa	49.00	56.54	86.66	3
Punjab	47.00	74.78	62.85	16
Rajasthan	49.00	55.81	87.79	2
Tamil Nadu	49.50	73.52	67.33	12
Uttar Pradesh	49.10	76.59	64.10	14
West Begal	49.40	59.94	82.42	6

Sources: Estimated and National University of Educational Planning and Administration 2002–03 to 2011–12.

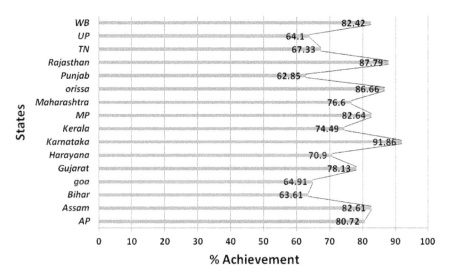

■ % Achieved to Frontier Norms in Primary School Girls Enrolment

Figure 6.4 Percentage achieved of frontier norms in primary school girls' enrolment

Sources: Estimated and National University of Educational Planning and Administration 2002–03 to 2011–12.

Table 6.73 Girls'enrolment at the upper primary level (actual and estimated values)

State	Upper primary GE actual	Upper primary GE estimated	% achieved	Ranks
Andhra Pradesh	1.00	3.97	25.18	15
Assam	52.70	121.26	43.46	3
Bihar	46.00	196.48	23.41	16
Goa	46.20	127.85	36.14	12
Gujarat	46.10	136.66	33.73	13
Harayana	52.50	130.75	40.15	4
Karnataka	58.60	126.24	46.42	2
Kerala	46.80	124.27	37.66	9
Madhya Pradesh	53.30	134.74	39.56	5
Maharashtra	49.80	130.75	38.09	8
Orissa	48.50	133.86	36.23	11
Punjab	46.20	120.78	38.25	7
Rajasthan	74.30	114.03	65.16	1
Tamil Nadu	45.10	120.82	37.33	10
Uttar Pradesh	51.70	134.80	38.35	6
West Bengal	56.80	170.89	33.24	14

Source: Estimated and National University of Educational Planning and Administration 2002–03 to 2011–12.

which include girls' toilets, pupil-teacher ratio, number of female teachers and age of the schools. Pertaining to girls' enrolment at the upper primary level, the highest achiever for girls' enrolment emerges as Rajasthan (65%), followed by Karnataka (46.42%), and with the lowest being Bihar (23%). The reasons for this difference in performance between Rajasthan and Bihar seem to be lower magnitudes of four variables in the latter – girls' toilets, student classroom ratio, pupil teacher ratio and established older schools. In terms of enrolment in government schools at the primary level, Bihar tops the list with 97 per cent achievement. This is followed by West Bengal (92%) and Orissa (91%), and Kerala (27.46) has the lowest value relative to the frontier norm. Thus interstate variations at different levels are due more to the availability of basic facilities in either government or private-sector schools.

Convergence in the health care sector in India

The objective of this section is to test the development paradigm that the inequity across states will converge and the adjustment period will be lowered for equitable outcomes in health. It may require a change in focus of health policy and the budgetary emphasis of states.

Earlier studies

Generally convergence has been discussed in the context of growth models and per capita income across regions and countries.[5] More recent work on explaining the process of helping lagging regions catch up is extensive and advocates three

Table 6.74 Toilets and drinking water facilities in primary schools in India (percentages)

	pICT	upICT	asICT	pIGT	upIGT	asIGT	pIDW	upIDW	asIDW
Andhra Pradesh	25	100	44	75.3	1	70.3	85.9	1	89.0
Assam	34	38	17	65.9	62.2	93.2	76.3	75.9	77.3
Bihar	60.6	89.1	71.8	59.1	82.4	99.7	88.7	99.6	93.0
Goa	10.0	1.0	4.0	91.4	100.0	96.5	99.5	100.0	99.4
Gujarat	1	1	4	99.6	100.0	98.4	100.0	100.0	100.0
Harayana	4	12	8	96.5	88.3	92.1	99.3	99.2	99.5
Karnataka	2	3	14	98.2	97.1	86.9	99.3	99.5	99.4
Kerala	9	3	8	91.4	96.7	92.5	96.9	99.7	95.9
Madhya Pradesh	14	17	21	86.9	83.4	79.9	97.9	97.4	98.0
Maharashtra	73.0	92.2	80.7	91.0	93.1	98.0	91.5	98.7	94.3
Orissa	1	1	1	76.0	79.3	95.6	92.9	92.5	94.4
Punjab	1	1	1	97.2	97.6	92.1	100.0	100.0	99.9
Rajasthan	1	1	1	93.2	96.8	89.2	92	98.9	95.1
Tamil Nadu	1	1	1	91.0	92.2	88.1	100.0	100.0	100.0
Uttar Pradesh	1	1	1	89.1	88.9	1.0	99.3	96.2	98.5
West Bengal	1	1	1	88.2	73.5	1.0	97.4	91.3	97.2

Source: Estimated and National University of Educational Planning and Administration 2002–03 to 2011–12.

CT = % schools with common toilets; GT = % schools with girls' toilets; DW = % schools with drinking water facility.

Table 6.75 Pupil-teacher ratio, student class room ratio, female teachers (%) and established older schools since 1994 in India (primary and upper primary schools)

	P1PTR	up1PTR	as1PTR	p1SCR	up1SCR	as1SCR	p1FT	up1FT	as1FT	p1sage	up1sage	as1sage
Andhra Pradesh	24	20	20	25	23	23	50.9	47	47.0	34.6	37.9	38.3
Assam	33	18	25	33	34	31	34.9	22.0	31.8	30.4	15.6	27.4
Bihar	52	52	59	78	72	79	44.6	25.1	39.9	44.1	1.7	29.8
Goa	21	19	22	19	26	24	89.3	63.5	78.8	4	10.7	5.1
Gujarat	25	30	31	25	30	33	47.9	55.0	54.7	33.4	33.7	23.2
Harayana	33	20	26	32	26	27	45.9	34.6	49.5	13.3	21.4	23.7
Karnataka	17	25	22	15	28	22	51.1	62.7	52.8	42.2	54.1	28.9
Kerala	19	19	21	20	28	24	79.5	73.7	77.2	3	5.4	3.6
Madhya Pradesh	34	43	34	26	31	27	33.8	31.9	41.2	45.3	60.1	50.7
Maharashtra	27	23	30	27	28	31	46.5	45.6	43.8	25.7	52.2	23.6
Orissa	25	30	25	24	33	27	42.0	29.6	38.5	27.8	8.7	19.8
Punjab	28	16	19	23	22	21	67.9	54.9	71.1	7.4	76.7	23
Rajasthan	27	17	26	21	21	23	31.8	62.4	30.7	73.8	65.5	55.5
Tamil Nadu	23	24	29	21	25	26	82.2	57.2	78.1	19.1	53	19.7
Uttar Pradesh	44	38	44	37	26	34	44.1	30.6	40.1	44.8	70.8	49.9
West Bengal	28	32	28	34	62	41	44.3	21.9	41.0	32.5	79	31.8

Source: Estimated and National University of Educational Planning and Administration 2002–03 to 2011–12.

PTR = pupil teacher ratio; SCR = student classroom ratio; FT = % female teachers; Sage = % schools established since 1994.

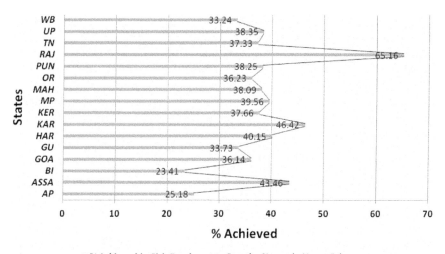

▨ % Achieved in Girls Enrolment to Frontier Norms in Upper Primary

Figure 6.5 Percentage achieved in girls' enrolment of frontier norms in upper primary

Sources: Estimated and National University of Educational Planning and Administration 2002–03 to 2011–12.

Table 6.76 Enrolment in government schools at the primary level in India (actual and estimated)

	Primary EGS actual	Primary EGS estimated	% achieved	Ranks
Andhra Pradesh	58.50	96.16	60.83	11
Assam	81.70	94.05	86.87	5
Bihar	100.00	103.56	96.56	1
Goa	49.50	112.91	43.84	14
Gujarat	87.20	100.13	87.09	4
Harayana	93.70	110.04	85.15	6
Karnataka	74.40	98.94	75.20	10
Kerala	29.80	108.50	27.46	16
Madhya Pradesh	88.60	108.05	82.00	7
Maharashtra	57.80	99.37	58.16	12
Orissa	94.30	102.79	91.74	3
Punjab	89.90	111.93	80.32	8
Rajasthan	84.20	106.17	79.30	9
Tamil Nadu	46.30	111.59	41.49	15
Uttar Pradesh	63.30	112.17	56.43	13
West Bengal	89.50	97.23	92.05	2

Source: Estimated and National University of Educational Planning and Administration 2002–03 to 2011–12.

possible and sometimes related forms of convergence: beta convergence, conditional beta convergence and sigma convergence. Beta convergence postulates that poorer countries will tend to grow faster than richer countries. This is because of the diminishing marginal returns to capital in the richer countries, as their level of capital per labour is relatively high. Moreover, the further down a country is below its balanced growth path and the higher the lags in access to new technology, the higher will be the expected growth when the country gains access to such technology (Romer 1990).[6]

The second type of convergence, conditional beta convergence, mainly takes into consideration the steady-state growth path of the country. If the structural conditions of countries were different, the respective long-run growth rates would be different, which may result in divergence or at best a very weak convergence.[7] The third type, sigma convergence, envisages that the cross-country dispersion of per capita income levels across economies tends to decrease over time, implying a tendency amongst countries to equalization of per capita income in the long run. That is, over time the dispersion around the steady-state value decreases. Beta convergence is a necessary condition for sigma convergence but not a sufficient condition (Barro and Sala-I-Martin 1995).

Thus the basic idea of convergence originates in growth models and is discussed more in the context of per capita incomes. Applications in the context of health care are very limited.[8] Most of these studies are focused on income or other economic variables. Relating to income variables, the study by Arbia, Basile and Piras (2005) highlights the convergence of per capita income in the Italian provinces over 40 years. Eckey, Kosfeld and Türc (2005) on regional convergence of German labour markets derives equations to estimate the speed of convergence on the basis of an extended Solow model. Researchers provide surveys on the European level (see e.g. Neven 1995, Thomas 1996, Engel and Rogers 1996, Helliwell 1998, Nitsch 2000, Martin 2001, Niebuhr 2002, Fingleton 2003, Arbia and Paelinck 2003, Greunz 2003 and López-Bazo, Vayá and Artis 2004). In the Indian context, a review of state-level studies pertaining to some important macroeconomic variables indicates that divergence across states may be a serious issue for India (Cashin and Sahay 1996). Another study by Rao and Sen (1997) argues that the inclusion of four special-category states in the Cashin-Sahay sample has distorted the results. A study by Marjit and Mitra (1996), however, argues that the evidence for convergence is weak. Indeed, Ghosh, Marjit and Neogi (1998) also find evidence for divergence across states, over the period 1961–62 to 1995–96. In contrast, evidence for absolute convergence was not found in an attempt by Nagaraj, Varoudakis and Véganzonès (2000) which covers 17 states for 1970–94 (including three special-category states). Rao, Shand and Kalirajan (1999) examine data for the 14 major states, for the period 1965–95, using state domestic product as the output measure. An attempt by Subrahmanyam (1999) emphasizes inclusion of capital formation, work participation and technology as factors influencing growth across states. Bajpai and Sachs (1999) also examine data for a sample of 19 states for 1961–93. For the subperiod 1961–71, they find some evidence of convergence, but not for later subperiods or for the period as a whole. Singh and Srinivasan (2005) examine the effects of foreign direct investment (FDI), as well as credit availability, in state-level convergence regressions and remain inconclusive for either convergence or divergence. Adabar (2005) uses data for the 14 major states of India from 1976–77 to 2000–01 and employs a dynamic fixed effects panel growth regression. Ahluwalia (2000) indicates using Gini coefficient for the 14 major states in which interstate inequality, after being stable for most of the 1980s, increased, starting from the late 1980s and into the 1990s. In a later analysis Ahluwalia (2002) also adds some simple regressions, but these do not change the overall analysis or conclusions. Dasgupta, Maiti, Mukherjee, Sarkar, and Chakrabarti (2000), covering a period from 1960–61 to 1995–96, find a clear divergence amongst the states in terms of the coefficient of variation of per capita SDP as also the growth in per capita SDP. Reviewing a multitude of demographic indicators such female literacy, SDP, poverty, development and nondevelopment expenditure by state government, shares in plan outlay, investments, banking activities and infrastructure development, Kurian (2000) concludes an aggravated regional disparity. Dhongde (2004), by using a nonparametric kernel density for poverty estimation and decomposing the changes in poverty across regions for the year 1999–2000, has concluded that differences in state and national poverty levels can largely be explained by differences in the state and national mean income levels rather than differences in the state and national distributions. Lall and Chakravorty (2004) suggest that spatial inequality of industry location is the primary cause of spatial income inequality in developing nations. Dholakia (2003) has examined the trends in regional disparity in economic and human development in India over the last two decades. Using NSS data on consumption for the 13th to the 53rd rounds, Jha (2000) examines the relationship between economic inequality, poverty and economic growth in the Indian states.

Among some of the studies restricted to the health care sector, Annigeri (2003), while estimating the district health accounts in Karnataka for the year 1997–98, observes that in terms of sources of funds, private funds account for about 52 per cent of the resources flowing into the district. Using population aged 0–6 years as observed in 2001, Guilmoto and Rajan (2002) estimate district-level indirect birth and fertility rates for all districts of India. Based on six indicators – poverty ratios, hunger, infant mortality rate, immunization, literacy rate and enrollment ratios – Debroy and Bhandari (2003) identify 69 backward districts. Using the estimation procedure of the NSS 55th round on variables of monthly household consumer expenditure and household size, Sastry (2003) shows that it is feasible to derive valid distributions for a majority of districts on the basis of relative standard errors criteria. Finally, using two sets of data including National Sample Survey (NSS) and district-level data to conduct a convergence analysis of growth focusing on six variables – consumption expenditure, petrol sales, diesel sales, bank credit, bank deposits and cereal production – and thus restricting to nine states, Singh, Kendell, Jain and Chander (2010) find no evidence for divergence, but do find evidence for conditional convergence in some cases. At the region level, partial measures of economic activity do not indicate any strong evidence for conditional convergence or divergence. However, there is clear evidence of conditional convergence in per capita consumption levels. The study by Chaurasia (2005) computes indexes of state-mean differences (SMD) and inter-state differences (ISD) in infant mortality rate across states. The analysis reveals that with declining levels of infant mortality, the absolute interstate inequality in the probability of death during infancy has also decreased for the country and for its rural and urban populations. In terms of relative interstate inequality, however, the declining trend in inequality can be observed in rural areas only; in urban India, the relative interstate inequality in infant mortality has tended to increase during the 20 years under reference.

The study by Banik and Banerjee (2011) has refuted the popular perception in India that economic reforms have benefited the rich more than the poor, leading to unequal income distribution as in Quah's twin peaks hypothesis. A study by Gächter and Theurl (2011) focuses on within-country convergence of health status for the local community level in Austria for 1969–2004. Using age-standardized mortality rates from 2,381 Austrian communities as an indicator for health status, they analyze the convergence/divergence of overall mortality for (i) the whole population, (ii) females,(iii) males and (iv) the gender mortality gap. Regarding sigma convergence, they find mixed results. However, they find highly significant coefficients for absolute and conditional beta convergence between the periods. Shankar and Shah (2003) examine whether decentralized fiscal arrangements would lead to ever-widening regional inequalities. They conclude that regional development policies have failed in almost all countries, federal and unitary alike. Still, federal countries do better in restraining regional inequalities, because of the greater political risk these disparities pose for such countries. Their findings also suggest that countries experiencing divergence tend to focus on interventionist policies, while those experiencing convergence have taken a hands-off approach to regional development and instead focus on promoting an economic union by removing barriers to factor mobility and ensuring minimum standards in basic services across the country. A study by Duraisamy and Mahal (2005) examines the determinants of economic growth and health using a panel data of 14 major Indian States for the period 1970–71–2000–01. Their findings indicate that states with a higher initial income have grown faster than states with a lower initial income. This has the effect of widening the gap between the rich and poor states. There is also a strong association between per capita income and health status life expectancy at birth (LEB) and IMR of the population. There is a two-way causation between economic growth and health status. The effect of health measured by life expectancy is positive and significant on economic growth even after controlling for initial income levels. There is evidence of a significant effect of per capita income and per capita public health expenditure on LEB. Average number of years of schooling emerges as the most significant determinant of LEB. The production function estimates indicate that the effect of health (LEB) on NSDP is very high, in fact much higher than the effect of the conventional inputs of capital and labour. A study by Noorbakhsh (2006) indicates that the extension of conversion hypothesis to the non-income components of HDI could be validated conceptually and empirically. The growth regression for the medium- and low-development countries shows an evidence of weak absolute convergence in development over 28 years. The same is established for subsamples of medium- and also low-development countries. The measures of sigma convergence are in line with those for weak beta convergence. When the population sizes of countries are taken into account, the results differ. The Gini coefficient for medium- and low-development countries shows a worsening of inequality while in the case of all countries sampled we see little change in inequality over the 28-years span of this study. To ensure improvements in human development in poorer countries, a reduction in inequality, far more effort under the Millennium Development Goals (MDG) is needed. Given that poorer countries on their own lack the required resources for this purpose, far more rigorous efforts are required by international aid agencies and donor countries to change the current trends.

Methodology and database

To study health status convergence and divergence we use life expectancy as an indicator. We apply two widely recognized concepts in economics to study convergence and divergence, namely (i) absolute convergence (or beta convergence) and (ii) conditional beta convergence.

   The concept of (absolute and conditional) beta convergence relates the change in life expectancy to the starting level, implying an inverse correlation between the starting values and the rates of change.[9] These concepts were first developed within the framework of neoclassical growth models to explain the convergence in aggregate output between states (regions). In these models a common steady state in economic development (absolute convergence) results from the law of diminishing returns of capital inputs. Similarly, health status convergence across regions could be caused by diminishing returns to factor inputs in a regional health production function. The empirical work on beta convergence (Sala-I-Martin 1997) stresses the role of differences in the characteristics of countries (e.g. productivity, quality of education) resulting in the concepts of conditional convergence and convergence clubs. Both concepts deny common steady states in the economic development. This basically leads to two questions: (i) why regions may differ in their health status, and (ii) why such regional differences are expected to decrease (i.e. converge) over time. We expect life expectancy differences between regions due to disparities in terms of the input factors in the regional health production function, such as education, income, household structures, institutional aspects, health care provision, economic development (particularly urban vs. rural areas) and environmental factors. Further, external shocks may lead to such differences, such as deviations in immigration rates across regions. In regard to the second question, with the increasing emphasis of health policy on Health for All, we expect convergence of life expectancy (i.e. health status) across states over time. Moreover, the diminishing returns of the input factors in the health production function might lead to convergence, as the general conditions (e.g. income, education) improve over time. The mobility of people across regions might also have a similar effect, as people tend to move to regions or communities which exhibit more favorable living conditions.

To measure absolute beta convergence in a cross section of Indian states, we employ the following statistical model:

$$\ln(y_{i,T}/y_{i,0}) = \alpha + \beta\ln(y_{i,0}) + \varepsilon_i \tag{1}$$

where, $y_{i,T}$ is the life expectancy at birth (gap) in the state i at final time T, and $y_{i,0}$ is the level of life expectancy in the starting period. i corresponds to the state as the cross sectional unit, β pictures the convergence coefficient and ε_i represents an error term. Equation (1) examines absolute convergence/divergence in the cross section. Conditional beta convergence is estimated by the following equation:

$$\ln(y_{i,T}/y_{i,0}) = \alpha + \beta * \ln(y_{i,0}) + \gamma * z_{i,0} + \varepsilon_i \tag{2}$$

Thereby $z_{i,0}$ features characteristics such as education level and socio-economic level at time t = 0 as further explanatory variables. Thus, they allow the convergence of regions to different steady states due to differences in the input factors of the health production function with respect to the level of education, household structures, economic development, income or population origins. Thus, we assume that differences in the environmental conditions at time t = 0 influence the dynamics of convergence across states.

Data sources and estimation

To study convergence, we have used life expectancy, per capita income, education, budgetary expenditure on health and infant mortality rates. The information is obtained from official publications of the Government of India (1997, 2001a, 2007a), Government of India: Ministry of Health (2001b, 2001a, 2003, 2004, 2007b, 2008, 2009a, 2010, 2011, 2012b), Government of India: Registrar General of India (2001a, 2012a), RBI (2012) and National Family Health Survey 3 (International Institute for Population Sciences and Macro International 2007). The period of coverage ranges from 1996–2010. The analysis covers 19 major states, including Andhra Pradesh, Assam, Bihar, Harayana, Gujarat, Madhya Pradesh, Maharashtra, Punjab, Karanataka, Kerala, Rajasthan, Orissa, Tamil Nadu, Uttar Pradesh and West Bengal. The convergence results make use of cross section and panel data. The estimation accordingly follows OLS and MLE methods.

Results and discussion

Results of our analysis are presented in the tables below. The cross section results for absolute convergence relating to life expectancy for two cross sections of states for the period 1996–2001 and 2001–06, presented separately for males and females, indicate an evidence of convergence for both the cross sections for both the males and females (Table 6.77). However, the statistical significance for the second period for males is not observed. The speed of convergence with the

Table 6.77 Absolute convergence: regression results

	Male LEXP Cross section		Female LEXP Cross section	
Explanatory variable \statistic↓	1996–2001	2006–11	1996–2001	2006–11
Intercept	−.090	.027	.082	−.103
	(−2.75)	(0.82)	(2.11*)	(−3.59*)
Life expectancy	−.0207	−.005	−.0185	−.023
initial period	(−2.75*)	(−0.71)	(−1.98**)	(−3.59*)
R^2	.318	.0375@	.172	.459
F statistic and DF	7.54*, 15	.51,15	3.91**, 15	12.92†, 15

Source: Estimated.

* = 5% level of significance; ** = 10% level of significance; † = denotes significance at 1% level; @ = R2.

estimated coefficients is observed to be annually respectively .410 and .10 (for males) and .367 and .455 (for females).[10]

The results for special category states and non–special category states are also presented in Table 6.78. Further, the results for the fixed effect panel model relating to life expectancy for males and females (Tables 6.79 and 6.80) indicate significant convergence, with the speed being 1.428 and .823 (Table 6.87; this table is common for speed of convergence for all the results discussed from 6.79 onwards). The conditional convergence for males pertaining to life expectancy indicates the significance of education and budgetary health expenditure by the government (Table 6.80). In the presence of these conditional variables the speed of convergence for males is estimated as 3.412. Likewise for females, with the same variables as significant (Table 6.81), results indicate a speed of convergence as 2.033 (Table 6.87).

Further, across non–special and special category states the results of absolute convergence for budgetary health expenditure (as percentage of total budget of the respective state government) indicate convergence for the non–special category states for both the cross sections of 2005–06 and 2010–11 (Table 6.83). The speed of convergence is estimated as 2.208 and 2.033 (Table 6.87). The results of special category states, however, indicate divergence in cross sections (Table 6.84). In the case of fixed effect panel data models a similar convergence is observed, with speed now being as 2.287 for the non–special category of states (Table 6.87). Divergence is again indicated for the special category of states with fixed effect model (Table 6.84).

Panel results for per capita budgetary expenditure for revenue expenditure indicate convergence only for average-income and rich states (Table 6.85 and 6.86), with the speed of convergence as 0.162 (Table 6.87). For poor states the statistical significance is not observed (Table 6.86). A similar result pertaining to capital expenditure is observed, with both rich as well as poor states not indicating a statistically significant coefficient.

Table 6.78 Absolute convergence: regression results HEXP

Explanatory variable \statistic↓	Non-special category states cross section		Special category states cross section	
	2000–05	2006–11	2000–05	2006–11
Intercept	.118	.163	−.215	−.149
	(1.54)	(4.23†)	(−3.13*)	(−1.82)
Life expectancy	−.1167	−.107	.127	.116
initial period	(−2.32*)	(−3.84†)	(2.66*)	(2.11**)
R^2	.214	.462	.377	.257
F statistic and DF	5.37*, 17	14.74†, 17	7.06*, 11	4.46**, 11

Source: Estimated.

† = 1% level of significance; * = 5% level of significance; ** = 10% level of significance.

Table 6.79 Convergence fixed-effect model (numbers in brackets refer to the t-values)

LEXP males unconditional convergence (1996–2001)	
Constant	315 (4.00*)
Initial level	−.074 (−3.94*)
Sigma-u	.0003
Sigma-e	.0001
Rho	.8810
F-test that all $u_i = 0$	2.18**
R^2 within	.526
R^2 between	.271
R^2 overall	.225
Correlation (u_i, x_b)	−.923
Observations	30
Number of groups	15
Observations per group	2

Source: Estimated.

* = significance at 5%; ** = significance at 10%.

This result is further substantiated if we plot the mean deviations of per capita public expenditure on health for both categories of states, which indicate convergence for average-income and rich states and divergence for poor states (Figures 6.6 and 6.7).

Policy recommendations

Keeping in view the preceding results, we suggest four policy measures to overcome divergence in poorer states and speed up convergence for average-income and rich states. These include:

1   Utilizing the Thirteenth Finance Commission's incentive grants
2   Making use of NRHM resources as additional resources and not supplementing them for state government budgetary expenditure

Table 6.80 Convergence fixed-effect model (numbers in brackets refer to the t-values)

LEXP males conditional convergence (1996–2001)

Constant	.802 (4.10*)
Initial level LEXP	–.186 (–4.26†)
LN PCI	–0036 (–1.17)
LN HEXP	.004 (1.85**)
LN EDU	.001 (2.11**)
Sigma-u	.0111
Sigma-e	.0001
rho	.9900
F-test that all ui = 0	2.98*
R² within	.773
R² between	.349
R² overall	.228
Correlation (u$_i$, x$_b$)	–.988
Observations	30
Number of groups	15
Observations per group	2

Source: Estimated.

† = significance at 1%; * = significance at 5%; ** = significance at 10%.

Table 6.81 Convergence fixed-effect model (numbers in brackets refer to the t-values)

LEXP Females unconditional convergence (1996–2001)

Constant	.180 (2.72*)
Initial level	–.042 (–2.65*)
Sigma-u	.0025
Sigma-e	.0012
rho	.8038
F-test that all ui = 0	5.08†
R² within	.3341
R² between	.360
R² overall	.341
Correlation (u$_i$, x$_b$)	–.616
Observations	30
Number of groups	15
Observations per group	2

Source: Estimated.

† = significance at 1%; * = significance at 5%; ** = significance at 10%.

3 Increasing the level of per capita health expenditure as envisaged in the national health policy (GoI 2002b)
4 Improving efficiency of resource use

According to the Thirteenth Finance Commission recommendations, the Sample Registration System (SRS) measuring IMR for 2009 will be the baseline from

Table 6.82 Convergence fixed-effect model (numbers in brackets refer to the t-values)

LEXP Females conditional convergence (1996–2001)	
Constant	.416 (2.04**)
Initial level LEXP	−.107 (−1.86**)
LN PCI	.0008 (0.70)
LN HEXP	−.0002 (−0.08)
LN FEEDU	.007 (0.80)
Sigma-u	.0060
Sigma-e	.0013
rho	.9556
F-test that all ui = 0	4.00*
R^2 within	.459
R^2 between	.271
R^2 overall	.253
Correlation (u_i, x_b)	−.921
Observations	30
Number of groups	15
Observations per group	2

Source: Estimated.

† = significance at 1%; * = significance at 5%; ** = significance at 10%.

Table 6.83 Convergence fixed-effect model (numbers in brackets refer to the t-values)

HEXP Non–special category states unconditional convergence (2000–11)	
Constant	.390 (6.59†)
Initial level	−.286 (−6.97†)
Sigma-u	.0424
Sigma-e	.0317
rho	.641
F-test that all ui = 0	2.18**
R^2 within	.752
R^2 between	.228
R^2 overall	.437
Correlation (u_i, x_b)	−.6243
Observations	34
Number of groups	17
Observations per group	2

Source: Estimated.

† = significance at 1%; * = significance at 5%; ** = significance at 10%.

which improvement of each state will be measured. The annual improvement in these indicators, as determined from the SRS bulletin, for the succeeding years will be measured from that base line. It is suggested that reward for performance in such cases be based upon a formula with two components: the first is to reward positive movement in the value of the parameter, and the second is to provide a

Table 6.84 Convergence fixed-effect model (numbers in brackets refer to the t-values)

HEXP special category states unconditional convergence (2000–11)	
Constant	−.347 (−3.64†)
Initial level	.236 (3.59†)
Sigma-u	.0396
Sigma-e	.0487
rho	.3981
F-test that all ui = 0	0.79
R^2 within	.563
R^2 between	.199
R^2 overall	.349
Correlation (u_i, x_b)	−.6356
Observations	22
Number of groups	11
Observations per group	2

Source: Estimated.

† = significance at 1%; * = significance at 5%; ** = significance at 10%.

Table 6.85 Convergence fixed-effect model (numbers in brackets refer to the t-values)

Per capita budgetary expenditure on health (rich and average-income states) unconditional convergence (1990–2010)	
Constant	.265 (3.15†)
Initial level	−.033 (−2.06*)
Sigma-u	.0306
Sigma-e	.0510
Rho	.2652
F-test that all ui = 0	0.97
R^2 within	.127
R^2 between	.045
R^2 overall	.026
Correlation (u_i, x_b)	−.5257
Observations	40
Number of groups	10
Observations per group	4

Source: Estimated.

† = significance at 1%; * = significance at 5%; ** = significance at 10%.

premium if such change is made above the median value of the parameter for all states. Thus, states are rewarded for both improvement in the parameter as well as the level at which the improvement is made. Each state's eligibility will be determined annually, based upon improvement in the IMR index. An amount of INR 5,000 crores for this grant over a 3-year period between 2012 and 2015 has been recommended. Details of scheduling this grant are presented in Table 6.88. Data pertaining to 2009–10, available in 2010, is the baseline for computing eligibility for all the succeeding years. Disbursal of grants will commence from

Table 6.86 Convergence fixed-effect model (numbers in brackets refer to the t-values)

Per capita budgetary expenditure on health (poor states) unconditional convergence (1990–2010)	
Constant	.152 (1.13)
Initial level	−.013 (−0.48)
Sigma-u	.0210
Sigma-e	.0610
rho	.1064
F-test that all ui = 0	0.42
R^2 within	.0132
R^2 between	.0194
R^2 overall	.0001
Correlation (u_i, x_b)	−.348
Observations	24
Number of groups	6
Observations per group	4

Source: Estimated.

† = significance at 1%; * = significance at 5%; ** = significance at 10%.

Table 6.87 Calculation for speed of convergence: absolute and conditional convergence

	beta	Speed of C(λ) (ln1–beta/years)	A. Rate of C	Half-life (ln hal/lambda)
Male LEXP (1996–2001)	0.021	0.004	0.410	169.154
Male LEXP (2006–11)	0.005	0.001	0.100	694.879
Female LEXP (1996–2001)	0.019	0.004	0.367	189.065
Female LEXP (2006–11)	0.023	0.005	0.455	152.410
Non-special category states				
HEXP (2000–05)	−0.117	0.022	2.208	31.399
HEXP (2006–11)	−0.107	0.020	2.033	34.094
Calculation for speed of convergence for fixed effect models				
Absolute convergence				
Male LEXP (1996–2001)	−0.074	0.014	1.428	48.547
Female LEXP (1996–2001)	−0.042	0.008	0.823	84.239
Conditional convergence				
Male LEXP (1996–2001)	−0.186	0.034	3.412	20.317
Female LEXP (1996–2001)	−0.107	0.020	2.033	34.094
Absolute convergence non-special category states				
HEXP (2000–01–2010–11)	−0.286	0.023	2.287	30.312
PC BEXH (1990–2010)				
Rich and average-income states	−0.033	0.002	0.162	426.983
Poor states	−0.013	0.001	0.065	1,073.297

Source: Estimated.

A = annual; C = convergence; BEXH = budgetary expenditure on health.

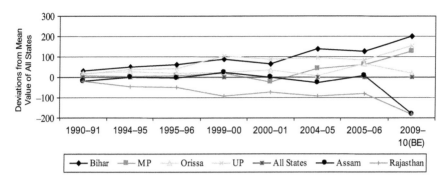

Figure 6.6 Deviation of per capita public expenditure (from mean value across all states) in poorer states

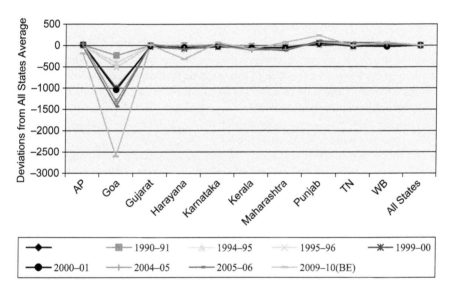

Figure 6.7 Deviation of per capita public expenditure (from the mean value across states) in average-income and rich states

Table 6.88 Scheduling of IMR incentive grant

Year	Amount (Rs. crore)	Calendar year of measurement baseline	Year of release of SRS report
2010–11		2009	2010
2012–13	1,500	2011	2012
2013–14	1,500	2012	2013
2014–15	2,000	2013	2014

Sources: GoI (2009a, 2009b); Thirteenth Finance Commission, 2010–2015, vol. 1, p. 219.

2012–13. This will give the states a period of 2 years to make improvements. During 2012–13, the cumulative change in IMR between the years 2009, 2010 and 2011 for each state will be applied to the Thirteenth Finance Commission formula (presented in Annex 12.10 to the Report). For 2013–14, the cumulative change between 2009 and 2012 will be applied to the formula. The same procedure will be followed for the succeeding year. The grant will be released in three annual installments between 2012–13 and 2014–15. This will be after the publication of the annual SRS bulletin/report incorporating statewide IMR statistics for the relevant year (Table 6.88).

In addition, some other states will also be given special grants as per their memorandum submitted to the Thirteenth Finance Commission. These include an amount of Rs. 250 crores to Madhya Pradesh for critical infrastructure in the state to improve the health care delivery system in the state, an amount of Rs. 275 crores to Orissa for upgrading its health infrastructure and a grant of Rs. 300 crore to Rajasthan for the construction of subcenters, primary health centers and additions to the subdivisional and district hospitals.

It is pertinent that the states should increase their health expenditure along with NRHM grants. However, at present, despite the fact that states should provide matching contributions, the lack of any such stipulation that this contribution be additional makes the states follow a policy of substituting expenditure on health in other areas rather than as it is envisaged under NRHM priorities. This thus defeats the very purpose of reducing deficiency in poorer districts and therefore does not lead to an improvement in reducing divergence.

As mentioned in the health policy document, the need for increasing funds has not been captured in actual implementation. As such, this public spending as percentage of GDP in India has remained almost stagnant, varying from 0.9 per cent to 1.2 per cent of GDP in the period 1990–2010. Thus an additional budgetary effort is a necessity to cope with increasing requirements for the important area of health care. Moreover, even out of this low public expenditure about 28 per cent has been on tertiary health care, which in fact was targeted at 10 per cent in the national health policy.

Lastly, within the states, a further analysis by us earlier at the district level in Madhya Pradesh and West Bengal (poorer states) and Karnataka, Maharashtra and Punjab (richer states) indicates that outcomes in the health sector are being influenced by inefficient utilization of limited budgetary resources due to various factors comprising misallocation of funds across inputs, low productivity and local political bureaucratic hurdles (Purohit, 2010a, 2010b, 2010c, 2010d). Thus any financing strategy aiming at reducing disparities should also take into account overcoming not only inadequacy but also inefficiency in allocation and utilization of health care inputs (Purohit, 2010e).

Notes

1 BIMARU means 'sickly' in the Hindi language.
2 http://in.news.yahoo.com/070308/43/6d09p.html
3 We also tried the alternative model using random effects. However, the results of the Hausman test indicated a fixed effect model.

4 We also tried the alternative model using random effects. However, the results of the Hausman test indicated a fixed effect model.

5 According to the neoclassical growth model, given the fully competitive markets and the availability of similar technology, for the same rate of investment every economy would grow at a similar rate determined by the exogenous technical progress and population growth. Assuming a production function with constant returns to scale and the diminishing returns of capital, economies with lower levels of initial productivity enjoy a higher rate of growth in productivity and as such will catch up with the more developed economies.

6 In the empirical literature, running a cross section regression of the time-averaged per capita income growth rate on the level of per capita income in the initial period tests this. A negative sign for the respective coefficient reflects the existence of convergence.

7 This type of convergence may be tested in the same way except that the regression should also include a set of explanatory variables which would define the steady-state growth path for per capita income. A negative coefficient for the per capita income in the initial period, in the presence of the extra conditional variables, suggests the existence of conditional beta convergence.

8 For a detailed review of these studies see, for instance, Purohit 2012.

9 Thus, beta convergence is a necessary condition for the existence of sigma convergence, while sigma convergence might not accompany beta convergence.

10 Speed of adjustment for all the results in Tables 6.77–6.86 are given in Table 6.87.

7 Executive summary and policy imperatives for social sector efficiency in India

The social sector has an important place in the state budgetary expenditure. From around 5.8 per cent, its share in total state expenditure has varied between 36.8 per cent (in 1990–95) to 39.2 per cent (2010–11; RBI 2012). Within the social sector, the major chunk (nearly 57%) is being spent on Education, Sports, Art and Culture (46.1%) and Medical and Public Health (10.5%). The other items, such as Family Welfare and Water Supply and Sanitation; Housing; Urban Development; Welfare of Scheduled Castes (SC), Scheduled Tribes (ST) and Other Backward Castes (OBC); Labour and Labour Welfare; Social Security and Welfare, Nutrition, Natural Calamities and the rest, make up a low percentage, which varies from 1.3 per cent (Natural Calamities) to 9.6 per cent (Social Security and Welfare) of the total social sector.

Utilizing UNDP's 1991 report terminology, which introduced three indicators, namely public expenditure ratio, social allocation ratio and social priority ratio (UNDP 1991), we find that two of these ratios considering the scenario for all the Indian states from 1990 to 2012–13, viz., overall public expenditure ratio remains 15 per cent, and the social allocation ratio has touched 40 per cent but remained lower than UNDP's optimal level and varied over the years from 33 per cent to more than 39 per cent. Overall, excluding central government expenditure, the Indian states have spent 5.2 per cent to 6.4 per cent of their GDP.

Focussing on two major segments of the social sector – health and education – it is observed that India has indeed achieved important milestones. In the former of these two segments, during 1947 to 2004 life expectancy doubled from 32 years to 64.6 years. In addition, other indicators, such as declining IMR, reduced malaria incidence and eradication of diseases like smallpox and guinea worm are highlights of the health sector. Despite all these achievements, there are numerous disconcerting features and emerging issues concerning the health care sector in India, which include: our large total population (16.5% of global total) accounting for one-fifth of the world's share of diseases; a third of the diarrhoel diseases, TB, respiratory and parasitic infections; a quarter of maternal conditions, a fifth of nutritional deficiencies, diabetes and venereal diseases; and the second largest number of HIV/AIDS cases after South Africa (GoI 2005d).

In addition to these observations, there are a number of undesirable outcomes of the health system. These are: widespread disparity across rural and urban areas as well as poor and rich states, neglect of some of the society's emerging health needs and inefficient functioning of public health sector (Purohit 2004, 2008). Thus, instead of playing a major role, public sector investment is providing a major impetus to the private sector for an investment that is more inequitable and less regulated. Even the low public investment and its largest chunk (nearly 70%) goes towards recurring expenditures, including wages and salaries. Thus, only a small percentage is spent on medicines and drugs for patients' care. With increasing prices, this amounts to a real per capita expenditure of only Rs. 120. This is reflected also in the availability and quality of care in the public sector. According to a study carried out by the National Commission on Macroeconomics and Health (NCMH; GoI 2005c), in terms of IMR and safe deliveries, poorly performing states (e.g. Madhya Pradesh, Orissa and Uttar Pradesh) actually spent more on primary care relative to better-performing southern states. In terms of international comparison, even countries such as Bangladesh and Indonesia, spending relatively less on health care than India, have lower IMR (World Bank 2003). Corroborated further by *World Health Report* (WHO 2005), India's health-related indicators are indeed lower than those in similarly placed countries like Bangladesh, Sri Lanka and Nepal. In fact, India has higher infant mortality per thousand and a lower life expectancy than countries like Sri Lanka and China.[1]

Thus, not only inefficiency but also overall inadequate and inequitable availability of resources in the public sector have had an adverse impact on the poor.[2]

Consequently, within the country, considerable inequity has emerged in terms of health achievements: higher infant mortality rate, for instance, in rural areas (62.2 per thousand live births) relative to urban areas (41.5 per thousand live births); a notable disparity between better-performing states like Kerala (IMR = 15.3), Maharashtra (37.5) and Tamil Nadu (30.4) and lower performers like Orissa (IMR = 64.7), Bihar (61.7), Rajasthan (65.3), Uttar Pradesh (72.7) and Madhya Pradesh (69.5; NFHS-3); uneven benefits across different segments of the society particularly women, children and socially disadvantaged populations such as scheduled castes (IMR = 66.4) and scheduled tribes (62.1) (NFHS-3, International Institute for Population Sciences and Macro International 2007).

Thus, over the years, the inefficiency and inadequacy of public sector health care services has also propelled the expansion of private sector services. Indeed, the private sector in India has gained prominence, particularly after liberalization (Purohit 2001a; GOI 2005a). It has catered to every segment of health sector and an estimated 98.68 per cent of private institutions, remain in the for-profit sector (GoI 2005a). In terms of total investment, a study by CII-McKinsey (CII and McKinsey & Company 2002) estimated it to be of overall worth of Rs. 69,000 crores, which was projected to double by 2012, and supported by an additional health insurance of Rs. 39,000. As such, the private sector currently absorbs nearly three-quarters of human resources and technology, 68 per cent of 15,047 hospitals and 37 per cent of 623,819 beds in the country (GoI 2005c).

A considerable investment is actually also being made by NRIs and industrial/pharmaceutical companies (Purohit 2001a). These private providers are fast becoming a provider for upper-income groups and with high-tech care, these providers are also making India a potential hub of medical tourism. However, the trend in insurance and the growing role of corporate hospitals may result in an overall increase in the cost of care. This may further lead to increased dependence of the majority of poor and lower-middle-income groups on the public health sector.

There also has been a major policy directive that curative care can be left to the market forces and resources thus released can be dedicated to primary care. This could be observed in both the National Health Policies (GoI 1983, 2002b). The same emphasis in health policy is seen from the central and state governments, which have extended a number of exemptions in the last decade and half. These have been mainly in the form of excise and import duty exemptions, land subsidy and concessional bank credit. However, an empirical study by NCMH (GoI 2005a) indicates that encouragement and sole reliance on only the private sector for even curative care could be contrary to the objective of health policy. It suggests that private health care is marked by fragmentation of the provider market; near absence of private sector providers in the poorest blocks; an overall small size of private OPD clinics; an urban concentration; abysmally low per capita ratio of doctors; a high proliferation of technology-intensive machines; low bed occupancy ratio in relation to public facilities; substandard treatment; high cost of care and concentration of three-quarters of specialists and technology in few towns (GoI 2005a). If we presume that the private, for-profit sector is going to be a replacement for the public sector provider in the delivery of curative health care, these features indeed restrict such optimism and possibly indicate a high cost even in the presence of universal insurance. Given the equity, efficiency and cost implications of sole dependence on the private sector, it is pertinent to look into the possibility of enhancing efficiency in the public sector or achieving an optimal mix of public and private sector funding as well as other alternatives, such as not-for-profit community-based organizations charged with bringing better health outcomes to the country.

An overview of health care sector outcomes in India thus conveys a need to dwell in greater detail on the pertinent issue of the efficiency of the system and other factors that have led to the current situation marked by lack of availability, accessibility and affordability of healthcare facilities in the country.

India's education system is divided into pre-primary, primary, elementary and secondary levels as well as undergraduate and postgraduate levels. The government has laid emphasis on primary education up to the age of 14 years, referred to as elementary education. In fact, 80 per cent of all recognized schools at the elementary stage are government run or supported, making it the largest provider of education in the country. Owing to quality or availability factors, nearly 27 per cent of Indian children are privately educated, and this percentage is much higher in urban areas. However, the number of private schools in India is still low; the share of private institutions is 7 per cent (upper primary being 21% and secondary 32%). Improving public sector education efficiency in elementary education thus helps achieve literacy at a higher pace.

Generally, health system or education performance can be monitored with either efficiency, effectiveness, or economy. Efficiency is defined as the extent to which a health agency or health system maximizes the outputs produced from a given set of inputs or minimizes the input cost of producing a given set of outputs. Effectiveness is the extent to which programs and services (outputs) of a system achieve the desired outcomes. Economy refers to buying appropriate quality resources or inputs in the most economic manner (or at least cost).

However, use of any performance measure requires defining robust measures of outputs and inputs. Public health agencies (e.g. hospitals, primary health centres, government primary schools and the like) which provide unpriced services outside the market mechanism bristle with the conceptual difficulty of such a precise definition of outputs and inputs.

More often we discuss that how well the service delivery units of general government agencies convert inputs of labour, materials and capital into outputs of services. This is captured by means of the concept of the production function. It describes the relationship between the output (number of treatments) and the input (number of labour hours). The nature of the output-input relationship depends on the particular production technology or the skills of the labour input that is used to convert the inputs into the outputs. Generally, we measure efficiency by developing an idealized yardstick against which the overall or individual health set-up is compared. This has been done by deploying frontier efficiency measurement techniques which involve a production possibility frontier depicting a locus of potentially technically efficient output combinations that an organization or health system is capable of producing at a point in time. An output combination below this frontier is termed as technically inefficient.

Empirical studies in the healthcare sector have laid emphasis on the overall health system performance and its impact on health outcomes. Our review of studies indicates that there have been numerous attempts by researchers across the globe in recent years to address the empirical measurement of efficiency in health care institutions. These attempts focus on system endowments and the efficient utilization of resources within the system which could produce health outcomes that can be appropriately measured by a suitable method. Thus the studies pertaining to health care sector efficiency for both developed and developing countries have frequently used the data envelopment technique or stochastic frontier models within a system framework of a multicountry[3] or country-specific analysis. At the latter level, the studies have been carried out in the countries across different continents including America,[4] Europe,[5] Asia,[6] Africa[7] and Australia.[8] Most of these studies have covered either a country-specific or state-specific health system. They have focused on different set-ups encompassing hospitals, nursing homes, HMOs and district health authorities. Country-level analysis has also been done by many researchers. Despite exhaustive literature which provides us in detail the steps and empirical problems researchers face, very few studies focus on the developing countries' context. Particularly in the Indian context, there is a paucity of literature on such studies for recent periods. The available literature on the subject relates only to an all-India or a state-level analysis. The few studies in the Indian context mostly have remained focused at either the sectoral level, i.e. the all-India rural or urban sector, or the analysis has been carried out up to state-level aggregates only and the period of coverage is up to the year 2005. None have so far attempted a substate-level analysis. In this regard, our study makes a new attempt to extend health system efficiency analysis to focus on the health care system at the substate level (i.e. district level) in India and also at the state-level aggregate covering the period from 2000 to 2010. In the attempt to fill this gap, our study involves the measurement and analysis of health system performance in India focusing at three levels: all-India, state and substate (or district) levels. In the education sector no published study on India provides efficiency estimates for elementary education. Our study covers this gap. The major Indian states included in state-level coverage are Gujarat, Haryana, Maharashtra and Punjab (all high-income States); Karnataka, Kerala, Andhra Pradesh and Tamil Nadu (all middle-income States); and Bihar, Madhya Pradesh, Orissa, Rajasthan, Uttar Pradesh and West Bengal (all low-income States). For a substate-level analysis, the focus of this study is on five states: two better-off States, Punjab and Maharashtra; two low-income states, Madhya Pradesh and West Bengal; and one middle-income State, Karnataka.

Database

This study is based on secondary data. At the all-India level, main variables used in the study are life expectancy (LEXP), infant mortality rates (IMR), per capita income and other parameters related to health infrastructure, health manpower (medical and paramedical), and other variables relevant for depicting healthcare facilities, their utilization and health outcomes, and socio-economic parameters such as income, education, and basic amenities. In the case of education, the major source is *State Report Cards for Elementary Education in India* published annually by the National University of Educational Planning and Administration (NUEPA), New Delhi. Major variables used in the estimation for education sector efficiency include enrolment at primary level and upper primary level, enrolment of girls at primary and upper primary level and enrolment in government schools and other variables like facilities: toilets, and drinking water, student classroom ratio; manpower variables, availability of female teachers; ages of schools, utilization of school development or teaching learning material grants or enrolment of students from the categories of scheduled castes and scheduled tribes.

At the substate level for the health sector, information is collected from *Human Development Reports* of Punjab (GoP 2004), Maharashtra (GoM 2002), Karnataka (GoK 2006), Madhya Pradesh (GoMP 2002) and West Bengal (GoWB 2004).Websites of the states and other published sources have also been used. The information relates to the district level for each of the five states.

Our hypothesis and results

We use two types of techniques, namely nonparametric and parametric, that allow for a direct measurement of the relative efficiency of government spending among states. In the former type we apply free disposal hull (FDH) analysis, which assesses the relative efficiency of production units in a market environment. The major advantages of FDH analysis are that it imposes only weak restrictions on the production technology while allowing for a comparison of efficiency levels among producers. The only assumption made is that inputs and/or outputs can be freely disposed of, so that it is possible with the same production technology to lower outputs while maintaining the level of inputs and to increase the inputs while maintaining outputs at the same level. Thus, FDH analysis provides an intuitive tool that can be used to identify best practices in government spending and to assess how governments are faring in comparison with these best practices.[9] Depending upon the availability of latest and comparable information, we have applied this technique for data on major and smaller Indian states for education covering different cross sections from 2003 to 2011 and for health covering the period 2001–10. This analysis covers fifteen major Indian states (Andhra Pradesh, Assam, Bihar, Gujarat, Harayana, Karnataka, Kerala, Madhya Pradesh, Maharashtra, Orissa, Punjab, Rajasthan, Tamil Nadu, Uttar Pradesh, and West Bengal) and ten smaller states (Arunachal Pradesh, Chhattisgarh, Goa, Himachal Pradesh, Jammu and Kashmir, Jharkhand, Manipur, Meghalaya, Mizoram and Nagaland).

For the parametric approach, we cover the same fifteen major states as in the nonparametric approach and use panel data for 2000–05 and 2005–11. We extend our estimation to the second stage, which presumes that differences in technical efficiency pertaining to health systems can be discerned at the health facility planning level from non-health-related parameters. In our estimation of health system efficiency, our specification is based on a general stochastic frontier model which considers the health output (life expectancy or inverse of IMR) produced by a health system as a function of vector of factor inputs. This implies that technical efficiency of the jth health system is a relative measure of its output as a proportion of the corresponding frontier output. A health system is technically efficient if its output level is on the frontier which in turn means that q/q^* equals 1 in value.

It is presumed that estimated efficiency parameters should help the makers of health policy to improve district-level and thereby state-level health system performance. We hypothesize that districts differ in their technical efficiency pertaining to the health system due to factors which require emphasis in planning health facilities at the district level. It is also hypothesized that these factors differ among states according to their level of development.

The results of the frontier model, using panel data for fourteen major Indian states pertaining to the years 2000–05, indicate that the efficiency of the public health delivery system remains low. There is considerable disparities across states in terms of per capita availability and utilization of hospitals, beds and manpower inputs and this had an adverse impact on improving life expectancy in the states. Overcoming these factoral disparities and improvement in efficiency may result in an improved life expectancy at a higher rate and more equitably in the poorly performing states of Bihar, Madhya Pradesh, Orissa, Rajasthan and Uttar Pradesh. In the regression results using dispersion in health system efficiency (DISPERSION), endogeneity[10] was doubted for per capita income. To identify this possible endogeneity, we used per capita budgetary expenditure on health as instrument. The results using instrumental variable method and two stage least square methods (2SLS) indicated that per capita budgetary expenditure on health could be used as an instrument for per capita income, and this is retained in the final regression.

It is suggested from our results that the efforts to overcome factoral disparities within the health system at the state level have to be supplemented with other adequate infrastructure facilities (e.g. safe drinking water supply in rural habitats) to improve the outcomes in deficient states. It may require a considerable reorientation of the current healthcare set-up and a reallocation of surplus manpower. Part of low availability of medicines and materials due to different budgetary expenditure of the states may be overcome by NRHM funds and other efforts like better coordination between economic and social sector policies may also lead to optimal results The results from our district-level analysis have indicated that health sector efficiency in the five states, namely Punjab, Maharashtra, Karnataka, Madhya Pradesh and West Bengal can be improved by overcoming disparities in performance at the district level. There are specific factors for each of the states which should be tackled by using the results of our district-level analysis. Generally across the states, this would require policy initiatives to help the poorer-performing districts through adequate support and specifically different measures discussed in the context of individual states.

The frontier estimation for education was carried out using a set of explanatory variables – facilities such as common toilets, girls' toilets, drinking water facilities and student classroom ratio; manpower variables such as pupil teacher ratio, availability of female teachers and age of schools in terms of older schools established since 1994; and other policy inputs such as utilization of school development or teaching learning material grants, or enrolment of students in the categories of scheduled castes and scheduled tribes. These variables explain enrolment at the primary and upper-primary levels, enrolment of girls at the primary and upper-primary levels and enrolment in government schools.

There are notable interstate variations in terms of achieved efficiency relative to the norm established by frontier estimation. For instance, in primary level enrolment, a high-income state like Maharashtra ranks highest and is followed by Uttar Pradesh and Rajasthan. The lowest performer appears to be Orissa. The major difference between Maharashtra and Orissa is in the numbers of private schools and enrolment in private schools (per 1,000 population), which are very low for the latter (.02 and 1.984 respectively) relative to Maharashtra (at .05 and 14.69). In upper-primary enrolments Kerala is highest, with Orissa at the bottom. The reasons are traced back in the availability of facilities (schools) and manpower variables (teachers) in these two states. In particular, the extent of private teachers per capita is much higher in Kerala (.19) relative to Orissa (.08). In primary-level enrolments of girls, Karnataka is the highest achiever, with Punjab being the lowest. This difference could be due in part to different values of determining variables in these states, which include girls' toilets, pupil-teacher ratio, number of female teachers and age of the schools. Pertaining to girls' enrolment at the upper-primary level, the highest achiever for girls' enrolment emerges is Rajasthan (65%), followed by Karnataka (46.42%), and the lowest is Bihar (23%). The reasons for this difference in performance between Rajasthan and Bihar seem to be lower magnitudes of four variables in the latter – girls' toilets, student classroom ratio, pupil teacher ratio and established older schools. In terms of enrolment in government schools at the primary level, Bihar tops the list with 97 per cent achievement. This is followed by West Bengal (92%) and Orissa (91%); Kerala (27.46) has the lowest value relative to frontier norm. Thus interstate variations at different levels are due more to availability of basic facilities in either government or private sector schools.

Thus, overall our analysis indicates that disparities are prevalent not only across the states but also at the substate level, in both the richer and poorer states. It is imperative that these be accounted for in any state-level planning exercise, and resource allocation at the district level should be fine-tuned to remove such disparities. Without this, improvement in the performance of the health care system may not be easily feasible. Even the education sector needs more budgetary resources to enhance basic facilities in primary schools in the Indian states to improve the various enrolment ratios.

Further, we also test the development paradigm that the inequity across states will converge and the adjustment period will be lowered for equitable outcomes in health. It may require a change in focus of health policy and the budgetary emphasis of states. This result is substantiated as we plot the mean deviations of per capita public expenditure on health for two categories of states which indicate convergence for average- and high-income states and divergence for poor states.

Policy recommendations

Keeping in view the results discussed previously, we suggest four policy measures to overcome divergence in poorer states and speed up convergence for average and rich category of states. These may include: Improving the efficiency of resource use in light of our estimates both at the state and substate levels and also taking state specific factors into account; better adherence to policy directives envisaged in the national health policy (GoI 2003) and policy emphasis on elementary education by increasing the level of per capita health and education expenditures; use of NRHM resources as additional inputs instead of supplementing them for state governments increased budgetary expenditure and better utilization of other supplementary resources which are based on Thirteenth Finance Commission's incentive grants. These steps may speed up the convergence across the Indian states and bring about the desirable outcomes of equity and growth in social sectors.

Notes

1 Under-five mortality in India is 87 compared to corresponding figures of 69, 82, 15 and 37 for Bangladesh, Nepal, Sri Lanka and China. Likewise, life expectancy in India is 62 years in comparison to 63, 61, 71 and 71 for these countries respectively (UNDP 2006).

2 As indicated by the 52nd round of NSS, among the poor (in 1995–96), 61 per cent used public facilities compared to 33 per cent among the rich. Besides, overall utilization of government hospitals by the upper quintiles accounted for a higher share of total care, and utilization by the rural poor declined between 1986–87 and 1995–96.

3 See for instance Evans et al. 2000; Tandon et al. 2000; Spinks and Hollingsworth 2005; Greene 2002; Richardson, Robertson and Wildman 2001; Hollingsworth and Wildman 2002b; Jayasuriya and Wodon 2002.

4 Schmacker and McKay 2008; Jeffrey and Coppola 2004; Knox et al. 2001; Bates et al. 2006; Rosko 2001.

5 Kontodimopoulos et al. 2003; Gannon 2004; St. Aubyn 2002; Puig-Junoy1998; Farsi et al. 2007; Mainardi 2007; Kittelsen and Magnussen 1999; Magnussen 1996; Mirmirani 2008; Hofmarcher et al. 2002.

6 Li and Wang 2008; Sankar and Kathuria 2004; Mathiyazhgan 2006; Purohit 2010b; Suraratdechaac and Okunadeb 2006; Hajialiafzali et al. 2007.

7 Masiye 2007.

8 Wang et al. 2006; Yong and Harris 1999; Mortimer and Peacock 2000.

9 Some of the studies which have employed FDH analysis include, for instance, Deprins et al. 1984, Tulkens and Vanden Eeckaut 1995 and Fakin and de Crombrugghe 1997.

10 Some of our variables used as explanatory variables might have been influenced by endogeneity, said to occur in models in which economically endogenous variables are determined by each other and some additional economically exogenous variables. The simultaneity gives rise to empirical models with variables that do not satisfy the zero conditional mean assumption (Baum 2006, pp. 186–215). To derive consistent estimates we generally use an instrument variable method (IVM). This method consists in finding an instrument variable (IV) that satisfies two properties: the IV must be uncorrelated with error term and must be highly correlated with the variable which is influenced by endogeneity. Keeping in view this problem, we identified the endogenous variable by using the instrument variable method.

References

Abel-Smith, B. (1992). Health insurance in developing countries: Lessons from experience. *Health Policy Plan, 3,* 215–226.

Abel-Smith, B. (1993). *The health insurance system in Vietnam.* Stockholm: Assignment report for SIDA.

Abel-Smith, B., and Dua, A. (1988). Community financing in developing countries: The potential for the health sector. *Health Policy Plan, 3,* 95–108.

Ahluwalia, Montek S. (2000, May 6). Economic performance of states in post-reforms period. *Economic and Political Weekly, 35* (19), 1637–1648.

Ahluwalia, Montek S. (2002). State level performance under economic reforms in India. In Anne Krueger (Ed.), *Economic policy reforms and the Indian economy.* Chicago: University of Chicago Press.

Adabar, K. (2005). *The regional dimensions of economic growth in India's federalism* (unpublished doctoral dissertation). Bangalore: Institute for Social and Economic Change.

Afonso, A., and Fernandes, S. (2006). Local government spending efficiency: DEA evidence for the Lisbon region. *Regional Studies, 40* (1), 39–53.

Afonso, A., and St. Aubyn, M. (2005a). *Cross-country efficiency of secondary education provision: A semi-parametric analysis with non-discretionary inputs* (Working Paper No. 494). European Central Bank.

Afonso, A., and St. Aubyn, M. (2005b). Non-parametric approaches to education and health efficiency in OECD countries. *Journal of Applied Economics, 8* (2), 227–246.

Afonso, A., Schuknecht, L., and Tanzi, V. (2005). Public sector efficiency: An international comparison. *Public Choice, 123* (3–4), 321–347.

Ahmed, R. (2012). The public sector efficiency in the education department. *Public Policy and Administration Research, 2* (3). ISSN 2224-5731 (Paper), ISSN 2225-0972 (Online). www.iiste.org.

Akin, J. (1987, July–August). Health insurance in developing countries: Prospects for risk sharing. In *Health care financing: Proceedings of regional seminar on health care financing,* pp. 191–236. Manila, Philippines: Asian Development Bank.

Alam, Moneer. (2004). Aging old age income security and reforms: An exploration of Indian situation. *Economic and Political Weekly, 39* (33), 3731–3740.

Anderson, R. I., Lewis, D., Webb, J. R. (1999). The efficiency of nursing home chains and the implications of non-profit status. *Journal of Real Estate Portfolio Management, 5* (3), 235–245.

Annigeri, V. B. (2003, May 17). District health accounts: An empirical investigation. *Economic and Political Weekly, 38* (20), 1989–1993.

Arbia, G., Basile, R., and Piras, G. (2005, September). *Using spatial panel data in modelling: Regional growth and convergence* (Working Paper No. 55). Rome, Italy: Istituto Di Studi E Analisi Economica.

Arbia, G., and Paelinck, J.H.P. (2003). Economic convergence or divergence? Modeling the interregional dynamics of EU regions. *Journal of Geographical Systems, 5,* 291–314.

Arhin, D. (1994). The health card insurance scheme in Burundi: A social asset or a nonviable venture. *Social Science and Medicine, 39,* (8), 861–870.

Arrow, K. J. (1963). Uncertainty and welfare economics of medical care. *American Economic Review, 53,* 941–973.

Bajpai, N., Dholkia, R. H., and Sach, J. (2005, November). *Scaling up primary health services in rural India* (CGSD Working Paper No. 29). New York: The Earth Institute at Columbia University.

Bajpai, N., and Sachs, J. (1999, November). *The progress of policy reform and variations in performance at the sub-national level in India* (Development Discussion Paper No. 730). Cambridge, MA: Harvard Institute for International Development.

Banik, N., and Banerjee, A. (2011, September). *The rich keep getting richer in India! Says who?* (Working Paper Series No. 10511). Asia-Pacific Research and Training Network on Trade.

Banker, R. D., Conrad, R. F., and Strauss, R. P. (1986). A comparative application of data envelopment analysis and translog methods: An illustrative study of hospital production. *Management Science, 32* (1), 30–44.

Barro, R., and Sala-I-Martin, X. (1990, August). *Economic growth and convergence across the United States* (Working Paper No. 3419). Cambridge, MA: National Bureau of Economic Research.

Bates, L. J., Mukherjee, K., and Santerre, R. E. (2006). Market structure and technical efficiency in the hospital services industry: A DEA approach. *Medical Care Research and Review, 63* (4), 499–524.

Battese, G. E., and Coelli, T. J. (1995). A model for technical inefficiency effects in a stochastic frontier production function for panel data. *Empirical Economics, 20,* 325–332.

Bauer, P. W. (1990, October–November). Recent developments in the econometric estimation of frontiers. *Journal of Econometrics, 46* (1), 39–56.

Baum Christopher F. (2006). *An introduction to modern econometrics using stata.* New York: Stata Press.

Bennett, S. (1989). The impact of the increase in user fees: A preliminary investigation. *Lesotho Epidemiological Bulletin, 4,* 29–37.

Bennett, S. (1992). Promoting the private sector: A review of developing country trends. *Health Policy Plan, 7* (2), 97–110.

Bennett, S., and Mills, A. J. (1993). Health insurance and the private sector. In *Report of the Workshop on the Public/Private Mix for Health Care in Developing Countries.* London: Department of Public Health and Policy, LSH&TM.

Bhat, R. (1996). Regulating the private health care sector: The case of the Indian Consumer Protection Act. *Health Policy Plan,11* (3), 265–279.

Bogg, L., Dong, H., Wang, K., Cai, W., and Vinod, D. (1996). The cost of coverage: Rural health insurance in China. *Health Policy Plan, 11* (3), 238–352.

BPO Watch. (2012, November 27). India emerging as hub for Healthcare BPO. *BPO Watch,* www.bpowatchindia.com/Trends/9/India-emerging-as-hub-for-Healthcare-BPO.

Broomberg, J. (1994). Managing the health care market in developing countries: Prospects and problems. *Health Policy Plan, 9* (3), 237–251.

Burgess, J. F., and Wilson, P. W. (1998). Variation in inefficiency among US hospitals. *INFOR, Canadian Journal of Operational Research and Information Processing, 36* (3), 84–102.

Byrne, D. J., and Gertlar, P. J. (1990). *An analysis of the impact of user fees on outpatient utilisation in Lesotho* (Draft Report). Santa Monica, CA: The Rand Corporation.

Byrnes, P., and Valdmanis, V. (1993). Analysing technical and allocative efficiency of hospitals. In A. Charnes, W. W. Cooper, A. Y. Lewin and L. M. Seiford (Eds.), *Data envelopment analysis: Theory, methodology and applications.* Boston: Kluwer.

Cashin, P., and R. Sahay. (1996). Internal migration, centre-state grants and economic growth in the states of India. *IMF Staff Papers, 43* (1), 123–171.

Caves, D. W., Christensen, L. R., and Diewert, W. E. (1982). The economic theory of index numbers. *Econometrica, 50,* (6), 1393–1414.

Charnes, A., Cooper, W. W., Lewin, A. Y., and Seiford, L. M. (1995). *Data envelopment analysis: Theory, methodology and applications.* Boston: Kluwer.

Charnes, A., Cooper, W. W., and Rhodes, E. (1978). Measuring the efficiency of decision making units. *European Journal of Operational Research, 2* (6), 429–444.

Chattopadhyay, S., and Ray, S. C. (1996). Technical, scale and size efficiency in nursing home care: A nonparametric analysis of Connecticut homes. *Health Economics, 5* (4), 363–373.

Chaurasia, A. R. (2005). *Inter-state Inequality in infant mortality in India, 1981–2000* (Studies in Population and Development No. 00-05). Datia, MP, India: SHYAM Institute.

Chilingerian, J. A. (1993). Exploring why some physicians' hospital practices are more efficient: Taking DEA inside the hospital. In A. Charnes, W. W. Cooper, A. Y. Lewin and L. M. Seiford (Eds.), *Data envelopment analysis: Theory, methodology and applications*. Boston: Kluwer.

Chirikos, T. N. (1998). Identifying efficiently and economically operated hospitals: The prospects and pitfalls of applying frontier regression techniques. *Journal of Health Politics, 23* (6), 879–904.

CII and McKinsey & Company. (2002). *Healthcare in India: The road ahead. Confederation of Indian Industry,* New Delhi.

Clements, B. (2002). How efficient is education spending in Europe? *European Review of Economics and Finance, 1* (1), 3–26.

Coelli, T., Rao, D.S.P., and Battese, G. (1998). *An introduction to efficiency and productivity analysis.* Boston: Kluwer.

Collins, D., Quick, J. D., Musau, S. N., Kraushaar, D., and Hussein, I. M. (1996). The fall and rise of cost sharing in Kenya: The impact of phased implementation. *Health Policy Plan, 11* (1), 52–63.

Cook, P., and Kirkpatrick, C. (1988). Privatisation in less developed countries: An overview. In P. Cook and C. Kirkpatrick (Eds.), *Privatisation in less developed countries.* London: Harvester Wheatsheaf.

Cornia, G. A., Jolly, R., and Stewart, F. (1988). *Adjustment with a human face.* 2 vols. Oxford, UK: Oxford University Press.

Creese, A. (1991). User charges for health care: A review of recent experience. *Health Policy Plan, 6* (4), 303–319.

Cunha, M., and Rocha, V. (2012, July). *On the efficiency of public higher education institutions in Portugal: An exploratory study* (Working Paper). Portugal: University of Porto.

Dasgupta, D., Maiti, P., Mukherjee, R., Sarkar, S., and Chakrabarti, S. (2000, July 1). Growth and interstate disparities in India. *Economic and Political Weekly, 24,* 13–22.

Dave, P. (1991). Community and self-financing in voluntary health programmes in India. *Health Policy and Planning, 6,* 20–31.

De Bethune X., Alfani S., and Lahaye, J. P. (1989). The influence of an abrupt price increase on health service utilisation: Evidence from Piyaratn Zaïre. *Health Policy Plan*, 4, 76–81.

De Borger, B., and Kerstens, K. (1996). Cost efficiency of Belgian local governments: A comparative analysis of FDH, DEA, and econometric approaches. *Regional Science and Urban Economics, 26,* 145–170.

De Borger, B., Kerstens, K., Moesen, W., and Vanneste, J. (1994). Explaining differences in productive efficiency: An application to Belgian municipalities. *Public Choice, 80,* 339–358.

Debroy, B., and Bhandari, L. (2003). *District-level deprivation in the new millennium.* Delhi: Konark.

Defelice, L. C., and Bradford, W. D. (1997). Relative inefficiencies in production between solo and group practice physicians. *Health Economics, 6* (5), 455–465.

Deprins, D., Simar, L., and Tulkens, H. (1984). Measuring labor-efficiency in post offices. In M. Marchand, P. Pestieau, and H. Tulkens (Eds.), *The performance of public enterprises: Concepts and measurement.* Amsterdam: North-Holland.

Dholakia, R. H. (2003, September 27). Regional disparity in economic and human development in India. *Economic and Political Weekly, 38,* 4166–4172.

Dhongde, S. (2004, August). *Decomposing spatial differences in poverty in India* (WIDER Research Paper No. 2004/53). United Nations University.

Duggal, R., Nandraj, S., & Vadair, A. (1995a). Health expenditure across states – part I. *Economic and Political Weekly, 30,* 834–844.

Duggal, R., Nandraj, S., & Vadair, A. (1995b). Health expenditure across states – part II. *Economic and Political Weekly, 30,* 901–908.

Duraisamy, P., and Mahal, A. (2005). *Health, poverty and economic growth in India: Financing and delivery of health care services in India.* New Delhi: Commission on Macroeconomics and Health, Government of India, pp. 3–17.

Eckey, H.-F., Kosfeld, R., and Türc, M. (2005). *Regional convergence in Germany: A geographically weighted regression approach* (Working Paper No. 76/05). Volkswiertschaftlich Diskussionsbeitrage. www.uni-kassel.de/fb07/fileadmin/datas/fb07/5-Institute/IVWL/Forschungskolloquium/diskussionen/papier7605.pdf.

The Economic Times. (2005, September 5). Regional disparity widens; rich states corner benefits of reform. *The Economic Times,* p. 9.

The Economic Times. (2007, November 8). Age no bar: Senior citizens may now enjoy healthy aging. *The Economic Times,* p. 23.

The Economic Times. (2009, January 6). Indian medical tourism to touch Rs 9,500 cr by 2015:Assocham.*TheEconomicTimes.*http://economictimes.indiatimes.com/articleshow/3943611.cms?utm_source=contentofinterest&utm_medium=text&utm_campaign=cppst.

Ellis, R. P., and McGuire, T. G. (1993). Supply side and demand side cost sharing in health care. *Journal of Economic Perspectives, 7* (4), 135–151.

Ellis, R. P., McInnes, D. K., and Stephenson, E. H. (1994). Inpatient and outpatient health care demand in Cairo, Egypt. *Health Economics, 3* (3), 183–200.

Emanuele, B., Guin-Siu, M., and De Mello, L. (2003). More on the effectiveness of public spending on health care and education: A covariance structure model. *Journal of International Development 15,* 709–725. Published online in Wiley InterScience (www.interscience.wiley.com). doi:10.1002/jid.1025.

Engel, C., and Rogers, J. H. (1996). How wide is the border? *American Economic Review, 86,* 1112–1125.

Evans, D. B., Tandon, A., Murray C.J.L., and Lauer, J. A. (2000). *The comparative efficiency of national health systems in producing health: An analysis of 191 countries* (GPE Discussion Paper Series No. 29). Geneva: EIP/GPE/EQC, World Health Organization.

Evans, D. B., Tandon, A., Murray, C.J.L., and Lauer, J. A. (2001). *Measuring overall health system performance for 191 countries* (GPE Discussion Paper Series: No. 30). Geneva: EIP/GPE/EQC, World Health Organization.

Express Healthcare. (2008). Diagnosing Growth. http://healthcare.financialexpress.com/200806/labwatch01.shtml

Express Healthcare. (2011). Money, Dreams & Opportunities. http://healthcare.financialexpress.com/201106/labwatch01.shtml.

Fakin, B., and de Crombrugghe, A. (1997). *Fiscal adjustment in transition economies: Social transfers and the efficiency of public spending: A comparison with OECD countries* (Policy Research Working Paper No. 1803). Washington, DC: World Bank.

Färe, R., Grosskopf, S., Lindgren, B., and Roos, P. (1993). Productivity developments in Swedish hospitals: A Malmquist output index approach. In A. Charnes, W. W. Cooper, A. Y. Lewin and L. M. Seiford (Eds.), *Data envelopment analysis: Theory, Methodology and applications.* New York: Springer.

Farrell, M. J. (1957). The measurement of productive efficiency. *Journal of the Royal Statistical Society, 120*, 253–281.

Farsi, M., Filippini, M., and Lunati, D. (2008, January). *Economies of scale and efficiency measurement in Switzerland's nursing homes* (Working Paper No. 08-01). Lugano, Switzerland: Department of Economics, University of Lugano.

Ferrier, G. D., and Lovell, C. A. K. (1990, October–November). Measuring cost efficiency in banking: Econometric and linear programming evidence. *Journal of Econometrics, 46* (1), 229–245.

Fingleton, B. (2003). Models and simulations of GDP per inhabitant across Europe's regions. A preliminary view. In B. Fingleton (Ed.), *European regional growth* (pp. 11–53). Berlin: Springer-Verlag.

Fizel, J. L., and Nunnikhoven, T. S. (1992). Technical efficiency of for-profit and non-profit nursing homes. *Managerial and Decision Economics 13* (5), 429–439.

Forsberg, C. B., et al. (1992). *Health expenditures and attitudes in sub-Saharan setting.* Stockholm: Karolinska Institute.

Fried, H. O., Lovell, C. A., and Schmidt, S. S. (1993). *The measurement of productive efficiency: Techniques and applications.* New York: Oxford University Press.

Fuento, A. de la. (2000, January). *Convergence between countries and regions: Theory and empirics* (Working Paper No. 447). Barcelona: Instituto de Analisis Economico (CSIC).

Gächter, M., and Theurl, E. (2011). Health status convergence at the local level: Empirical evidence from Austria. *International Journal for Equity in Health, 10,* 34.

Gannon, B. (2004, November). *Technical efficiency of hospitals in Ireland* (Working Paper No. 18). Dublin, Ireland: Economic and Social Research Institute.

Ghosh, B., Marjit, S., and Neogi, C. (1998, June 27–July 3). Economic growth and regional divergence in India, 1960 to 1995. *Economic and Political Weekly, 33* (26), 1623–1630.

Ghuman, B. S., and Mehta, A. (2006). Health care for the poor in India with special reference to Punjab State. In R. Ahmad (Ed.), *The role of public administration in building a harmonious society.* Manila: Philippines: Asian Development Bank and Network of Asia-Pacific Schools and Institute of Public Administration and Governance.

Gonzalez Lopez-Valcarcel, B., and Barber Perez, P. (1996). Changes in the efficiency of Spanish public hospitals after the introduction of program-contracts. *Investicaionnes Económicas, 20* (3), 377–402.

Gopalakrishnan, R., and Agnani, M. (2001, March). *'Swasth Jeevan Sewa Guarantee Yojana': Moving towards decentralized management of health care in Madhya Pradesh* (Occasional Papers No. 8). Madhya Pradesh: Rajiv Gandhi Mission.

Government of India. (1946). *Report of the Health Survey and Development Committee* (chairman, Joseph Bhore). New Delhi: Manager of Publications.

Government of India. (1983). *National health policy, 1983.* New Delhi: Ministry of Health and Family Welfare.

Government of India. (1986–87). *Morbidity and utilization of medical services, 42nd round* (Report No. 364). New Delhi.

Government of India. (1991). Results on socio-economic profile of the aged persons, NSS 42nd round (July 1986–June 1987). *Sarvekshana, 15* (2), S-81-S379. New Delhi: National Sample Survey Organisation.

Government of India. (1992a). *Eighth Five Year Plan, 1992–97 Planning Commission.* New Delhi.

Government of India. (1992b). Morbidity and utilisation of medical services, NSS 42nd round (1986–87). *Sarvekshana 51st issue, 15* (4). New Delhi: National Sample Survey Organisation, Department of Statistics.

Government of India. (1996). *The constitution of India.* New Delhi.

Government of India. (1997). *Economic survey.* New Delhi: Ministry of Finance.

Government of India. (1998a). *The aged in India: A socio-economic profile.* New Delhi: National Sample Survey Organisation, Department of Statistics.

Government of India. (1998b). *Morbidity and utilisation of medical services, 52nd Round, July 1995–June 1996.* New Delhi: National Sample Survey Organisation, Department of Statistics.

Government of India. (1998c). National policy on education, 1986 (as modified in 1992). New Delhi: Department of Education, Ministry of Human Resource Development.

Government of India. (2001a). Census of India. New Delhi: Registrar General of India.

Government of India. (2001b). *Health information of India, 2000–01.* New Delhi: Central Bureau of Health Intelligence, Directorate General of Health Services, Ministry of Health and Family Welfare.

Government of India. (2002a). *Health information of India, 2002.* New Delhi: New Delhi: Central Bureau of Health Intelligence, Directorate General of Health Services, Ministry of Health and Family Welfare.

Government of India.(2002b). *National health policy, 2002.* New Delhi: Ministry of Health and Family Welfare.

Government of India. (2002c). *National human development report.* New Delhi: Planning Commission.

Government of India. (2002d). *National population policy 2000.* New Delhi: Ministry of Health and Family Welfare.

Government of India. (2002e). *Project OASIS complete report.* New Delhi: Ministry of Social Justice and Empowerment.

Government of India. (2003). *Health information of India, 2003.* New Delhi: Central Bureau of Health Intelligence, Directorate General of Health Services, Ministry of Health and Family Welfare.

Government of India. (2004). *Health information of India, 2004.* New Delhi: Central Bureau of Health Intelligence, Directorate General of Health Services, Ministry of Health and Family Welfare.

Government of India. (2005a). Financing and delivery of health care services in India. Background papers, National Commission on Macroeconomics and Health. New Delhi: Ministry of Health and Family Welfare.

Government of India. (2005b). *Health information of India, 2005.* New Delhi: Central Bureau of Health Intelligence, Directorate General of Health Services, Ministry of Health and Family Welfare.

Government of India. (2005c). *National commission on macroeconomics and health (NCMH): Background papers.* New Delhi: Ministry of Health and Family Welfare.

Government of India. (2005d). *Report of the National Commission on Macroeconomics and Health (NCMH).* New Delhi: Ministry of Health and Family Welfare.

Government of India. (2006a). *Health information of India, 2006.* New Delhi: Central Bureau of Health Intelligence, Directorate General of Health Services, Ministry of Health and Family Welfare.

Government of India. (2006b, March). *Morbidity, health care and condition of the aged.* NSS 60th round (January–June 2004). Report No. 507 (60/25.0/1). New Delhi: National Sample Survey Organisation, Ministry of Statistics and Programme Implementation.

Government of India. (2006c). *Reproductive and child health survey, 2006.* New Delhi: Ministry of Health and Family Welfare.

Government of India. (2007a). *Economic survey 2007.* New Delhi: Ministry of Finance.

Government of India. (2007b). *Health information of India, 2006.* New Delhi: Central Bureau of Health Intelligence, Directorate General of Health Services, Ministry of Health and Family Welfare.

Government of India. (2008). *Health information of India, 2007.* New Delhi: Central Bureau of Health Intelligence, Directorate General of Health Services, Ministry of Health and Family Welfare

Government of India. (2009a). *Health information of India, 2008.* New Delhi: Central Bureau of Health Intelligence, Directorate General of Health Services, Ministry of Health and Family Welfare.

Government of India. (2009b). *Report of the thirteenth finance commission (2010–2015).* New Delhi: Ministry of Finance.

Government of India. (2010). *Health information of India, 2009.* New Delhi: Central Bureau of Health Intelligence, Directorate General of Health Services, Ministry of Health and Family Welfare.

Government of India. (2011). *Health information of India, 2010.* New Delhi: Central Bureau of Health Intelligence, Directorate General of Health Services, Ministry of Health and Family Welfare.

Government of India. (2012a). Census of India, 2011. New Delhi: Registrar General, India.

Government of India. (2012b). *Health information of India, 2011.* New Delhi: Central Bureau of Health Intelligence, Directorate General of Health Services, Ministry of Health and Family Welfare.

Government of Karnataka. (2004). *Health facility survey, Karnataka health system development project (KHSDP).* Bangalore: Government of Karnataka.

Government of Karnataka. (2006). *Karnataka human development report 2005.* Bangalore: Government of Karnataka.

Government of Madhya Pradesh. (2002). *The Madhya Pradesh human development report 2002.* Bhopal: Government of Madhya Pradesh.

Government of Maharashtra. (2002). *Human development report, Maharashtra, 2002.* Mumbai: Government of Maharashtra.

Government of Punjab. (2004). *Punjab human development report, 2004.* New Delhi: Government of Punjab.

232 *References*

Government of the Republic of Namibia. (2004, July). *The technical efficiency of district hospitals in Namibia.* Ministry of Health and Social Service.
Government of West Bengal. (2004). *West Bengal human development report 2004.* Kolkata: Government of West Bengal.
Greene, W. (2002, October). *Fixed and random effects in stochastic frontier models.* Department of Economics, Stern School of Business, New York University.
Greunz, L. (2003). Geographically and technologically mediated knowledge spillovers between European Regions. *Annals of Regional Science, 37,* 657–680.
Griffin, G. C. (1987, July–August). User charges for health care in principle and practice. In *Health care financing: Proceedings of regional seminar on health care financing.* Manila: Philippines: Asian Development Bank.
Griffin, G. C. (1990). *Health sector financing in Asia* (World Bank Report No. IDP-68). Washington, DC: World Bank.
Griffin, G. C. 1992. *Health care in Asia.* Washington, DC: World Bank.
Grosskopf, S., and Valdmanis, V. (1987). Measuring hospital performance: A non-parametric approach. *Journal of Health Economics, 6* (1), 89–107.
Guilmoto, C. Z., and Rajan, S. I. (2002, February 16–22). District level estimates of fertility from India's 2001 census. *Economic and Political Weekly, 37* (7), 665–672.
Gupta, S., Honjo, K., and Verhoeven, M. (1997, November). *The efficiency of government expenditure: Experiences from Africa* (Working Paper No. 971153). Washington, DC: International Monetary Fund. www.imf.org/external/pubs/ft/wp/wp97153.pdf.
Gupta, I., and Trivedi, M. (2005.) Social health insurance redefined: Health for all through coverage for all. *Economic and Political Weekly, 39,* 4132–4140.
Gupta, S., and Verhoeven, M. (2001). The efficiency of government expenditure experiences from Africa. *Journal of Policy Modelling, 23,* 433–467.
Gwynne, G., and Zschock, D. 1989. *Health care financing in Latin America and the Caribbean, 1985–1989, findings and recommendations.* Stony Brook: Department of Economics, State University of New York.
Hadley, J., and Zuckerman, S. (1994). The role of efficiency measurement in hospital rate setting. *Journal of Health Economics, 13* (3), 335–340.
Hajialiafzali, H., Moss, J. R., and Mahmood, M. A. (2007). Efficiency measurement for hospitals owned by the Iranian Social Security Organisation. *Journal of Medical Systems, 31* (3),166–172.
Halstead, S. B., Walsh, J. A., and Warren K. S. (Eds.). (1985). *Good health at low cost.* New York: Rockefeller Foundation.
Hamine, P. (1998, October 2). Committee issues guidelines for privatization of health centers. *Free Press Journal.*
Hardeman, W., Van Damme, W., Van Pelt, M., Por, I., Kimvan, H., and Meessen, B. (2004). Access to health care for all? User fees plus a health equity fund in Sotnikum, Cambodia. *Health Policy and Planning, 19* (1), 22–32.
Health Policy Network (HPN). 1995. *In practice: The NHS market.* National Health Service Support Federation: UK.
Helliwell, J. F. (2000). How much do national borders matter? *Canadian Journal of Economics/Revue canadienne d'Economique, 33* (1), 288–292.
The Hindu. (1997, July 31). Crucial role of corporate hospitals in health care.
The Hindu. (1998, January 29). IMA to monitor free service by corporate hospitals.
The Hindustan Times. (1997a, November 4). Government demand in violation of contract.
The Hindustan Times. (1997b, November 16). Government dithers at cost of poor patients.

Ho Lok, S. (1995). Market reforms and China's health care system. *Social Science Medicine, 41,* 1065–1072.

Hodgkin, D., and McGuire, T. G. (1994). Payment levels and hospital response to prospective payment. *Journal of Health Economics, 13,* 1–29.

Hofler, R. A., and Rungeling, B. (1994). US nursing homes: Are they cost efficient? *Economics Letters, 44* (3), 301–305.

Hofmarcher, M. M., Paterson, I., and Riedel, M. (2002). Measuring hospital efficiency in Austria – a DEA approach. *Health Care Management Science, 5* (1), 7–14.

Hollingsworth, B., and Wildman, J. (2002a, May). *Efficiency and cross efficiency measures: A validation using OECD data* (Working Paper No. 132). Australia: Centre for Health Program Evaluation, Monash University.

Hollingsworth, B., and Wildman, J. (2002b, May). *The efficiency of health production: Re-estimating the WHO panel data using parametric and nonparametric approaches to provide additional information* (Working Paper No. 131). Australia: Centre for Health Programme Evaluation, Monash University.

Hollingsworth, B., Dawson, P. J., and Maniadakis, N. (1999). Efficiency measurement of health care: A review of non-parametric methods and applications. *Health Care Management Science, 2* (3): 161–172.

Hsiao, W. C. (1984). Transformation of health care in China. *New England Journal of Medicine, 310,* 932–936.

Hughes, A. (2002). Guide to the measurement of government productivity. *International Productivity Monitor, 5,* 64–77.

Hurst, J. W. (1991, Fall). Reforming health care in seven European nations. *Health Affairs,* pp. 7–21.

India Brand Equity Foundation (IBEF). (2006). *Healthcare.* www.ibef.org/artdisplay. aspx?cat_id=161&art_id=13814.

Indian Council of Social Science Research/Indian Council of Medical Research (ICSSR/ICMR). (1981). *Health for all: an alternative strategy.* Pune: Indian Institute of Education.

Indian Institute of Management. (1987). *Study of health care financing in India.* Ahmedabad: Indian Institute of Management.

India Investment Centre. (2007). *Statistics (sector-wise foreign investment).* http://iic.nic. in/iic2_c02.htm.

India Briefing. (2012, May 10). India's medical technology industry. www.india-briefing. com/news/indias-medical-technology-industry-5376.html/.

International Institute for Population Sciences and Macro International. (2007). *National family health survey (NFHS-3), 2005–06: India,* vol.1. Mumbai: International Institute for Population Sciences.

International Rescue Committee (IRC). (2012). *Access to health care and the elimination of user fees: Experience with fully subsidized health care for targeted groups in the Democratic Republic of Congo* (Position Paper). London.

James, C. D., Hanson, K., McPake, B., Balabanova, D., Gwatkin, D., Hopwood, I., . . . Xu, K. (2006). To retain or remove user fees? Reflections on the current debate in low- and middle-income countries. *Applied Health Economics and Health Policy, 5* (3), 137–153.

Jamison, D. T., Sandbu, M., and Wang, J. (2001). *Cross country variation in mortality decline, 1962–87: The role of country specific technical progress* (CMH Working Paper Series Paper No. WGI: 4), Commission on Macroeconomics and Health, WHO.

Jayasuriya, R., and Wodon, Q. (2002, April). *Measuring and explaining country efficiency in improving health and education indicators*. Washington, DC: World Bank.

Jeffrey, P., and Coppola, M. N. (2004). Efficiency of federal hospitals in the United States. *Journal of Medical Systems, 28* (5), 411–422.

Jesani, A., and Anantharam, S. (1989, May). *What it is and how to fight it: A report of a workshop by Medico Friend Circle* (Bombay group). Mumbai: Medico Friends Circle Bulletin.

Jha, R. (2000, March 11–17). Growth, inequality and poverty in India – spatial and temporal characteristics. *Economic and Political Weekly, 35* (11): 921–928.

Kittelsen, S.A.C., and Magnussen, J. (1999). *Testing DEA models of efficiency in Norwegian psychiatric outpatient clinics* (Health Services Research Working Paper No. 4). Oslo: University of Oslo Health Economics Research Programme.

Knox K. J., Blankmeyer E. C., Stutzman J. R. (1999). Relative economic efficiency in Texas nursing facilities: A profit function analysis. *Journal of Economics and Finance, 23* (3), 199–213.

Knox, K. J., Blankmeyer, E. C., and Stutzman, J. R. (2001, April–June). Efficiency of nursing home chains and the implications of nonprofit status: A comment. *Journal of Real Estate Portfolio Management, 7* (2), 177–182.

Knox, K. J., Blankmeyer, E. C., and Stutzman, J. R. (2007, Spring). Technical efficiency in Texas nursing facilities: A stochastic production frontier approach. *Journal of Economics and Finance, 31* (1), 75–86.

Kontodimopoulos, N., Nanos, P., and Niakas, D. (2003). Balancing efficiency of health services and equity of access in remote areas. *Health Policy, 76* (1), 49–57.

Kooreman, P. (1994a). Data envelopment analysis and parametric frontier estimation: Complementary tools. *Journal of Health Economics, 13* (3), 345–346.

Kooreman, P. (1994b). Nursing home care in the Netherlands: A nonparametric efficiency analysis. *Journal of Health Economics, 13* (3), 301–316.

Kumar, S. E. (2010, April 14). Welcome, high-end patients! *Business Today*. http://businesstoday.intoday.in/bt/story/5489/1/welcome,-highend-patients!.html

Kurian, N. J. (2000, February 12). Widening regional disparities in India: Some indicators. *Economic and Political Weekly, 35* (7), 538–550.

Lakhotia, S. (1997, September 14). A clean bill of health. *The Economic Times*.

Lall, S. V., and Chakravorty, S. (2004, August). *Industrial location and spatial inequality: Theory and evidence from India* (WIDER Research Paper No. 2004/49). United Nations University.

Lagarde, M., and Palmer, N. (2008). The impact of user fees on health service utilization in low- and middle-income countries: How strong is the evidence? *Bulletin of the World Health Organization, 86,* 839.

Le Grand, J.(1991). Quasi markets and social policy. *Economic Journal, 101,* 1256–1267.

Le Grand, J. (1994). Evaluating the NHS Reforms. In R. Robinson and J. Le Grand (Eds.), *Evaluating the NHS reforms*. London: King's Fund Institute.

Lewis, M. A., and Kenney, G. (1988). *The private sector and family planning in developing countries: Its role, achievements and potential*. Washington, DC: The Urban Institute.

Lewis, M. A., and Miller, T. R. (1987). Public-private partnership in water supply and sanitation in sub-Saharan Africa. *Health Policy Plan, 2* (1): 70–79.

Ley, E. (1991). Eficiencia productiva: Un estudio aplicado al sector hospitalario. *Investic-aionnes Económicas, 15* (1), 71–88.

Li, L., and Wang, J. (2008). *Relative efficiency of the Chinese public acute hospitals: An empirical data envelopment analysis application.* Hong Kong: Department of Management, Hong Kong Polytechnic University.

Linna, M., Häkkinen, U., and Linakko, E. (1998). An econometric study of costs of teaching and research in Finnish hospitals. *Health Economics, 7* (5), 291–305.

Litvack, J. I., and Bodart, C. (1993). User fees and improved quality of health care equals improved access: Results of a field experiment in Cameroon. *Social Science Medicine, 37* (3), 369–383.

Liu, Y., Hsiao, W.C.L., Li, Q., Liu, C., and Ren, M. (1995). Transformation of China's rural health care financing. *Social Science Medicine, 41*, 1085–1093.

Lo, J. C., Shih, K-S., and Chen, K.-L. (1996). Technical efficiency of the general hospitals in Taiwan: An application of DEA. *Academia Economic Papers, 24* (3), 275–296.

López-Bazo, E., Vayá, E., and Artis, M. (2004). Regional externalities and growth. *Journal of Regional Science, 44,* 43–73.

Luoma, K., Järviö, M-L., Suoniemi, I., and Hjerppe, R. T. (1996). Financial incentives and productive efficiency in Finnish health centres. *Health Economics, 5* (5), 435–445.

Magnussen, J. (1996). Efficiency measurement and the operationalisation of hospital production. *Health Services Research, 31* (1), 21–37.

Mainardi, S. (2007). Unequal access to public healthcare facilities: Theory and measurement revisited. *Surveys in Mathematics and Its Applications, 2,* 91–112.

Marjit, S., and Mitra, S. (1996, August 17). Convergence in regional growth rates: Indian research agenda. *Economic and Political Weekly, 31* (33), 2239–2242.

Martin, R. (2001). EMU versus the regions? Regional convergence and divergence in Euroland. *Journal of Economic Geography, 1,* 51–80.

Masiye, F. (2007). Investigating health system performance: An application of data envelopment analysis to Zambian hospitals. *BMC Health Services Research, 7* (58). doi:10.1186/1472-6963-7-58.

Mathiyazhgan, M. K. (2006, 27 January). *Cost efficiency of public and private hospitals: Evidence from Karnataka State in India* (Working Paper No. 8). Institute of South Asian Studies.

McGreevey, W. P. (1990). *Social Security in Latin America: Issues and options for the World Bank.* World Bank Report No. 8456-LAC. Washington, DC: World Bank

McKinsey & Company and CII (Confederation of Indian Industry). (2012). *Inspiring possibilities and challenging journey.* New Delhi: CII.

McPake, B., Hanson, K., and Mills, A. (1993). Community financing of health care in Africa: An evaluation of the Bomako Initiative. *Social Science Medicine, 36* (1), 1383–1395.

McPake, B., and Ngalanda Banda, E. E. (1994). Contracting out of health services in developing countries. *Health Policy Plan, 9* (1), 25–30.

Meessen, B., Hercot, D., Noirhomme, M., Ridde, V., Tibouti, A., Bicaba, A., Tashobya, C. K., and Gilson, L. (2009). *Removing user fees in the health sector in low-income countries: A multi-country review.* New York: United Nations Children's Fund.

Meessen, B., Hercot, D., Noirhomme, M., Ridde, V., Tibouti, A., Tashobya, C. K., and Gilson, L. (2011). Removing user fees in the health sector: A review of policy processes in six sub-Saharan African countries. *Health Policy and Planning, 26,* ii16–ii29.

Menzel, P. T. (1983). *Medical costs, moral choices.* New Haven, CT: Yale UniversityPress.

Mirmirani, S. (2008). Health care efficiency in transition economies: An application of data envelopment analysis. *International Business and Economics Research Journal, 7* (2), 47–56.

Mortimer, D., and Peacock, S. (2000, August). *Hospital efficiency measurement: Simple ratios vs. frontier methods* (Working Paper No. 135). Australia: Monash University Centre for Health Program Evaluation.

Murray, C.J.L., and Frenk, J. (1999). *A WHO framework for health system performance assessment.* Washington, DC: Global Programme on Evidence and Information for Policy, World Bank.

Mwabu, G., and Wang'ombe, J. (1995, February). *Health service pricing reforms in Kenya: 1989–93* (Working Paper). New York: International Health Policy Program.

Nagaraj, R., Varoudakis, A., and Veganzones, M.-A. (2000). Long-run growth trends and convergence across Indian states. *Journal of International Development, 12* (1), 45–70.

Nanda, P. (2002). Gender dimensions of user fees: Implications for women's utilization of health care. *Reproductive Health Matters, 10* (20), 127–134.

National Family Health Survey (NFHS-3), 2005–06: India. Vol. 1. Mumbai: International Institute for Population Sciences (IIPS).

National Institute of Public Finance and Policy (NIPFP). (1993). *Structural adjustment programme – its impact on the health sector.* New Delhi: National Institute of Public Finance and Policy.

National University of Educational Planning and Administration. (2002–03 to 2011–12). *State report cards: Elementary education in India.* Various issues. New Delhi: National University of Educational Planning and Administration.

Neven, D. (1995). Regional convergence in the European Community. *Journal of Common Market Studies, 33,* 47–65.

Niebuhr, A. (2002). *Spatial dependence of regional unemployment in the European Union* (Discussion Paper No. 186). Hamburg: HWWA.

Nitsch, V. (2000). National borders and international trade: Evidence from the European Union. *Canadian Journal of Economics, 33,* 1091–1105.

Nonneman, W., and Van Doorslaer, E.K.A. (1994). The role of the sickness funds in the Belgian health care market. *Social Science Medicine, 39,* 1483.

Noorbakhsh, F. (2006, February). *International convergence or higher inequality in human development? Evidence for 1975 to 2002* (Research Paper No. 2006/15). Finland: World Institute for Development Economics Research, United Nations University.

Organisation for Economic Co-operation and Development (OECD). (1990). *Health care systems in transition: The search for efficiency.* OECD Social Policy Study. Paris: Organisation for Economic Co-operation and Development.

Organisation for Economic Co-operation and Development (OECD). (1992). *The reform of health care: A comparative analysis of seven OECD countries.* Health Policy Studies No. 2, Paris: Organisation for Economic Co-operation and Development.

Organisation for Economic Co-operation and Development (OECD). (1993). *Health systems: Facts and trends.* Health Policy Studies No. 3. Paris: Organisation for Economic Co-operation and Development.

Pal, P. (1997, October 8). The right diagnostics. *Business Standard,* p. 3.

Pal, P., and Viswanathan, V. (1997, October 8). Cashing in on health. *Business Standard,* p. 3.

Pandit, J. (2006). Unwanted medicines and nation's health. www.dailyexcelsior.com/web1/06apr28/edit.htm.

Parker, P. N. (2007, July 6). Parents and senior citizens bill, 2007. http://indiatogether.org/seniors-laws.

Parkin, D., and Hollingsworth, B. (1997). Measuring production efficiency of acute hospitals in Scotland, 1991–94: Validity issues in data envelopment analysis. *Applied Economics, 29* (11), 1425–1433.

The Pioneer. (1998, January 31). Indian medical industry takes off, p. 3.

Pitt, M. M., and Lee, L.F. (1981). The measurement and sources of technical inefficiency in the Indonesian weaving industry. *Journal of Development Economics, 9,* 43–64.

Piyaratn, P.J.W.S. (1994, October). *Health insurance in Thailand.* Paper presented at the National Seminar on Health Sector Development, Hanoi, Vietnam.

Powell, M., and Anesaki, M. (1990). *Health care in Japan.* London: Routledge.

Prabhu, K. S. (1996). The impact of structural adjustment on social sector expenditure: Evidence from Indian states. In C.H.H. Rao and H. Linnemann (Eds.), *Economic reforms and poverty alleviation in India.* New Delhi: Sage.

Prinja, S., Aggarwal, A. K., Kumar, R., and Kanavos, P. (2012). User charges in health care: Evidence of effect on service utilization and equity from north India. *Indian Journal of Medical Research, 136,* 868–876.

Puig-Junoy, J. (1998). Technical efficiency in the clinical management of critically ill patients. *Health Economics, 7* (3), 263–277.

Purohit, B. C. (1995). The cost benefit analysis of a loan scheme: A case study of Rangabelia Project. *Community Development Journal,* 30 (1), 66–72.

Purohit, B. C. (1996a). Private voluntary health sector in India. *Asian Economic Review, 37* (2), 297–311.

Purohit, B. C. (1996b, June). *Private voluntary health sector in India: Some issues in sustainability* (IDSJ Working Paper No. 68). Jaipur: Institute of Development Studies.

Purohit, B. C. (1996c, May–June). Sustainability of voluntary sector in India. *Health for the Millions, 22,* 19.

Purohit, B. C. (1997, April). *Structural adjustment and health care sector in India: Some policy issues in financing* (QEH Working Paper No. 2). Oxford: University of Oxford. www2.qeh.ox.ac.uk/research/qehwp.

Purohit, B. C. (2001a). Private initiatives and policy options: Recent health system experience in India. *Health Policy and Planning, 16* (1), 87–97.

Purohit, B. C. (2001b). *Resource mobilization for health care sector in Andhra Pradesh-I (user charges).* Background paper for DFID/IHSD under APIER Review of Health Sector, Hyderabad.

Purohit, B. C. (2003). Social security for the aged in India: Some policy issues. *Journal of Aging and Social Policy, 15* (4), 49–79.

Purohit, B. C. (2004). Inter-state disparities in health care and financial burden on the poor in India. *Journal of Health and Social Policy, 18* (4), 37–60.

Purohit, B. C. (2008). Health and human development at sub-state level in India. *Journal of Socio-Economics, 37,* 2248–2260.

Purohit, B. C. (2008a). Efficiency of health care system: A sub-state level analysis for West Bengal (India). *Review of Urban and Regional Development Studies, 20* (3), 212–225, 20th anniversary special issue, Blackwell, Singapore.

Purohit, B. C. (2009). *Economic and policy issues in health care sector in India.* Ideaindia. com. London: Cooperjal Limited (digital book).

Purohit, B. C. (2010a). Efficiency of health care sector at sub-state level in India: A case of Punjab. *Online Journal of Health Allied Sciences, 8* (3).

Purohit, B. C. (2010b). Efficiency of health care system at sub-state level in Madhya Pradesh (India). *Social Work in Public Health, 25,* 42–58.

Purohit, B. C. (2010c). Efficiency variation at sub-state level: The health care system in Karnataka. *Economic and Political Weekly, 45* (19), 70–76.

Purohit, B. C. (2010d). *Health care system in India.* New Delhi: Gayatri Publications.

Purohit, B. C. (2012). Health policy, inequity and convergence in India. *International Journal of Development Studies, 4,* 104–118.

Purohit, B. C., and Mohan, R. (1996). New directions for public health, financing. *Economic and Political Weekly, 31* (8), 450–453.

Purohit, B. C., and Rai, V. (1992). Operating efficiency in inpatient care: An exploratory analysis of teaching hospitals in Rajasthan, India. *International Journal of Health Planning and Management, 7,* 149–162.

Purohit, B. C., and Siddiqui, T. A. (1995a). Cost recovery in diagnostic facilities. *Economic and Political Weekly, 30,* 1700–1705.

Purohit, B. C., and Siddiqui T. A. (1995b). Socio-economic correlates of outpatient care in a factor analytic framework. *Journal of Health and Social Policy, 7* (1), 1–18.

Quick, J. D. et al. (1993, October). *Monitoring methods for user fees in Kenya: Assessing impact on patients, access, quality and revenue.* Paper presented at American Association Annual Conference, San Francisco, California.

Rao, M. G., and Sen, K. (1997). Internal migration, centre-state grants, and economic growth in the state of India: A comment on Cashin and Sahay. *International Monetary Fund Staff Papers, 44* (2), 283–288.

Rao, M. G., Shand, R. T., and Kalirajan, K. P. (1999, March 27–April 2). Convergence of income across Indian states: A divergent view. *Economic and Political Weekly, 34* (13), 769–778.

Research Group. (2006, September). *User fees policy and equitable access to health care services in low- and middle-income countries with the case of Madagascar.* Institute for International Cooperation, Japan International Cooperation Agency.

Reserve Bank of India. (2012). *State finances 2011.* Mumbai: Reserve Bank of India.

Richardson, J., Robertson, I., and Wildman, J. (2001, October). *A critique of the World Health Organization's evaluation of health system performance* (Working Paper No. 125). Australia: Centre for Health Program Evaluation, Monash University.

Romer, P. M. (1990). Endogenous technological change. *Journal of Political Economy, 98* (5), S71–S102.

Rondinelli, D. (1981). Government decentralisation in comparative perspective: Theory and practice in developing countries. *International Review of Administrative Science, 47* (2),133–145.

Rosenman, R., Siddharthan, K., and Ahern, M. (1997). Output efficiency of health maintenance organisations in Florida. *Health Economics, 6* (3), 295–302.

Rosko, M. D. (2001). Cost efficiency of US hospitals: A stochastic frontier approach. *Health Economics, 10* (6), 539–551.

Sala-I-Martin, X. X. (1997). I just ran two million regressions. *American Economic Review, 87* (2), 178–183.

Salomon J. A., Mathers C. D., Murray C.J.L., and Ferguson B. (2001). *Methods for life expectancy and healthy life expectancy uncertainty analysis* (GPE Discussion Paper No. 10). Geneva: World Health Organization. www.who.int/evidence.

Sankar, D., and Kathuria, V. (2004, March 27–April 2). Health system performance in rural India: Efficiency estimates across states. *Economic and Political Weekly, 39* (13), 1427–1433.

Sappington, D., and Stiglitz, J. E. (1988). Information and regulation. In E. Bailey (Ed.), *Public regulation: New perspectives on institutions and policies.* Cambridge, MA: MIT Press.

Sastry, N. S. (2003, January 25–31). District level poverty estimates – feasibility of using NSS household consumer expenditure survey data. *Economic and Political Weekly, 38* (4), 409–412.

Sav, G. T. (2012). For-profit college entry and cost efficiency: Stochastic frontier estimates vs. two-year public and non-profit colleges. *International Business Research, 5* (3), 26–32.

Schmacker, E. R., and McKay, N. L. (2008). Factors affecting productive efficiency in primary care clinics. *Health Service Management Research, 21* (1), 60–70.

Schmidt, P., and Sickles, R. C. (1984). Production frontiers and panel data. *Journal of Business and Economic Statistics, 2* (4), 309–316.

Schulenburg, J.M.G. von der. (1994). Forming and reforming the market for third party purchasing of health care: A German perspective. *Social Science and Medicine, 39* (10), 1473–1481.

Scotton, R. B. (1994). Let us think seriously about managed competition. *Social Science and Medicine, 38,* 2.

Shankar, R., and Shah, A. (2003). Bridging the economic divide within countries: A scorecard on the performance of regional policies in reducing regional income disparities. *World Development, 31* (8), 1421–1441.

Sharma, S. (n.d.). *Reproductive and child health status in India: District level analysis.* Mimeograph, Population Research Center, Institute of Economic Growth, University Enclave, Delhi-8, www.sasnet.lu.se/EASASpapers/11SureshSharma.pdf.

Singh, N., and T. N. Srinivasan. (2005). Indian federalism, globalization and economic reform. In T. N. Srinivasan and Jessica Wallack (Eds.), *Federalism and economic reform: International perspectives.* Cambridge, UK: Cambridge University Press.

Singh N., Kendell J., Jain R. K., and Chander J. (2010). *Regional inequality in India in the 1990s: Trends and policy implications* (Study No. 36). Mumbai: Reserve Bank of India (RBI).

Spinks, J., and Hollingsworth, B. (2005, January). *Health production and the socioeconomic determinants of health in OECD countries: The use of efficiency models* (Working Paper 151). Australia: Centre for Health Economics, Monash University.

State Council of the Republic of China. (1985). *A report with respect to some policies of health work reform* (State Council Document 62). Beijing: State Council.

Stinson, W. (1984). Potential and limitations of community financing. *World Health Forum, 5* (2), 123–125.

St. Aubyn, M. (2002). Evaluating efficiency in the Portuguese health and education sectors. *Economica, 26.*

Subrahmanyam, S. (1999, November 20). Convergence of income across states. *Economic and Political Weekly, 34* (46 & 47), 3327–3328.

Sudhir, Uma. (1997, August 21). Government health care network starved of funds. *The Economic Times.*

Sulabh International Social Service Organization. (2007). *Study on disease burden to inadequate water & sanitation facilities in India.* New Delhi: SISSO.

Suraratdechaac, C., and Okunadeb, A. A. (2006, June). Measuring operational efficiency in a health care system: A case study from Thailand. *Health Policy, 77* (1), 2–23.

Sutherland, D., Price, R., Joumard, I., and Nicq, C. (2007), Performance indicators for public spending efficiency in primary and secondary education (Working Papers No. 546). Paris: OECD Economics Department. http://dx.doi.org/10.1787/285006168603.

Tandon, A., Murray, C.J.L., Lauer, J. A., and Evans, D. B.(2000). *Measuring overall health system performance for 191 countries* (GPE Discussion Paper Series No. 30). Geneva: EIP/GPE/EQC, World Health Organization.

Thanassoulis, E., Boussofiane, A., and Dyson, R. G. (1996). A comparison of data envelopment analysis and ratio analysis as tools for performance measurement. *OMEGA, International Journal of Management Science, 24* (3), 229–244.

Thomas, I. P. (1996). *Regional policy, convergence and subsidiarity in the European Community* (Kiel Working Paper No. 737). Kiel: Kiel Institute of World Economics.

Thomason, J. A., Newbrander, W. C., and Kolehmainen-Aitken, R-L. (Eds.). (1991). *Decentralization in a developing country: The experience of Papua New Guinea and its health service.* Pacific Research Monograph No. 25. Canberra: Australian National University.

Times of India. (1997, November 1). Tamil Nadu *Seeks Corporate Help in Maintaining Government Health Centres.*

Tulasidhar, V. B. (1993, November 6). Expenditure compression and health sector outlays. *Economic and Political Weekly, 28* (45), 2473–2477.

Tulkens, H., and Vanden Eeckaut, P. (1995). Non-parametric efficiency, progress and regress measures for panel data: Methodological aspects. *European Journal of Operational Research, 80,* 474.

UNDP. (1991). *Human development report 1991.* New York: Palgrave MacMillan.

UNDP. (2006). *Human development report 2006.* New York: Palgrave MacMillan.

Uneke, C., Ogbonna, A., Ezeoha, A., Oyibo, P., Onwe, F., and Ndukwe, C. (2008). User fees in health services in Nigeria: The health policy implications. *Internet Journal of Health, 8* (2). www.ispub.com.

UNICEF. (2008). *The drinking water and sanitation situation.*

Valdmanis, V. (1992). Sensitivity analysis for DEA models. An empirical example using public vs. NFP hospitals. *Journal of Public Economics, 48* (2), 185–205.

Viswanathan, V. (1997, October 3). The high premium on health. *Business Standard, 3.*

Viveros-Long, A. (1986). Changes in health financing: The Chilean experience. *Social Science and Medicine, 22,* 379–385.

Vogel, R. J. (1988a). *Cost recovery in the health care sector: Selected country studies in West Africa* (World Bank Technical Paper No. 82). Washington, DC: World Bank.

Vogel, R. J. (1988b). An analysis of the welfare component and intergenerational transfers under the Medicare Program. In M. V. Pauly and W. B. Kissick (Eds.), *Lessons from the first twenty years of Medicare.* Philadelphia: University of Pennsylvania Press.

Vogel, R. J. (1990a). *Health insurance in Sub-Saharan Africa: A survey and analysis* (Working Paper WPS 476, Africa Technical Department). Washington, DC: World Bank.

Vogel, R. J. (1990b). *Trends in health in health expenditures and revenue sources in Sub-Saharan Africa.* Background paper for African Health Policy. Washington, DC: World Bank.

von Otter, C., and Saltman, R. B. (1992). *Planned markets and public competition strategic reform in Northern European health systems.* Buckingham, UK: Open University Press.

Waddington, C., and Enyimayew, K. (1989). A price to pay, part I: The impact of user charges in Ashanti-Akin District, Ghana. *International Journal of Health Planning and Management, 4,* 17–47.

Waddington, C., and Enyimayew, K. (1990). A price to pay, part II: The impact of user fees in the Volta Region of Ghana. *International Journal of Health Planning and Management, 5,* 287–312.

Wagstaff, A. (1989). Estimating efficiency in the hospital sector: A comparison of three statistical cost frontier models. *Applied Economics 21* (5), 659–672.

Wang, J., Jamison, D. T., Bos, E., Preker, A., and Peaboy, J. (1999). *Measuring country performance on health: Selected indicators for 115 countries*. Washington, DC: Human Development Network, Health, Nutrition and Population Studies, IBRD/World Bank.

Wang, J., Zhao, Z., and Mahmood, A. (2006, December). *Relative efficiency, scale effect, and scope effect of public hospitals: Evidence from Australia* (IZA Discussion Papers No. 2520). http://nbn-resolving.de/urn:nbn:de:101:1-20080502103.

Winkler, D., and Sondergaard, L. (2008). *Uganda: The efficiency of public education in Uganda*. Washington, DC: World Bank. http://documents.worldbank.org/curated/en/2008/03/16453602/uganda-efficiency-public-education-uganda.

Wolszczak-Derlacz, J., and Parteka, A. (2011). Efficiency of European public higher education institutions: A two-stage multicountry approach. *Scientometrics 89*, 887–917. doi:10.1007/s11192-011-0484-9.

World Bank. (1987). *Financing health services in developing countries: An agenda for reform*. Washington, DC: World Bank.

World Bank. (1990). *China: Revenue mobilisation and tax policy*. Washington, DC: World Bank.

World Bank. (1993). *World development report, investing in health*. Washington, DC: Oxford University Press.

World Bank. (1995, May). *India: Policy and finance strategies for strengthening primary health care services* (Report No. 13042-IN, Population and Human Resource Division, South Asia Country Department II). Washington, DC: World Bank.

World Bank. (1996). *World development report*. Washington, DC: Oxford University Press.

World Bank. (2003). *World development report, 2003*. Washington, DC: World Bank.

World Health Organization (WHO). (1991, July). *The public/private mix in national health systems and the role of ministries of health*. Report of a meeting held at the Hacienda Cocoya, State of Morelos, Mexico, Director of Strengthening of Health Services. Geneva: World Health Organization.

World Health Organization (WHO). (2000). *The world health report, 2000. Health systems: Improving performance*. Geneva: World Health Organization.

World Health Organization (WHO). (2005). *World health report, 2005*. Geneva: World Health Organization.

Worthington, A. C. (2004). Frontier efficiency measurement in health care: A review of empirical techniques and selected applications. *Medical Care Research and Review, 61* (2), 135–170.

Yang, B. (1990). *Issues in health care delivery: The case of Korea*. Paper presented at World Bank Seminar on Health Financing and the Role of Health Insurance, Bali, Indonesia.

Yoder, R. A. (1989). Are people willing and able to pay for health services. *Social Science and Medicine, 29*, 35–42.

Yong, K., and Harris, A. (1999, June). *Efficiency of hospitals in Victoria under case mix funding: A stochastic frontier approach* (Working Paper No. 92). Australia: Centre for Health Program Evaluation, Monash University.

Zheng, X., and Hillier, S. (1995). The reforms of the Chinese health care system: County level changes: The Jiangxi study. *Social Science and Medicine, 41* (8), 1057–1064.

Zuckerman, S., Hadley, J., and Iezzoni, L. (1994). Measuring hospital efficiency with frontier cost functions. *Journal of Health Economics, 13* (3), 255–280.

Author Index

Subject Index

For Product Safety Concerns and Information please contact our EU
representative GPSR@taylorandfrancis.com
Taylor & Francis Verlag GmbH, Kaufingerstraße 24, 80331 München, Germany

www.ingramcontent.com/pod-product-compliance
Ingram Content Group UK Ltd.
Pitfield, Milton Keynes, MK11 3LW, UK
UKHW021118180425
457613UK00005B/142